Imaging the Chinese in Cuban Literature and Culture

UNIVERSITY PRESS OF FLORIDA

Florida A&M University, Tallahassee
Florida Atlantic University, Boca Raton
Florida Gulf Coast University, Ft. Myers
Florida International University, Miami
Florida State University, Tallahassee
New College of Florida, Sarasota
University of Central Florida, Orlando
University of Florida, Gainesville
University of North Florida, Jacksonville
University of South Florida, Tampa
University of West Florida, Pensacola

Also by Ignacio López-Calvo, from the University Press of Florida:

"God and Trujillo": Literary and Cultural Representations of the Dominican Dictator (2005)

Imaging the Chinese in Cuban Literature and Culture

Ignacio López-Calvo

University Press of Florida
Gainesville/Tallahassee/Tampa/Boca Raton
Pensacola/Orlando/Miami/Jacksonville/Ft. Myers/Sarasota

Copyright 2008 by Ignacio López-Calvo
Printed in the United States of America on acid-free paper
All rights reserved
First cloth printing, 2008
First paperback printing, 2009

Library of Congress Cataloging-in-Publication Data
López-Calvo, Ignacio
Imaging the Chinese in Cuban literature and culture/Ignacio Lopez-Calvo.
p. cm.
Includes bibliographical references and index.
ISBN 978-0-8130-3240-5 (cloth, alk. paper); 978-0-8130-3445-4 (pbk.)
1. Cuban literature—History and criticism. 2. Cuban literature—Chinese influences. 3. Cuba—Civilization—Chinese influences. I. Title.
PQ7372.L67 2008
860.9'35299519—dc22   2008001589

The University Press of Florida is the scholarly publishing agency for the State University System of Florida, comprising Florida A&M University, Florida Atlantic University, Florida Gulf Coast University, Florida International University, Florida State University, New College of Florida, University of Central Florida, University of Florida, University of North Florida, University of South Florida, and University of West Florida.

University Press of Florida.
15 Northwest 15th Street
Gainesville, FL 32611–2079
http://www.upf.com

To Yuli Chung, my dear friend, who opened my eyes to the world of the Chinese in Cuba.

Contents

Foreword by Evelyn Hu-DeHart ix
Acknowledgments xiii
A Note on the Translation xv
1. Introduction 1

Part 1. A Hostile Path to Hybridity

2. Chinese Bondage 29
3. Cuban Sinophobia 46

Part 2. Strategies for Entering and Leaving Chineseness

4. Orientalism 61
5. Chinese Women as Exotica 72
6. Self-Orientalization 80

Part 3. Cross-Cultural Heterogeneity and Hybridization

7. Religious Syncretism 93
8. Painful Transculturations 106

Part 4. Beyond Identity: Ongoing Identitarian Sedimentations

9. Self-Definition and the *Chinos Mambises* 119
10. Exclusion and (Mis)representation 134
11. Conclusion 145

Epilogue 155
Notes 165
Bibliography 209
Chronological List of Works 221
Index 223

Foreword

For most of history, Asians in Latin America and Asian–Latin American relations have not been topics of much serious discussion or scholarly attention in the U.S. academy, marginalized at best, with some infrequent token recognition. Yet, let us not forget Christopher Columbus's project that changed world history was all about finding a new route to link Asia to the known Western world, for the primary purpose of trade and commercial exchange. Although Columbus died clinging to a broken dream, his voyages did launch a period of feverish Spanish imperial expansion to Las Américas and across the Pacific to Las Filipinas. In fact, Spaniards established one of the modern world's first, biggest, and most enduring global trading systems, the Manila Galleon trade between the two antipodes of its far-flung empire: Acapulco on the Pacific side of Nueva España (Mexico) and Manila on the other side of this vast ocean.

For 250 years (1565–1815) every year without fail, at least one galleon fought off monsoon storms and pirates to sail round-trip between these two port cities, their trade made possible by the established community of largely Chinese (Fujianese and some Cantonese) and other Asian merchants, shopkeepers, and artisans in Manila. American silver poured into China for centuries, underwriting the Chinese economy through the nineteenth century, while Spanish American cities and their middle- and upper-class residents wore Chinese silk and used exquisitely crafted Chinese lacquer, porcelain, furniture, and decorative arts in their homes and daily lives. For the Europeans who ventured east and laid eyes on the Manila market, it was a sight to behold. Jesuit Father Colín was duly awed by what he saw:

> Manila is the equal of any other emporium of our monarchy, for it is the center to which flow the riches of the Orient and the Occident, the silver of Peru and New Spain; the pearls and precious stones of India; the diamonds of Narsinga and Goa; the rubies, sapphires and topazes, and the cinnamon of Ceylon; the pepper of Sumatra and the Javas, the cloves, nutmeg and other spices of the Mollucas and Banda; the fine Persian silks and wool and carpets from Ormuz and Malabar; rich hangings and coverings of Bengal [India]; fine camphor of Borneo; balsam and ivory of Abada and Cambodia . . . and from Great China, silks of all kinds, raw and woven in velvets and figured damasks, taffetas and other cloths of every texture, design and colors, linens and

cotton fabrics, gilt-decorated articles, embroideries and porcelains, and other riches and curiosities of great value and esteem; and from Japan, amber, varicolored silks, writing desks, boxes and tables of precious woods, lacquered and with curious decorations and very fine silverware. (Schurz 50)

In addition to this impressive array of trade goods, inevitably, people were exchanged as well. Of the Asians who went to America, their numbers were not large, but they were quite diverse in their makeup: servants, merchants, artisans, travelers, immigrants, and expatriates were noted in the historical records. We know that Chinese barbers in Mexico City in the early seventeenth century aroused the ire of Spanish barbers who, loathe to compete with the Chinese for business, petitioned the viceroy to banish the latter to the outskirts of the city. During this same period, Christian Japanese immigrant Luis de Encío, his son-in-law Juan de Páez, and a few other Japanese immigrants settled in Guadalajara, married local women, built successful businesses, and established intimate relationships with bishops and other city notables. Then there is the extraordinary story of Mirrha, a young girl captured somewhere in the Mughal empire (India), sold in the Manila slave market, and brought to Puebla, Mexico, around 1625. Baptized as Catarina de San Juan, this "Chinese foreigner," as she referred to herself, refused to consummate her marriage to a fellow slave from Asia, instead devoting herself entirely to a life of penitence, fasting, prayers, and divine visions; ministering to the poor and humble masses; making prophesies; and performing miracles that made her famous and revered in her own lifetime, the origin of *la china poblana* (Hu-DeHart; "Transpacific").

What we know about this early history of contact and exchange between Asia and Latin America and their peoples is incomplete and episodic, at least on the American side. Aside from the previously noted complaints lodged by Spanish barbers against their Chinese competitors, relationships appear to have been relatively harmonious, as exemplified by the Japanese in Guadalajara. On the Filipina side, however, the story was considerably more violent, driven by the ambivalence Spaniards felt towards the Chinese community, on whom they depended for food and other necessities of daily living as well as for building the galleons and supplying merchandise for the trans-Pacific voyages. Governor Niño de Tavares admitted in 1628 that "there is no Spaniard, secular or religious, who obtains his food, clothing, or shoes, except through [the Chinese]" (Dubs and Smith 389). At times as large as twenty thousand, the Chinese population in Manila (called *sangley*, a curious word that could be derived either from the Chinese word for "merchant" or from the expression meaning "come and go frequently") overwhelmed the handful of Spanish colonial officials, military officers, and trading company factotums. Out of fear and necessity, Spaniards tolerated the Chinese but tried to keep them under strict control, a favorite mechanism being periodic expulsions from Manila. Living with instability and under great stress, Chinese merchants and artisans traveled back and forth between home in South China and Manila, where they were confined to the special quarter called the Parián and burdened with excessive taxes, anticipating the next expulsion decree. Indeed, under these circumstances, Spaniards and Chinese were both sojourners with transnational lives and identities. Manila was truly home for neither, but both Spaniards and Chinese were kept there by the profits of the lucrative trans-Pacific trade, where many fortunes were made and an immense amount of wealth transferred across the Pacific in both directions.

Spanish relations with Chinese in Manila were a better forecaster of relationships to come in the nineteenth century than what had transpired in colonial New Spain or Peru, the core of the Spanish Empire. After the successful movements for independence in the early nineteenth century, Spain lost most of her overseas empire, but managed to hold on to sugar-producing Cuba, her jewel in the Caribbean, and Las Filipinas. No doubt their familiarity with Chinese laborers in Manila—their discipline, hard work, durability, experience, and ingenuity, and the seemingly bottomless pit of human reserves in a crowded south China—encouraged Spaniards to look to South China for good, cheap labor to supplement a rapidly dwindling African slave labor force on her flourishing Cuban sugar plantations. Thus began a sordid chapter in the history of Asia and Latin America.

Between 1847 and 1874, Cuban planters imported about 125,000 laborers, commonly known as *culíes* (following the British example of naming their East Indian contract laborers "coolies") under eight-year contracts. In his exemplary study, Ignacio López-Calvo examines this history through the lens of Cuban and Cuban American literature of the nineteenth and twentieth centuries and into the twenty-first. In so doing, he is bringing light to a history that has been overshadowed in Caribbean and Latin American studies. During the past quarter century, a handful of serious studies have been published on the topic, but few in English. For too long hidden in plain view, the Chinese in Latin America are finally brought in from the cold, enjoying daylight after all those overcast years. López-Calvo is helping to uncover and recover a story that others are also revealing; indeed, this book is among a rash of books on the Chinese in Cuba and in Latin America that have already been published, or soon will be, by scholars trained in a variety of disciplines—literature, history, anthropology, and sociology. Through the timely publication of his path-breaking work, López-Calvo is joining an academic movement in the United States to expand coverage of the Chinese diaspora to Spanish America.

Ironically, as this book makes clear, Cubans have always recognized the Chinese in their midst and in their history; otherwise, López-Calvo would never have identified so many rich sources in Cuban letters. As Suzanne Jill-Levine states in the "tranlator's Note" to Severo Sarduy's *From Cuba with a Song*: "Three cultures, at least, have been superimposed to constitute the Cuban—Spanish, African, and Chinese" (Sarduy. *From Cuba*). Or as Nicolás Guillén notes about the poetics of Regino Pedroso, who also claimed Chinese ancestry: "Here, one can see it flow like a wide and slow river whose waters pass through Asia and Africa before arriving in Cuba" (7). Or as Cuban American writer Cristina García explains when queried about why she chose to write a multigenerational saga about Chinese in Cuba in her latest novel, *Monkey Hunting*: the Cubans take Chinese Cubans "for granted" as a "huge part of the island that most people are not even aware of outside of Cuba" ("The Nature" n.p.). It is worth noting that Ignacio López-Calvo, a literary scholar, took his cue from Cuban and Cuban American writers, a legion of novelists, *cuentistas*, poets, and essayists, who, as it turns out, have duly recognized the Chinese in Cuban society, identity, and culture.

Evelyn Hu-DeHart
Professor of History and Ethnic Studies
Brown University

Acknowledgments

I want to express my deep gratitude to my friends Robert Rudder, José I. Suárez, and Mark Anderson for their careful proofreading of the manuscript and their invaluable suggestions. I also wish to thank Yuli Chung, one of the inspirations for this book and a person I will always keep very close to my heart. Likewise, I am very grateful to my research assistants, Mary Barnard and Sally Perret, who were also part of the proofreading process, and to all my colleagues, students, and friends who provided information, inspiration, and suggestions for this book, including Inés Anido, Gene Bell-Villada, Robert Bradley, Roberto Cantú, Jorge Luis Castillo, Juan de Castro, Kenya C. Dworkin, Chester Hu, Evelyn Hu-DeHart, Amado Lay, Tonya López-Craig, Teresa Marrero, Gabriela Miranda, Francisco Morán, Salvador Morán, José Neftalí Recinos, and Miriam Wenchang Lay. I am also grateful to Amy Gorelick, acquisitions editor at the University Press of Florida, Jacqueline Kinghorn Brown, project editor, and to the anonymous readers of my manuscript. I also wish to thank my wife, Tonya López-Craig, for all her love and support during the writing of this book, and to apologize to my baby daughter, Sofía, for the hours this book took away from my playing with her.

I would like to acknowledge the financial support provided by the University of North Texas to conduct research in Cuba and to attend two conferences in China. My participation in one of these conferences was also partially funded by the Chiang Ching-Kuo Foundation for International Scholarly Exchange. During my stay in Cuba, I was generously helped by Jorge Chao Chiu, María del Carmen Wong, and especially by María Luisa Chong Silva, without whose help I would not have had access to the Chinese societies and the Chung Wah Casino. I also want to thank Carlos Alay, Cristina Apón Peña, Luis Chao, Rolando Chion, Guillermo Chiu, Leandro Chiu, Alejandro Chiu Wong, León Choy, María del Carmen Li, Yrmina Eng Menéndez, José Fong Broomfield, Graciela Lau Quan, Ofede Lau Si, Eugenio Lee Wong, and Mirta J. Sam Echavarría.

A Note on the Translation

In all cases where no English-language edition of the text appears in the bibliography and there are no page numbers after the quotation in the text, the translation is mine. The original Spanish and the page number of the quotation appear in an endnote. Otherwise, quotations come from English-language sources. In a few cases, however, I felt compelled to provide amendments (which I enclosed in square brackets or explained in endnotes) for some passages that seemed either unidiomatic or wrongly interpreted. In cases where I consulted both the English and Spanish versions, the page number of the English edition appears after the quotation in the text and the page number of the corresponding passage in the Spanish edition appears in the note.

1
Introduction

> Understanding others is knowledge. . . .
> To die but not be forgotten is longevity.
>
> Lao-tzu

> "China" can no longer be limited to the more or less fixed area of its official spatial and cultural boundaries nor can it be held up as providing the authentic, authoritative, and uncontested standard for all things Chinese.
>
> Ien Ang

For the last several decades, academic circles in the humanities have been questioning the construction of binary oppositions when dealing with issues of gender, sexuality, race, ethnicity, class, or religion. This relatively new approach has brought a whole new spectrum into literary and cultural studies. Likewise, in the shadow of the so-called New World Order, another crucial line of research has led literary and cultural studies to problematize the old paradigm that contrasted "the Orient" versus "the West."[1] This paradigm of binary oppositions and dichotomies between Eastern and Western worldviews at the end of the Cold War in the late 1980s positions the People's Republic of China (PRC) in the minds of the U.S. political elite as the next military and economic superpower competing with the newfound undisputed supremacy of the United States. Thus, the great shadow of the recently awakened "sleeping giant" casts fear and resentment in the Western collective subconscious, particularly in the United States. As Chinese President Hu Jintao (1942–; president 2003–present) continues the campaign to build new commercial ties and to extend his country's influence in Latin America, so grows the resentment in the so-called First World. In fact, in 2005 the Pentagon considered the PRC for the first time a threat to U.S. interests in Asia. Secretary of State Condoleezza Rice (1954–) not only defined China as "a problem for the international economy," but also demanded changes to its economic policies.

Of course, today's network of geopolitical and hegemonic dynamics between East and West is preceded by a long history of interaction in every imaginable field (commercial, military, religious, artistic, political, human), which goes back many centuries. As early as 100 BCE, during the reign of Emperor Wu Ti (156–87 BCE; Chinese emperor 140–87 BCE) of the Han Dynasty (206BCE–220CE), the Chinese territorial conquests in central Asia allowed them to open the Silk Road that linked the Middle Kingdom (*Chung-kuo* in Mandarin) with the Roman Empire. Since then, China has informed the imaginations of Westerners, particularly after travelers like Marco Polo (1254–1324) and, before him, in 1253, the Franciscan friar William of Rubruck visited the Kublai Khan's territories and wrote about their observations.[2]

As surprising as it may seem to some readers, the island nation of Cuba is a crucial landmark in the history of Chinese interaction with the West. Its capital city, Havana, once boasted one of the first Chinatowns in Latin America and one of the most populous ones in the Americas, perhaps rivaled only by the one in San Francisco.[3] It was there that several interethnic societal experiments that would later be replicated in other nations in the Americas were put to the test. Therefore, the debates about "Chinatown" as a Western invention and as a frail simulacrum of the native land should start with Havana as a point of departure. Both the mistrust and the affinity that the Chinese generated within Cuban society resonate in the cultural production by Cubans and about Cuba since the last decades of the nineteenth century. As could be expected, the stereotypes about the Chinese and their Chinatowns (both hostile and positive) that abounded in the United States coincide, for the most part, with those that originated in Cuba. In most Latin American and Caribbean countries, including Cuba, however, racial classifications still seem to be more flexible than the ones that predominate in the United States.

The literary and cultural representation of the Chinese in Cuba is inseparable from the interpretation of racism before and after the Cuban Revolution (1956–1959).[4] Phenotype and heritage are not the only factors in this regard. Lok C. D. Siu has addressed these differences:

> While the term "Asian American" represents a panethnic collective identity encompassing all the different ethnic groups from Asia in the United States (Espíritu 1992), it is not well known, much less used, elsewhere in the Americas. The term derived from the history of the 1960s grassroots Asian American movement, and because no similar social movement took place elsewhere in the Americas, ethnicity remains the most salient form of self-identification (besides national identity) among Asians in Latin America. Nevertheless, the tendency

for panethnic racialization by the dominant society still exists. In many Latin American countries, with the exception of Brazil, the terms *chino* and *china* are often used broadly by non-Asians to refer to all people with an East Asian phenotype. (202)

In any case, the malleable conceptualization of race has not stopped the historic discrimination suffered by different ethnic groups.[5] Thus, it seems evident that, regardless of the improvements brought about by the revolution, the problem of racism is still very much present in Cuba.

Much has been written on the topic of race relations in Cuba. Among the scholars broaching the subject, we find anthropologists Rodrigo Espina Prieto and Pablo Rodríguez Ruiz, who, in an essay recently published in Cuba, state,

> Racial inequalities persist in Cuba, and they have become more visible mainly after the economic crisis of the 1990s. They are the result of the functionalization of the forms of racism that have remained hidden in the subjectivity of many people.... Concerning racial representations, a negative evaluation of blacks and a positive one of whites predominates, which configures one of the fundamental barriers that limit the mobility of blacks toward the more advantaged sectors.[6]

Henley C. Adams has also addressed black Cubans' limited access to the island's most important governing institutions:

> The under-representation of nonwhites among Cuba's leadership can be understood only by recognizing the crucial effect of the rates at which nonwhites are retained and replaced during periods of elite turnover. Because few blacks are members of the Politburo or Council of Ministers, and also have a proportionately greater presence among the Central Committee and Council of State's lesser categories, nonwhites tended to be disadvantaged during membership rotations. (181)

The Cuban exile Carlos Moore, in his book *Castro, the Blacks, and Africa* (1988), is much more critical of the Cuban Revolution. He argues that not only is racism against blacks still prevalent and even fostered, but also that Fidel Castro himself is racist and that the race card has been used by the Cuban government to accomplish its own political objectives. His analysis, however, has been widely refuted by Lisa Brock and Otis Cunningham, Pedro Pérez Sarduy, and other critics, who accuse him, among other things, of not providing enough evidence to support his claims. Along these lines, in a collection of fourteen interviews titled *Afro-Cuban Voices: On Race and*

Identity in Contemporary Cuba (2000) editors Pedro Pérez Sarduy and Jean Stubbs address the issue of racial discrimination against nonwhites in today's Cuba, the changes brought about by the revolution, and the progressive erosion of those changes. Previously, in an essay entitled "What Do Blacks Have in Cuba?" (1995), Pedro Pérez Sarduy had warned about the resurgence of racism:

> Compared with most countries of the world, the state of race relations in Cuba is by no means alarming, but postponing attention might allow them to worsen considerably and risk possible repeat occurrences of 1994. Then, in the sweltering summer heat, in the waterfront neighborhood of Central Havana, there was what the international media described as "the biggest antigovernment protest" in Cuba's 35 years of revolutionary regime. It followed a string of hijackings of government boats by Cubans trying to flee to the United States. Crowd frustration was vented primarily on shops selling dollar-priced goods in an underclass area heavily populated by families of all races, but predominantly black. It was a warning signal. (n.p.)[7]

Most academic works, therefore, coincide in pointing out that, although the revolution eliminated official discrimination and, overall, social conditions improved for blacks, there are still remnants from the times when white supremacy thrived in Cuba. In this context, this book explores several Cuban cultural and aesthetic practices dealing with the Chinese, with the wider goal of revealing the etiology of today's prejudice and cultural animosities between East and West.

In the 1830s, Chinese men began to migrate in massive waves as a result of several push and pull factors. Among the latter were the increasing need for cheap labor in different parts of the world and the shifting of power relations between China and influential Western nations. Domestic problems, however, were equally important factors. Overpopulation, natural catastrophes, and the dreadful economic conditions of the country made the prospect of migration attractive. Along with these factors, the political instability invited workers to dream about a better life elsewhere. Wars and rebellions plagued China during the nineteenth century: the Opium Wars with Great Britain (1839–1843, 1856–1860), the Taiping Rebellion (1850–1864), the Sino-Japanese War (1894–1895), and the Boxer Rebellion (1898–1900) against the imperial government of the last Chinese dynasty, the Manchu (also Qing; 1644–1912). It has been estimated that about one million southern Chinese had migrated by 1875. Most of them went to the European plantations in Southeast Asia; British colonies such as the British Antilles (Trinidad and

Tobago, Jamaica, Barbados); Australia; Hawaii; or different regions of the Americas, including British Columbia, California, Guyana, Suriname, Peru, Cuba, Panama, Mexico, and Brazil.[8]

The so-called coolie trade (also known at the time as the "Yellow Trade") is intimately related to the Atlantic slave trade, which was banned by the British Parliament in 1807.[9] Eight years later, at the Congress of Vienna, Great Britain pressured Spain, Portugal, France, and the Netherlands to sign an agreement that prohibited the slave trade. However, Spain and Portugal were allowed two more years of slaving, since, as Bernard H. Nelson points out, "Spain felt that closing the Spanish slave trade would inconvenience her American colonies. Unlike England, she would not have twenty years to supply her colonies with slaves before cessation. Spanish statesmen felt that Spain would be 'signing away what constituted the very existence of her colonies'" (196). This resistance, Nelson points out, also had to do with the skepticism of European maritime powers about British motivations for these philanthropic laws.

On September 23, 1817, Great Britain and Spain signed the Treaty of Madrid abolishing the Atlantic slave trade, under which Spain agreed to end the slave trade north of the equator immediately and south of the equator on May 20, 1820. It continued to grow, however, due to the expanding plantation economy of Cuba and the legal limitations on British ships arresting foreign vessels suspected of slaving. In this sense, Duvon Clough Corbitt points out that the treaty was ineffective during its early years:

> Its enforcement was in the hands of both countries, but Spain soon began to regret having signed the Treaty and left its execution to Britain. Spanish officers in Cuba, to please the planters and to increase their left-handed incomes, connived at slave smuggling to such an extent as to exasperate the English officers. In 1835, Britain obtained a second Treaty designed to put teeth into the enforcement of the first. (2)

Indeed, the renewal of the anti–slave-trade agreement between Great Britain and Spain on June 28, 1835, tightened the surveillance of ships on the high seas. British vessels were authorized to arrest suspected Spanish slavers and to bring them before mixed courts in Havana and Sierra Leone. Although this new treaty made the continuation of the human trade more difficult, it did not eradicate it. Therefore, the Chinese coolies, in many cases, had to work side by side with African slave labor, labor conditions that coolies considered extremely humiliating. As Hu-DeHart puts it, "the Chinese were imported while African slavery was still in effect though undergoing 'gradual abolition,' and worked alongside this traditional form of plantation labor" ("Opium" 170). The situation changed after the arrival of Captain General Juan de la Pezuela in Havana in December 1853, however. As David Sartorius explains, he "imposed stricter penalties for individuals attempting to import slaves, authorized the search of properties that might be using the labor of illegally purchased slaves, and demanded better record-keeping of slave workforces in order to differentiate *bozales*, or African-born slaves, from *criollos*, or island-born slaves" (n.p.). In 1880, the Spanish *Cortes* (the national legislative assembly) passed a new abolition law called the Ley de Patronato that included a transition period of eight years:

> The slaves became *patrocinados* (the slaves that were promised freedom eventually, but still had to remain under a system of supervision by their masters), but their labor was still controlled by their masters. This change in terminology can be viewed as semantic freedom, but without the reality of emancipation. (Galván 226)

In the end, Spain ended this process two years early and declared slavery officially ended on October 7, 1886. As Hu-DeHart explains, the goal of the importation of coolies was to find a substitute for the vanishing black slave labor:

> It can be seen from these figures that as the African slave trade wound down, ending with the last shipments in 1865 and 1866 of just 145 and 1,443 slaves, the size of the coolie imports rose correspondingly, reaching the high marks of 12,391 and 14,263 in 1866 and 1867. From 1865 to the end of the coolie trade in 1874, 64,500 coolies, or over 50% of the total volume, entered Cuba.
>
> During this period, sugar production climbed steadily, reaching a high of 768,672 metric tons in 1874. Clearly then, coolies constituted the source of labor replenishment, delaying the crisis that would have set in with the end of the slave trade, and making it possible for the plantation economy to continue to prosper. ("Race" 83)

Cuba was the last colony in the Americas to abolish slavery; Brazil, which became an independent nation in 1822, abolished it in 1888.

Concerned by British pressure and the failure of official programs to attract free, white immigration from Spain (white immigrants refused to work side by side with African slaves), Cuban planters made new plans for the importation of Chinese labor. Despite initial complaints by several planters about the Chinese laborers' laxity in their work; lack of discipline; and disposition to quarrel among themselves, run away, and kill the overseers, Urbano Feijoo de Sotomayor, one of the Cuban planters, justified importing more Chinese in a typically Orientalist way: "We need men to work side by side with the slaves, and for this only the sons of a country governed with the rod will serve" (qtd. Corbitt 10).

This mentality connects with a long tradition of European thought in which Asians are seen as servile, lazy, and natural-born slaves due to the climate of their land. Thus, the Greek physician Hippocrates (460?–377? BCE), in his study *On Airs, Waters, and Places* (400s BCE), maintained "the principal reason the Asiatics are more unwarlike and of gentler disposition than the Europeans is the nature of the seasons, which do not undergo any great changes either to heat or cold [. . .] For these reasons, [. . .] men are not their own masters nor independent, but are the slaves of others" (Adler 31–32).

The same type of environmental determinism resurfaces in the works of French philosopher Charles de Montesquieu (1689–1755). In the seventeenth book of his discourse on government, *The Spirit of Laws* (1748), titled "How the Laws of Political Servitude Bear a Relation to the Nature of the Climate," he states: "Power in Asia ought, then, to be always despotic; for if their slavery was not severe they would soon make a division inconsistent with the nature of the country" (124).

Cuban planters and officers frequently made various other assumptions about the Chinese. For instance, in the 1852 stipulations governing the importation of new Chinese laborers, more humane measures were planned, requiring ships to "carry two pounds of rice per day for each coolie for a voyage of 160 days' duration" (Corbitt 16). Apparently, as one of the characters in Cristina García's *Monkey Hunting* (2003) laments, they were not well informed about the Chinese diet: "Devil ships. On one journey, there was nothing to eat on board except rice. They thought we ate only rice!" (62).[10]

Interestingly, the importation of Chinese labor "was considered officially as White colonization" (Corbitt 5). Yet once the Chinese arrived in the Spanish colony of Cuba, they met with a deep-seated culture of slave labor that would not be easily changed. At a time when more than half of the population of the island was black (including free blacks), Chinese migrant workers were not easily accepted into the privileged sectors of society. As previously stated, the timing and purpose of the coolies' arrival, that is, as preparation for the inevitable abolition of the infamous Middle Passage, probably contributed to the perception of these workers as the new slaves. Although Chinese were often considered white colonists in legal terms, the planters and most of the population saw them not as wage laborers but as the continuation of the slave trade (this time from another distant, strange race). Contrary to the official discourse, their recruitment did not really respond to an attempt to transform the plantation-based economic structures, but rather to the Creoles' efforts to safeguard a capitalist economy that had made Cuba the world's leading producer of sugar since the second decade of the nineteenth century.

In the introduction to the fascinating testimonial *The Cuba Commission Report: A Hidden History of the Chinese in Cuba* (1877), Denise Helly acutely interprets Chinese emigration to Cuba within the context of British imperialism: "Great Britain desired not only to destroy the slave-based system of sugar production in order to dominate the world sugar market but also to seize Cuba from Spain" (6). These attempts at sabotage, along with competition from the new large-scale production of sugar in other regions, became a serious threat to the Cuban economy. In these circumstances, and fearing new slave rebellions that could bring about another black republic like the one in neighboring Saint-Domingue (today's Haiti), Julián Zulueta's suggestion in 1845 of using purportedly docile labor from the overpopulated southern Chinese provinces of Guangdong and Fujian was seen as a lesser evil than black slavery. Over time, the use of Chinese labor, along with the mechanization of sugar factories, would become increasingly lucrative investments.

As the leading sugar-producing country in the world, Cuba was in a unique position to attract new labor. While some of these newcomers traveled of their own will, others were slaves or contract workers. The importation of coolies placated, to a certain degree, the anxiety caused by the treaties calling for the gradual abolition of the Atlantic slave trade that Spain and Great Britain had been signing since 1817.[11] At the same time, it led to the founding of the oldest Chinese community in the Western Hemisphere. Although the figures vary significantly depending on the historian, most agree that, counting illegal immigration, approximately 150,000 immigrants from China had been taken to the Spanish colony by the time the coolie trade effectively ended in 1874 (and officially in November 1877). The end of this human trade was brought about by the investigation carried out by Chinese imperial commissioner Ch'en Lan Pin into the enforced recontracting and inhumane living conditions of indentured workers.[12] Surprisingly, in spite of the significance of the Chinese presence for Cuban national identity and cultural memory, the number of historical studies on the Chinese colony (i.e., community) in Cuba is limited.[13]

As to the first stages of this massive migration, Evelyn Hu-DeHart has found that there were "318 [Chinese coolies] recruited from Saigon and 304 from Manila in 1860" ("Chinese Coolies" n.p.). Antonieta César has also noted that, according to oral tradition, by 1830 some Chinese men had already arrived in Cuba from the Philippines, "where a great number of Cantonese people had been residing for many generations. They spoke Spanish, were familiar with Spanish customs, and worked as domestic servants, farmers, or florists."[14] However, the first official record of the importation of Chinese labor from mainland China dates from seventeen years later. On June 3, 1847, 207 contract workers from Amoy (today Xiamen), the survivors of the 300 that had been brought aboard the Spanish brigantine *Almirante Oquendo* arrived after a 131–day voyage at the Port of Regla on Havana Bay.[15] There, they were consigned to the Real Junta de Fomento (Royal Board of Public Works and Economy), the association of Cuban planters. Ten days later, 365 additional coolies, also from Amoy, disembarked from the English ship *Duke of Argyle*.

The trafficking of Chinese workers from 1847 to 1874 was an international enterprise carried out by ships (many of which had previously been used to transport black African slaves), companies, and crew members from various countries.[16] In this light, Evelyn Hu-DeHart has stated that this lucrative business "constituted a prime example of nineteenth century globalization or global capitalism" ("Chinese Coolies" n.p.). The ships, clippers, and steamboats that brought these *colonos contratados*, or hired colonists, underwent a long and perilous voyage, which was, obviously, much longer than that of the slave ships coming from Africa; it took roughly 120 days to travel the approximately 13,000 nautical miles. The length of the journey, together with the crew's cruelty, frequent mutinies, and suicides, accounted for the high mortality rate: approximately one-fifth of the men recruited died before arriving at their destination. Despite these difficulties, ships with young, single men from southern China would continue to arrive in Havana until 1874. As Jesús Guanche Pérez points out, "most of the Chinese population (more than 80 percent) settled in the western provinces, mainly in Havana and Matanzas."[17] These provinces, along with Villa Clara and Oriente, had the most robust sugar industries on the island. Later, however, the Chinese spread out to other provinces, moving mainly to the cities. The majority of these men were hired or, more accurately, deceived[18] or kidnapped in the southeastern agricultural provinces of Fujian and Guangdong, in the Pearl River Delta, where the city of Canton (today Guangzhou) is located.[19]

As happened with the Leyes de Indias (Laws of the Indies) during the Spanish conquest of the Americas, the documents and treaties signed by the Spanish government (many of them ostensibly benevolent) regarding the treatment of Chinese workers became dead letter when it came to their application in the colony. This is clearly reflected in *The Cuba Commission*

Report: "Thus the Spanish Government distinctly limited the penal powers conferred on employers, and never intended to sanction the arbitrary infliction of chastisements and fines. The action of the Cuban proprietors has been however totally at variance with the course thus prescribed" (59). Along the same lines, Corbitt mentions the royal order of July 3, 1847, by which the captain general Leopoldo O'Donnell was asked "to take particular pains to see that from the moment of their arrival in the country, they were distinguished with all attention and consideration that good treatment, religion and humanity demand and that their contracts were fulfilled to the letter" (5). The captain general was also instructed to have prosecuting attorneys defend the interests of the coolies, to avoid mixing them with black slaves, and to recruit a "proportionate number of females of the proper age and hardihood to promote marriages within the same class" (Corbitt 5). These orders had no effective means of enforcement and were seldom respected by Cuban planters.

Therefore, thousands of Chinese contract workers trusted the promises of unscrupulous countrymen (known as *contratistas* or *enganchadores*) that great riches would be obtained in the lands of the Spanish Empire. Their signature committed them to twelve hours a day of labor in the sugarcane fields (or even more hours of domestic work), for eight consecutive years.[20] In addition to their salary, they were to receive food and two sets of clothing per year. Although nominally the Chinese coolies (who followed in the steps of many Filipinos and Mayans from the Yucatan Peninsula, and even some Apaches from New Mexico) were contract laborers who went to Cuba voluntarily, the harsh working conditions and the barracks they shared with African slaves turned them into de facto slaves.[21] This is quite evident in the valuable eyewitness account provided by the North American lawyer and writer Richard Henry Dana (1815–1882). His particular choice of vocabulary leaves little doubt about their humiliating circumstances. Dana describes, for instance, "the coolie jail, or market, where the imported coolies are kept for sale," the "heartless-looking" dealer, and the driver armed with a whip ("The Trade" 79). Some of them look unhappy, Dana explains, while others are stolid. One of the indentured workers, he tells us, suffered from leprosy, even though the dealer would not admit it. Since the coolie trade in Cuba was not regulated (unlike in the British possessions), Dana wonders whether they would be able to go back to China or be permitted to remain in Cuba. After his conversations with locals, he wisely assumes that "they will be brought in debt, and bound over again for their debts, or in some other way secured to a lifelong servitude" (81). Dana's interpretation of the scenes he witnessed provides powerful insight into the beginnings of the Chinese presence in Cuba: "a strange and striking exhibition of power. Two or three white men, bringing hundreds of Chinese thousands of miles, to a new climate and people, holding them as prisoners, selling their services to masters having an unknown tongue and an unknown religion, to work at unknown trades, for inscrutable purposes!" (79).

Although most of the indentured workers had initially planned to be sojourners in a faraway foreign land (those who knew where they were going, of course), they eventually saw their transitory presence become permanent. For some time, they fell into the category of social pariahs, an underclass isolated from the rest of the Cuban collectivity by both externally and self-imposed rules. Although they were supposed to serve only an eight-year term, most were forced to sign new contracts with the same planters; those who refused to do so were either imprisoned or sent to work without pay at a depot alongside criminals.[22] This type of enforced recontracting became a sort of legal neo-slavery that entrapped most of the coolies. The fraudulent system prevented them from saving the necessary money for their return to China. The colonists themselves provided personal testimonies of this outrageous treatment. Of course, critics must always be cautious about the veracity of first-person, autobiographical, and testimonial narratives, especially when they respond to ulterior motives. Yet the strong coincidences in many of these depositions by different people make them quite credible. Thus, Wu A-fa and thirty-nine others reported, "After the eight years are completed they refuse us the identification cards and we are forced to remain slaves in perpetuity" (*Cuba Commission Report* 53). Even more pitiable, two elderly men begged the commission to procure them a mendicant's pass so that they could beg for food after seventeen years of hard labor. In fact, in section 27, several Chinese declare they had been begging for many years, having no alternative after becoming old or seriously injured.

It was at this heavy human cost that Cuba found a temporary solution to the upcoming abolition of the Atlantic slave trade. Although the workers had been promised a salary of four Spanish pesos, if paid at all, they were paid in Mexican pesos, a weaker currency. Moreover, they were often not paid the full amount that they had been promised. These wages destined them for semi-slavery or slavery. In many cases, they had no alternative but to rebel. While the first documented coolie revolt took place as early as 1847, there were previous plots to abolish slavery, such as the Aponte Conspiracy of 1812. José Antonio Aponte y Ubarra (?–1812), a free black who had been a first corporal in the Batallón de Milicias Disciplinadas de Pardos y Morenos (Battalion of Disciplined Militia of Mulattos and Blacks) and who belonged to the *cabildo* (council) of "Shango Tedum," organized a revolt that included slaves and free people of color.[23] The revolt began in Havana, but other enslaved and mixed-race people who suffered exploitation joined it in other Cuban locations. Aponte's goal was to abolish slavery and put an end to Spanish colonialism. In Eugène Godfried's words, "Aponte and his followers aspired to a rupture with the metropolis in order to create an independent society based on equality" (n.p.). On April 7, 1812, Aponte and other leaders of the revolt were hung. This rebellion is particularly significant because, as Lena Delgado de Torres points out, "the free colored class (a subaltern class with minimal privileges) and its 'intellectuals' (Gramsci 1971) led the fight for abolition, drawing in white abolitionists but relying primarily on Black participation" (41).

After this uprising, there were other slave rebellions. One of the most celebrated is the so-called Ladder Conspiracy (Conspiración de la Escalera; 1843–1844), in which the black Cuban poet Gabriel de la Concepción Valdés, known as "Plácido" (1809–1844), allegedly participated. As Robert Freeman Smith points out, there is a lot of controversy about whether this revolt, which allegedly also included slaves and free people of color, actually occurred:

> Vidal Morales and Francisco González del Valle have written that this conspiracy was a myth created by the Spanish to justify their harsh measures. On the other hand, Ramiro Guerra, Emeterio S. Santovenia, and the Spanish historian Mario Hernández y Sánchez-Barba support the view that the conspiracy did exist and that David Turnbull—the British Consul—was involved. José Manuel Ximeno has gone further and hailed the conspiracy as the first major example of a secessionist movement with implications all over Cuba. (58–59)

In spite of the common assertion that the Chinese participated in the Ladder Conspiracy, this is highly improbable, since it predates the arrival of the first Chinese coolies. Perhaps the confusion arises from the fact that, in colonial times, the word *chino* was used to designate the child of an Indian woman and a mulatto.[24] In any case, these revolts probably encouraged Cuban planters to find new sources of cheap labor.

Other coolies chose to flee the plantations rather than rebelling. In fact, a large percentage of the runaway slaves captured in the mid-nineteenth century were of Chinese origin. Others committed suicide. Despite the years of exploitation and opprobrium, however, many Chinese immigrants succeeded in outliving their contracts and survived by becoming street vendors. Some of them used their hard-earned savings from working in these humble occupations to open their own businesses in the cities. Thus, they founded the first Chinatowns.

Even after the coolie trade was terminated and the contracts of the last coolies had expired in 1883, ties with the sending communities in China continued to be strong. The fact that former coolies sent remittances and letters, and would occasionally make the voyage back to their homeland to marry or to make investments, prevented (or at least slowed) the uprooting process that would otherwise be expected. It also provided continuity to the history of the community and its unyielding resistance to oppressive forces, both national and international. Perhaps this ongoing contact with the homeland (and therefore with tradition and the past), which supports a collective cultural memory or lineage, is one of the main differences between the Chinese and the African slaveries in Cuba: the effects of forced uprootedness were undoubtedly more intense within the African community. Elaborate hometown and familial networks facilitated the continuation of migration patterns throughout the years. According to the map "Presencia china en Cuba" (Baltar Rodríguez et al.) there were 59,077 Chinese in Cuba by 1860, while, as Walton Look Lai reveals, only 34,334 were in the United States at the time (6).[25] It has also been calculated that in 1870, when Cuba's population was 1.4 million, there were more than 150,000 coolies there, compared to a similar number of Chinese (other sources say there were only 63,000) in the United States, which had a population of 38 million. In proportion to population, therefore, the Chinese diaspora in Cuba was the largest in the Western Hemisphere.

As occurred in other countries of the Americas, the Chinese in Cuba had to defend themselves against racial, social, and institutional exclusion and prejudice. "In the 1920s and 1930s," underscores Kathleen López, "a politically conservative, anti-immigrant nationalism developed in Cuba, reinforced by decades of North American– and European-dominated capitalist expansion" (117). In these circumstances, the foundation of *sociedades chinas*, or Chinese societies (social clubs or associations), for mutual aid and other purposes—which in many cases replicated those existing in China—contributed to an increased sense of security.[26]

Ironically, some overseas Chinese had seen Cuba as a haven where they could flee from widespread xenophobia and start a new life. Between 1860 and 1875, an estimated five thousand Chinese immigrants who had migrated to California following the gold rush or had been brought there to build railroads arrived in Cuba escaping the new outbreak of white nationalism and widespread racism in California. These newcomers to the United States opted for yet another migration, to Cuba, after 94 percent of the state's voters approved a referendum in 1880, the Chinese Exclusion Act, to bar Chinese laborers from entering the United States and to deny them naturalization. Although some of them had been living in Mexico, they came to be known in Cuba as the *chinos californianos*. Since many were wealthy, they were able to open businesses in Cuba, and these investments brought new life to the fledging *barrio chino* in Havana, which had begun to be built in the 1850s.

With time, however, the image of the Chinese in the national collective subconscious would improve dramatically, thanks to their contribution to the wars of independence (1868–1878 and 1895–1898). The existence of *chinos mambises* (Chinese rebels) opened the door for their integration into mainstream Cuban society. Yet they had to continue fighting spurts of anti-Chinese sentiment for years, particularly during the Great Depression of 1929. In contrast, the support that some of them provided to the revolution led by Fidel Castro and his July 26 Movement (1953–1959) would not much increase the acceptance of the remnants of the Chinese community in postrevolutionary Cuba. "The Chinese in Castro's Cuba," argues Andrew Wilson, "were in a particularly awkward position, given the tensions between Moscow (Havana's benefactor) and Beijing and the fact that petty entrepreneurship, which was the foundation of Havana's Chinese community, was anathema to the Communist regime" (xiii). Indeed, once the Cuban government began to lean toward the Soviet model of communism, the Chinese in Cuba became somewhat suspect and their activities were supervised. Considering language barriers and the secrecy of their societies, Castro's government probably felt compelled to monitor their alliances. As to the impact of the Cuban Revolution on the Chinese way of life, the Chinese Cuban Joaquín Li, in his testimony "Paper Son Meets Father," states, "The government took over the grocery stores in 1959. No more private business. Many Chinese, especially the young, left Cuba" (43). The Chinese ethnic, commercial, and "bourgeois" stance became an obstacle for Fidel Castro's nationalistic and homogenizing project, which was conceived along class lines.[27]

Moreover, the fact that the Cuban Revolution forbade the Chinese to send remittances to their families in China was unacceptable to many of them, as both Joaquín Li and Pedro, one of Frank Scherer's informants, explain in their testimonies ("Culture" 85). Scherer adds a further insight when he observes that their exodus had begun in the mid-1950s, during the violent regime of Fulgencio Batista (1901–1973; president of Cuba 1940–1944; dictator after staging a coup, 1952–1958) ("Culture" 82).[28]

At any rate, the unsatisfactory conditions that the new government imposed on the Sino-Cuban colony added, for many, another link to the long chain of migrations and virtually eliminated its presence in Cuba. While a few of the older members of the community stayed in Cuba and some migrated to Taiwan, Hong Kong, or the PRC or remigrated to other Caribbean and Latin American countries, the majority of them chose the United States (especially Miami and New York) and Canada (particularly Toronto) as their new homes.[29] Yet in *Our History Is Still Being Written* (*Nuestra historia aún se está escribiendo*; Choy, Chui, and Sío Wong 2005), general of the Revolutionary Armed Forces Moisés Sío Wong (1938–) introduces, both through his remarks and through his own biography, a new dimension to the history of the Chinese Cubans after 1959. He claims that most of them remained in Cuba and joined the revolution: "The wealthy Chinese merchants, as well as some of the smaller Chinese merchants, abandoned the country. The majority of the Chinese, however, joined the revolution" (70).

The last flow of Chinese immigrants arrived in Cuba in the late 1940s and 1950s, fleeing communism and poverty in China. As Antonieta César reports, the Chung Wah Casino carried out a census in 1980, establishing that there were only 4,300 Chinese on the island, most of them elderly people who were physically unable to migrate after the Castro takeover.[30] This number, of course, has become even smaller in recent years. "According to Casino Chung Wah President Alfonso Chao," reveals Kathleen López, "in 1998 there were about 430 remaining ethnic Chinese, with an average age of about 80, and about 3,200 descendents of Chinese" (222; endnote 119). In 2005, Choy, Chui, and Sío Wong provided even lower numbers: "There are only about 300 Chinese in Cuba who were born in China" (73). According to Cristina Apón Peña, a Chinese Cuban who runs the Havana Chinatown's social work program, as of December 8, 2005, there were only 143 natives of China registered in Havana. Interestingly, there are now more Chinese Cubans in the United States than in Cuba (Meyer 146). This gradual vanishing of the Chinese colony (community) in Cuba is nostalgically reflected in several works. In Zoé Valdés's *La eternidad del instante*, for example, the protagonist, Mo Ying/Maximiliano Megía, claims that he felt "very far from becoming a vegetable, as had happened to so many of his old countrymen, the ones that still lived."[31] Despite the diminishing number of Chinese Cubans, it is worth noting that in recent years there has been a revitalization of Havana's Chinatown. General Sío Wong, president of the Cuba-China Friendship Association, has explained how in 1993 he was approached by a group of Chinese descendents who requested his support for a restoration project that has two main objectives: "One is preserving the traditions, art, and culture of Chinese in Cuba. The other is to revitalize the Chinese barrio in Havana economically and commercially" (Choy, Chui, and Sío Wong 73).[32] From 1993 to 2005, the state-funded Havana Chinatown Promotional Group (Grupo Promotor del Barrio Chino), which for some time worked under the office of Eusebio Leal (the official historian of the city of Havana), was in charge of leading these changes. According to Frank F. Scherer, they were able to secure this support because of the Cuban government's interest in both tourism and improving relations with the PRC ("Sanfancón" 153). As a result of these efforts, continues Scherer, the Sino-Cuban community has been re-ethnicized through the practice of what he calls "strategic self-Orientalization": "The use of self-Orientalizing discourses (that is, Chinese-Cuban articulations of an essential and distinctive Chineseness, which allow for conceiving of 'difference' in ethnic and cultural terms) has (re)appeared in Cuba only very recently" ("Sanfancón" 161).[33] Although Eusebio Leal dissolved the Chinatown Promotional Group in December 2005, the official support provided by his office was part of a wider effort to restore all the historic sites of the capital city. It must be stated however that the original impetus to rebuild and revitalize Havana's Chinatown came not from the government but from the native Chinese and their descendents, who decided on their own to rescue a part of their history that was rapidly disappearing.

In any case, there is no doubt that, as Scherer points out, the Cuban government has recently tried to improve its political relations with the PRC. The recent history of the economic and political relations between communist China and Castro's Cuba is quite complicated. Cecil Johnson, in his study *Communist China and Latin America (1959–1967)*, posits that the main objective of the Chinese was to bring about different Latin American revolutions to undermine the power and influence of the United States in the region. To that end, during the mid-1960s they competed with Soviet revisionism to recruit Fidel Castro to their cause. In fact, Johnson claims that for some time Mao Zedong (1893–1976; head of state 1949–1959) saw Castro, despite their ideological differences, as a great model for other Latin American revolutionaries. Like Mao Zedong, Castro had a decidedly anti-imperialist stance against the United States. He had also used the path of armed struggle (guerrilla warfare) and had relied on the support of the peasantry. Although the Chinese government soon realized that it would be unable to compete with the military aid and economic support offered by the Soviet Union, it saw the Cuban Missile Crisis of 1962 as an opportunity to regain its influence in Cuba: "Castro felt that he had been betrayed and humiliated by the strongest socialist power in the bloc. Needless to say, the

Chinese intensified their efforts to expand their influence over Castro and thus enhance their standing in Latin American revolutionary circles" (Johnson 149). Part of this strategy was Mao Zedong's recognition of Castro's regime as socialist.

Johnson also underscores the fact that in Cuba Liu Ning-i, the head of the Sino-Cuban Association (established in 1962), "in an address to the newly created Association, referred to the 'leadership of *comrade* Fidel Castro' and also asserted that the Cuban people had established the first socialist country in Latin America and the Western Hemisphere" (152). This initial enthusiasm on the part of the Chinese government ended once Castro reconciled with the Soviets, who had recently increased their economic support to Cuba. Despite the Cubans' avowed intention to remain neutral in the Sino-Soviet conflict, two subsequent visits to the USSR by Fidel Castro made it clear that he felt closer either to Nikita Khrushchev's (1894–1971; premier 1958–1964) approach to socialism or to Soviet economic and military aid. Furthermore, Castro did not extend an invitation to the Chinese government to participate in the Havana Conference on Latin American Communist Parties, held in November 1964. All these events, in Cecil Johnson's view, "support the contention that Sino-Cuban relations deteriorated seriously in 1965, after reaching their high point in 1964" (164).

The rupture became even more serious when "on January 2, 1966, Fidel Castro made his first overt attack on the Chinese on the eve of the historic tricontinental Conference, a meeting attended by almost six hundred delegates representing eighty-two countries" (Johnson 164). The collapse of the Soviet Union in 1991 would however bring a new and constructive chapter in the bilateral relations between Cuba and the PRC, which has undoubtedly influenced the acceptance of Chinese subjectivity on the Caribbean island. Official visits between high-ranking politicians of the two countries have been frequent in recent years: Fidel Castro went to China in 1995 and 2003, and Raúl Castro, in 1997 and 2005; in turn, Jiang Zemin (1926–; president 1993–2003) visited Cuba in 1993 and 2001, and Hu Jintao, in 2004.

In fact, today the PRC is Cuba's second largest trading partner, behind Venezuela. Chinese-Cuban trade has recently soared to $1,800 million a year ("Castro se reúne" n.p.). Likewise, William Ratliff has stated that there is increasing bilateral cooperation in education, nickel mining, oil exploration, biotechnology, tourism, technological development, and transportation infrastructure. In this exchange, China benefits mostly "from obtaining intelligence on the U.S. through the Cuban government" ("Cuba and China" n.p.). On the political level, Ratliff continues, the cooperation has also increased due to the 'mirror' relationship of the Americans to Taiwan and the Chinese to Cuba: "The United States provides sophisticated military support for the island just off China's coast, while China, partly in response, gives similar but much more limited support to Cuba, a small, threatened island off the U.S. coast" ("Mirroring" n.p.).[34]

In any case, with or without the support of the PRC, the Chinese presence and heritage in Cuba challenge both the perceived binary opposition between black and white and the discourse of *mestizaje* as a nationalist project defended by Simón Bolívar, José Martí, José Vasconcelos, Roberto Fernández Retamar, and others. Of course, the same could be said about the heritages left by the Jewish Cuban community; the descendents of the native Cubans; and other ethnic groups on the island such as the Japanese, the Koreans, or the Arabs. In this sense, Rafael Rojas, discussing "Cuban difference," has argued that "what we call 'Cuban culture' is nothing but the symbolic construct, in the lapse of two centuries, of the meta-account of national identity. A meta-account that postulates a subject, the White, Masculine, Heterosexual, Catholic or Marxist Subject, whose historical values legitimate the discourses and the hegemonic practices of national elites" (105).[35]

Decades ago, the incorporation of African heritage as a key component of Cuban identity initiated by the poet Nicolás Guillén (1902–1989) and other Cuban intellectuals resulted in a revision of Eurocentric self-conceptions of the notion of *cubanía* or *cubanidad* (Cubanness). Yet in this process of reconsidering the false sameness of the national subject, historians and critics have studied the numerous contributions of the Chinese to Cuba's culture and identity over the last 150 years much less than those of Afro-Cubans. Even the native Siboneys and Tainos (or Caribs) of the island, whose numbers declined almost to the point of extinction during the first decades of the conquest due to disease and exploitation, have received more historical and literary attention than other representative communities in Cuba, such as the Chinese and the Jews.[36] The Cuban author Severo Sarduy, in an interview with Emir Rodríguez Monegal, has noticed this historic silence: "In Cuba, for many centuries, racial prejudice was openly exercised against blacks. But we didn't realize that, at the same time, there was another one, as serious as the first, against the Chinese. The Chinese have been very important in Cuba because, besides their influence on the cultural level, they are part of the Cuban worldview."[37]

From this perspective, in the introduction to the collection of essays *The Chinese in the Caribbean*, one of the few interdisciplinary studies on this topic, Andrew Wilson laments that "whereas Chinese migrations to Southeast Asia and North America receive significant attention, the experiences of

Chinese migrants in the Caribbean remain a poorly understood and largely unchronicled chapter in the region's history" (xv).

In the field of literary criticism the lacuna is perhaps greater, even though the Chinese community in Cuba has gained representation beyond Orientalist stereotypes through a compelling corpus of works. Fortunately, a few critics have recently begun to study the cultural production dealing with the presence of the *huaqiao* (overseas Chinese nationals) in Cuba.[38] The uninterrupted representation of the Chinese in different genres of popular and high culture attests to the fact that, for many years, Cuban society has accepted them as an integral part of the national identity. This has taken place despite nationalistic efforts by the official elite to silence and erase their ethnic mark and impose Creole (*criollo*) hegemony.[39] My study of the impact and heritage of this ethnic group is an attempt to partially fill the vacuum left by the historians' and literary critics' oversight.

The analysis of the (mis)representation and erasure of the Chinese presence in Cuban cultural production inevitably disrupts the official black-and-white discourse of the nation by underscoring alternative notions of ethnic difference. Moreover, though undoubtedly many of the Chinese workers who arrived in Cuba shared common motivations and traits, overall the works studied here challenge the temptation to homogenize them or to simplify their experience through historical reductionism. Instead, they explore, among other issues, the migrants' different reasons and motivations for leaving their native land (beyond abduction and deceit), the variety of places from which they came, and their different degrees of adaptation and assimilation in their adopted country.[40] They also examine their contact with the sending communities and the various levels of social agency they enjoyed once they arrived in Cuba. Inevitably, the literary and cultural representation of the Chinese also testifies to the subhuman conditions suffered by the indentured workers during their transportation and years of indentured servitude.

A conspicuous peculiarity of these works is that for the most part they were created by non-Chinese authors. Yet, even though most of these authors cannot trace their family lines back to China, their treatment of the topic suggests that they consider Chinese culture an intrinsic part of the Cuban identity. With the exception of the paintings by Wifredo Lam and Flora Fong; Pedroso's poems; and the testimonials in *The Cuba Commission Report*, *Apunte histórico de los chinos en Cuba* (Historical Note about the Chinese in Cuba; Chuffat Latour 1927), *La colonia china de Cuba 1930–1960* (The Chinese Community of Cuba 1930–1960; Seuc 1998), and *Our*

History is Still Being Written (Choy, Chui, and Sío Wong 2005), these are works by writers and artists who lack the epistemologically privileged perspective of being Chinese Cuban. Although some of these authors (Severo Sarduy, Cabrera Infante, and Zoé Valdés) have Chinese ancestors in their ethnic background, most of them identify themselves not as Chinese Cubans but as Cuban or Cuban American.[41] Therefore, even the counter-discourse against the official history has been formulated, for the most part, by a Creole or *mestizo* intelligentsia that is sympathetic to this racialized group. In this sense, Rey Chow maintains that "the émigrés who can no longer claim proprietorship of Chinese culture through residency in China henceforth inhabit the melancholy position of an ethnic group that, as its identity is being 'authenticated' abroad, is simultaneously relegated to the existence of ethnographic specimens under the Western gaze" (15). More importantly, the multiple representational strategies used in these works are not only a reflection of a cultural reality, but also an active component in the creation of a parallel fictional reality in the eyes of readers and viewers. For instance, it is interesting to note that, except for Cristina García's *Monkey Hunting*, these works rarely mention the abduction of Chinese workers as one of the main methods used by the recruiters.

The millennia of cultural heritage brought by the Chinese diaspora to this fledging country (China was born as a nation in approximately 2700 BCE) contributed greatly not only to its cuisine, art, language, music, and literature, but also to its aspirations for independence. For example, although according to Pedro Eng Herrera, Chinese food did not become popular in Cuba until the 1950s (Sariol n.p.), Chinese contributions to Cuban cuisine are echoed in the literature of José Lezama Lima and Severo Sarduy, among other authors. Along these lines, Beatriz Varela has studied, in *Lo chino en el habla cubana* (Chinese Influence in Cuban Spanish; 1980), Chinese influences in the Cuban dialect of Spanish. Likewise, Severo Sarduy considers the Chinese flute the center of the Cuban orchestra and of Cuban music (Rodríguez Monegal, *Arte de narrar* 277), and Alejo Carpentier, in *La música en Cuba* (Music in Cuba; 1946), points out the influence of the Chinese pentatonic scales in the Cuban *danzón*.[42]

It is obvious, then, that the indentured laborers' experiences, values, and beliefs did not merely survive but thrived and even influenced Creole traditions. Their cultural inheritance was later translated into a cultural capital that opened the doors to resources such as wealth, social status, and political influence. More than any other factor, their participation in the two wars of independence against Spain (1868–1898) provided this community with a powerful argument against nativist discourses and other forms of anti-Chinese prejudice.[43] Despite all of these contributions to national culture and independence, the degree of Creole and black acceptance and tolerance for the Chinese varied. Esteban Montejo explains in *Biography of a Runaway Slave* (*Biografía de un cimarrón*; Barnet and Montejo 1966) that blacks and Creoles participated in the activities organized during Chinese festivities. The Chinese subject was often met with ethnic hostility and mistrust, however, as he (and I use the masculine personal pronoun intentionally, since most of them were men) was perceived by the national elites as an obstacle to their project of national homogeneity. Likewise, Chinatowns were frequently conceived of in the national imaginary as spaces of decadence, barbarism, and corruption that threatened public health and morals.

On the other hand, the foreignness of Chinese culture (language, religion, clothing, beliefs) and their employment in professions traditionally ascribed to women often made them objects of mockery among Cubans. Furthermore, the employers' use of Chinese labor to break strikes and, later, the competition created by their frequent economic success as entrepreneurs caused clashes with the two dominant ethnic groups. There was also a great disparity between Chinese self-perception (as free, white, contract migrant workers) and the Creoles' notion that the coolies were merely replacements for black slaves. Just as occurred in other host countries of the Chinese diaspora, these cases of Sinophobia further "othered" and racialized their community. Whereas in some works these adversities actually strengthen individuals' self-identification as Chinese and encourage Chinese unity for the sake of self-protection, in others, they lead the characters to a path of self-denial, wherein they become alienated and ashamed of their own ethnicity and culture.

A feature common to many of these texts is their unveiling of the cultural differences that have traditionally dominated the lives of the Chinese and Chinese Cubans. In this light, rather than "identity," perhaps less fixed terms such as "liminality" and "hybridity" more effectively articulate the collective condition of communities such as the Chinese Cubans, which are not defined by the territorially based concept of the nation-state, preponderant since the nineteenth century. From the confluence of local (Cuban) and global (Chinese, Californian, and beyond) cultural fluxes, a newly created hybrid culture came to life. The works studied here re-create the hidden voices of these colonial subjects in their negotiation of what Homi Bhabha has termed the "third space"; that is, an in-between situation between home culture and receiving culture that, according to him, can generate a potentially subversive agency. Ultimately, rather than resulting in a perfect replica of their communities in China, the transculturation and *mestizaje* of Chinese cultures with those of both the Creole and black communities produced an entirely new Sino-Cuban hybrid reality with its own idiosyncrasies and institutions.[44] Indeed, despite the fact that Chinese immigrants tended to group together in their own communities, evidence of social and cultural mixing challenges traditional assumptions of Chinese separatism. One expression of the agency achieved by the Chinese in Cuba is precisely their appropriation of local mores, which mediated and transformed the ancient cultures they inherited.

Reflecting a historical reality, a common reaction to extreme adversity for many Chinese and ethnic Chinese characters is re-migration. As Denise Helly has explained, the Chinese in Cuba began to migrate after 1874 and "by 1899, only 15,000 free Chinese remained" (26). A second wave of re-migrations began in 1959, after the success of the Cuban Revolution hampered the small-scale entrepreneurship upon which their community had been founded. Obviously, this new migration (a blend of two different diasporas: the Chinese Cuban and the Cuban in general) increased the transnationalist spirit that had always characterized Cuba's Chinese community. At the same time, it brought the decline of the once-vibrant *barrios chinos*, or Chinatowns, in Havana and other Cuban towns. Consequently, some of the works by and about the Chinese in Cuba reflect an unmistakable nostalgia for that gradually disappearing world, which had succeeded in surviving previous historical forces, including wars and revolutions. They also reflect the malleability of so many marginal Sino-Cuban identities, forged in the gaps and interstices of at least two national cultures, which end up gaining new strength after being pushed beyond geographic and political borders by the advent of the Cuban Revolution. With the new migration (another in a seemingly perpetual series), we witness the creation of a diasporic version of national identity, which incorporates new strategies to contend with the Eurocentric hegemony that has negated and silenced the Chinese (at least at an official level) since the inception of the coolie trade. This book concentrates precisely on the challenge to both Creole and *mestizo* nationalistic discourses posed by those interstices and connections among biographies, local and global histories, and different sociopolitical units, such as ethnicities, nation-states, and other politically or territorially based spaces.

As could be expected, both fiction and reality are present not only in the cultural production dealing with the Chinese in Cuba, but also in other discursive practices such as historiographic and testimonial texts. For example, discrepancies exist regarding the estimated numbers of Chinese who migrated to Cuba and who left the country after 1959, the extent of their participation in the wars of independence, and the degree of insularity of the Chinese community. The claim to truth of testimonial texts must also be problematized. With *The Cuba Commission Report*, for example, if one considers the Chinese laborers' desperate need to elicit some sort of protective measures or reaction from the Chinese government, caution as to the veracity of some of their testimonies is warranted. Likewise, Antonio Chuffat Latour's obvious attempt to demonstrate the true Cubanness of the Chinese community in *Apunte histórico de los chinos en Cuba*, and the testimonialists' unconditional support of Castro's regime in *Our History Is Still Being Written* make some of their arguments questionable.

Several of these literary and cultural products provide new personal and collective histories that add to the oppositional counter-discourse of what used to be the third ethnic group on the island. At the same time, they reveal that sanctioned versions of Cuban history (based on either monolithically homogeneous cultural markers or the equally mythical binary opposition between blacks and Creoles) are mere ideological constructs. A next step, as Gustavo Geirola points out, would be to contrast these works with those written in China that also deal with the Chinese migration to Cuba: "One can conjecture that there must exist artistic texts in Chinese and Japanese; that is, a cultural production in the original languages that in some instance may give an account of the tribulations of their countrymen in Latin American lands, whether they returned to their countries of origin or not."[45] Equally interesting, I would add, would be to find more cultural creations (besides *The Cuba Commission Report*) produced in Cuba by Chinese migrant workers and their descendents in the Chinese language.

Ultimately, the analysis of these works must be framed within what Juan de Castro terms "the discourse of mestizaje." In his own words, this Latin American discourse celebrates "miscegenation or cultural mixture as the basis for conceiving a homogenous national identity out of a heterogeneous population [. . . it] uses that heterogeneity paradoxically to imagine a common past and a homogenous future" (9). Indeed, the recent political Sinophilia in Cuba, together with the Sinicization of Cuban and Cuban American aesthetic practices, responds in part to a project of national consolidation under the flag of a harmonic process of *mestizaje*. In a sense, it is a different type of homogenization which, as de Castro argues, should be problematized: "it is precisely these harmonic images that must be analyzed in order for the contradictions and aporias that lie hidden beneath the smoothness of identity to be brought into focus. The importance of the analysis of the discourse of mestizaje is rooted in the need to uncover the social and cultural oppositions hidden by its veneer of homogeneity" (10).

While the preceding information is a brief summary of the history of the

Chinese diaspora in Cuba, perhaps their true experience comes to life better when, instead of making generalizations, we focus on the biographies of individual members of the community on the island and abroad. This individual focus takes place in the epilogue to this study. The second chapter focuses on the topic of Chinese slavery as represented in the testimonials *Biography of a Runaway Slave* and *The Cuba Commission Report*, and in two other texts with some testimonial traits: *Apunte histórico de los chinos en Cuba* and *Our History Is Still Being Written*. The chapter also studies the way in which the indomitable nature of the Chinese, their nostalgia, and their resignation are portrayed in the documentary film *Nadie escuchaba* and in the novel *Monkey Hunting*.

The third chapter analyzes Sinophobic representations of the Chinese in Cuban popular jokes, the novel *La eternidad del instante*, the short stories "Los chinos" and "Cuarenta y nueve chinos," the testimonial novel *Gallego*, the play *El chino*, and the detective story *La cola de la serpiente*. In consonance with these questionable representations of the Chinese and focusing on the novella *The Mandarin*, the short story "Juego de las decapitaciones," the novels of Severo Sarduy, *La eternidad del instante*, and several poems, chapter 4 studies the way in which the Chinese in Cuba have been Orientalized or "Chinesized." Still within the framework of Orientalism, chapter 5 deals with the depiction of Chinese women and Chinese mulattas as exotica in the novels *Monkey Hunting*, *The Messenger*, *I Gave You All I Had*, *La cola de la serpiente* and *La eternidad del instante*, as well as in Severo Sarduy's opus.

The sixth chapter concentrates on the notions of double consciousness and self-exoticization as they appear in different cultural manifestations, including the poetry of Regino Pedroso the paintings of Sino-Cuban artists Flora Fong and Pedro Eng Herrera, and the photographs of María Lau. Chapter 7 studies religious syncretism, with a particular emphasis on the representation of Chinese witchcraft and religion in the novels *La eternidad del Instante, El hombre, la hembra y el hambre, The Messenger*, and *Cold Havana Ground*; the novella *La cola de la serpiente*; the collection of poems *El ciruelo de Yuan Pei Fu*; and the essays *El Monte* and *Apunte histórico de los chinos en Cuba*.

Chapter 8 covers issues dealing with transculturation and assimilation in the study *La colonia china de Cuba 1930–1960, Biography of a Runaway Slave, I Gave You All I Had, Monkey Hunting, La eternidad del instante*, and the works of Severo Sarduy. The ninth chapter rescues three texts in which Chinese Cuban subjectivity can be analyzed from a self-representational point of view: *Apunte histórico de los chinos en Cuba, Our History Is*

Still Being Written, and *La colonia china de Cuba 1930–1960*. It also places particular emphasis on the image of the Chinese at war that appears in *The Cuba Commission Report*, *Memorias de una cubanita que nació con el siglo*, and *La eternidad del instante*. The last chapter studies the erasure and (mis)representation suffered by the Chinese subject in José Martí's works, the novel *Carmela*, the essay "El mercader chino," *Biography of a Runaway Slave*, *The Messenger*, *La eternidad del instante*, *Cold Havana Ground*, *La cola de la serpiente*, the short story "Chino olvidado," and *Monkey Hunting*.

Altogether, these chapters paint a picture of the evolution and resistance of the Chinese community in Cuba. They also study the process of hybridization, which has transformed it into its contemporary expression, as well as its frequent misrepresentation in Cuban and Cuban American cultural production. In some cases, this misrepresentation is self-inflicted and takes the form of various self-Orientalizing and de-Orientalizing strategies for entering and leaving Chineseness.

1

A Hostile Path to Hybridity

2

Chinese Bondage

> Let there be a small state with few people,
> where military devices find no use;
> let the people look solemnly upon death,
> and banish the thought of moving elsewhere.
>
> Lao-tzu

A long tradition of colonialist and Orientalist discourses has resulted in the (mis)representation of Chineseness (a tenuous term in itself) not only by authors and artists, but also within academic circles. In this sense, Rey Chow has voiced her suspicion of Western academia's acceptance of non-Western testimonials:

> As in the case of representations by all minorities in the West, a kind of paternalistic, if not downright racist, attitude persists as a method of categorizing minority discourse: minorities are allowed the right to speak only on the implicit expectation that they will speak in the documentary mode, "reflecting" the group from which they come. (16)

Whatever the reason for the acceptance of this subgenre by Western academics, the influence of the *testimonio* in Latin American and Caribbean prose narrative and historiography is undeniable. Testimonials by political prisoners, indigenous people, *favela* (Brazilian shanty town or slum) dwellers, slaves, and runaway slaves have offered valuable alternative discourses to the official histories of each country. At the same time, they have presented a more accurate view of the ethnic diversity of the regions in question and of the contributions by minorities and marginalized ethnic groups to Latin American identities. The Cuban ethnographer Miguel Barnet, one of the leading experts on this subgenre, has noted the way in which it has contributed to improving the self-esteem of various sectors of the population: "It is useful when it rescues people's pride in being alive, and when it vindicates the values that were most concealed and reveals the true identity of the people in society" (Barnet and Montejo, *Biography* 206).

In the testimonial subgenre, ethical commitment and the impetus of urgent denunciation typically prevail over aesthetic excellence. In fact, the very nature of the testimonial account presupposes immediateness. However, in the case of *The Cuba Commission Report*, although the text was published in English and Chinese in 1876 and 1877, respectively, it was not widely available until the publication of the 1993 edition. Given that to this day this document has not been translated into Spanish, it never elicited the Cuban reader's sympathy as might be expected from a *testimonio*. In any case, its primary objective was achieved, since it did elicit empathy and a reaction from the Chinese government.

The testimonies in *The Cuba Commission Report* and *Apunte histórico de los chinos en Cuba* are mediated by sympathetic individuals from the same ethnic group. These mediators enjoy a greater degree of agency than the testifiers due to their political status, intellectual abilities, and access to publishing houses. In contrast, the three Sino-Cuban generals who produced *Our History Is Still Being Written* are not in a destitute position in their society. In all cases, however, the Chinese men interviewed are either witnesses to or victims of exploitation, oppression, and discrimination, and their main objective is to inform readers about the injustices committed against their people.

Critics have also debated the issue of the intellectual property of *testimonios*. This is particularly relevant in *Biography of a Runaway Slave* (*Biografía de un cimarrón*; 1966) by Miguel Barnet (1940–) and Esteban Montejo (1860–1973), the former slave Barnet interviewed.[1] For this reason, I will avoid the word "author," which is a function of the literary system, and will use the term "testimonialist" instead. In a sense, one could argue that this work is the result of the cooperation between Montejo, who provided most of the information, and Barnet, who directed the interviews, chose most of the topics, and edited the written version of the oral evidence.

Another widely debated issue concerning *testimonios* is their claim to objectivity and truth. Indeed, emulating at times the genre of the journalistic report, testimonial accounts usually claim to be nothing but the representation of historical truth. Yet, as in any first-person narrative text, including autobiographies and memoirs, certain views can be exposed as subjective or exaggerated. The debates among David Stoll, Arturo Arias, and other scholars about evidence of fraudulence and fiction in *I, Rigoberta Menchú* (*Me llamo Rigoberta Menchú y así me nació la conciencia*; 1982) immediately come to mind.

Although *I, Rigoberta Menchú* has nothing to do with the Chinese presence in Cuba, it is nonetheless an excellent example of the typical process of editing a *testimonio*. In the foreword, Elizabeth Burgos Debray, the editor who gave voice to the subaltern subject of the book, explains the strategies she used in both her research and the transcription of the data. As she explains, she prepared a chronological sketch for the interviews and later created a table of contents with theme-based chapters. To achieve narrative continuity, she avoided transcribing her own questions in the interviews and transformed the dialogue into a monologue by adding connecting passages. Finally, as Burgos Debray admits in the foreword, she eliminated unnecessary repetitions and corrected some grammatical mistakes to avoid picturesque effects. As William Luis explains, other factors determine the production of a testimonial text: "As a poet of Quiché memory, Menchú is aware of her present and of her public and she adjusts her discourse so that one time is reconciled with the other. If the past is important for the poet, the present determines how the previous time is commemorated."[2]

Likewise, Miguel Barnet explains his methodology in the brief introduction to the first edition of *Biography of a Runaway Slave* in 1966. Among other tactics used during the interviews, the ethnologist mentions that he allowed the interviewee to digress on different topics of his choosing. Later, he organized the information chronologically, avoiding unnecessary reiterations and presenting the account from a first-person narrative perspective. Barnet was thus able to insert Montejo's peculiar idioms and archaisms, thereby producing a sense of spontaneity. He also consulted other biographies and reference books and interviewed veterans of Montejo's generation to verify the data. At one point in the introduction, Barnet admits that by paraphrasing his informant's words, he was in some sense writing literature. Nonetheless, he claims that he was not trying to write a novel.

Interestingly, while Barnet insists on Montejo's bias when the latter praises the actions of blacks during wartime, he forgets to camouflage his own partiality when he ends the introduction by presenting the 105–year-old former runaway slave as a good example of revolutionary conduct. Montejo's rebelliousness, his membership in the Popular Socialist Party (Partido Socialista Popular), and his support of revolutionary principles are emphasized to the point where the ethnological study becomes tinted with political overtones. Therefore, neither of the two voices in the book may be considered impartial.

Undoubtedly, one of the most fascinating testimonial resources by and about the Chinese in Cuba is *The Cuba Commission Report: A Hidden History of the Chinese in Cuba* (1877). This extraordinary record of oral history and the history of international labor and migration has been surprisingly overlooked in the studies on Latin American testimonials. As Denise Helly has explained, in May 1873, after the imperial viceroy in Canton (Kwangtung) had been hindering the recruitment of Chinese workers in this region for years, two agents of Cuban companies decided to complain to the emperor (14). Subsequently, representatives of the Russian, British, French, and German embassies, who had been called to assist in the litigation, proposed to launch an investigation of the treatment received by Chinese emigrants in Cuba. After a six-week inquiry, the findings of Imperial Commissioner Ch'en Lan Pin (aided by A. MacPherson, commissioner of customs of Hankow, and A. Huber, commissioner of customs of Tientsin) not only provided Chinese laborers in Cuba with a voice, but also led to the official end of the coolie trade with the signing of a treaty between China and Spain in November 1877.[3] In addition, four Chinese consuls were named to different towns in Cuba to afford protection to Chinese citizens.

Anyone reading the hundreds of testimonies recorded in this document would have little doubt that most coolies became de facto slaves from the moment they were deceived or kidnapped. Its depiction of hate, punishment, torture, and suffering is even more gruesome than the atrocities detailed in the majority of published Latin American *testimonios*, including *I, Rigoberta Menchú* and *Never Again: A Report* (*Nunca más*; 1984) by the CONADEP (Argentine National Commission on the Disappearance of Persons). Despite the efforts of Cuban officials and planters to conceal the truth, the self-reports supplied in 1873 by the Chinese laborers draw an appalling picture of their ordeals. From these testimonies of suffering collected in Cuban labor camps, prisons, plantations, jails, and sugar warehouses, we learn about numerous demoralizing and dehumanizing patterns of abuse. According to *The Cuba Commission Report*, eight out of ten coolies claimed to have been deceived or abducted. On the sugar plantations, they had only about four hours a day of rest, and some denounced the insufficient and inappropriate food they received as yet another form of humiliation. Once their contracts expired, Chinese workers in Cuba were often coerced into renewing them; if they refused, they were sent to the labor camps to do unpaid hard labor. In fact, labor coercion was often cited as the main source of despair, as it prevented them from fulfilling their dream of returning to their homeland and condemned them to lifelong slavery. Overall, the 1,176 depositions and eighty-five petitions recorded by the commission, supported by 1,665 signatures, indicate that the coolies worked in conditions of slavery.

Of course, the process of editing a testimonial account should always be considered. In this case, it may even explain one of the most dubious peculiarities of this testimonial: along with various inconsistencies with regard to numbers and statistics, a number of coincidences in the vocabulary of the depositions and petitions abound. For instance, whenever the question,

"From what places does Cuba draw coolies?" is posed, some words become suspiciously recurrent in the translated answers: "snare," "decoyed," "misled," "entrapped," "forced," "kidnapped," "by force," "by violence," "sold as slaves," "removing queues [braids]," "vicious men." On the other hand, this vocabulary is testimony to the fact that from the beginning, the Chinese in Cuba were perfectly aware they were being considered not *colonos contratados* (hired colonists or settlers) but slaves. Thus, Chêng A-mou and eighty-nine others, after claiming to have been abducted and told that eight foreign years were equivalent to four Chinese years, declaim: "when on arrival at Havana, we were exposed for sale and subjected to appraisement in a most ruthless manner, it became evident that we were not to be engaged as labourers, but to be sold as slaves" (37). Several other laborers also declare that Cubans clearly want to enslave them for life and that "they have been converted into serfs, not of an individual but of the entire island" (92).

Contracts, if given at all, were often handed to the Chinese laborers in the barracoons or on board ships, when there was no longer a choice to refuse them. Similarly, recruiting methods included gambling, lies, abduction, contract signing on behalf of other laborers who were temporarily absent, and other deceptive ploys. Although it is not mentioned in the report, Evelyn Hu-DeHart has revealed that opium was also one of the tools used for recruiting: "Apparently opium was part of the coolie trade from its inception, as soon as Chinese men were decoyed in Canton and other cities along the south China coast and put on warehouses in Canton and Macao to await the coolie ships to Peru and Cuba" ("Opium" 174). The level of intimidation and violence described by Yeh Fu-chün and fifty-two other men who were asked about methods used to make them sign the agreements attest to the recruiters' disregard for the life of the Chinese: "The barracoon was of great depth, and, at the time of punishment, as an additional precaution to prevent the cries being overheard, gongs were beaten, and fireworks discharged, so that death even might have ensued without detection" (39). Likewise, when the commission asked whether recruiters had made sure agreements were understood, many Chinese men replied that much of the information was passed over, that they were told they were going to Annam (Vietnam) or Singapore, or that Havana was the name of a vessel. In other cases, the Chinese emigrants could not read and the contract was not read to them at all. They were also told that if they were dissatisfied once in Cuba, return fares to China would be provided to them. In addition, recruits were not allowed to notify their families about their departure or even to maintain correspondence with them. Therefore, as happened with the "disappeared" (missing citizens) during the twentieth-century dictatorships in South America, their families were never informed of their whereabouts, let alone whether they were alive.

One of the most noticeable contrasts between *The Cuba Commission Report* and fictional texts such as Zoé Valdés's *La eternidad del instante* (The Eternity of the Instant; 2004) is that in the former very few testimonialists (one or two out of every ten) acknowledge having emigrated voluntarily. Likewise, only a few petitioners considered the treatment and the food they received during the voyage appropriate. Even more disturbing is the fact that, although the emigration agreement with China stipulated that Chinese under twenty years of age were not allowed to emigrate without the written consent of their parents, many children under the age of twelve were contracted or kidnapped.[4]

In the end, the commission came to the conclusion that of the 140,000 Chinese who sailed to Cuba, more than 16,000 died during the voyages. However, among other inconsistencies, section 16 of the report places the number of coolies at 200,000 and the deaths in transit at 15,000, with the overall number of deaths reaching 53,502 (Helly 99). This extremely high mortality rate was due to frequent suicides, insufficient amounts of food and water, and harsh punishment constantly inflicted by the crew. The coolies were charged one or two pesos for a cup of water and were beaten so severely if they tried to steal one that many died or committed suicide. Some were also chained or imprisoned in bamboo cages, and the strongest ones were frequently flogged to set an example for the rest or placed in irons for the entire voyage. In sum, among the many reasons coolies were harshly beaten, both during the voyage and later in Cuba, were the following: asking for food or water, going on deck to get fresh air or to relieve themselves, being ill or seasick, asking for medicine when sick, objecting to having their queues cut, or smoking. Some also claimed to have been severely punished because they were suspected of mutiny, for resembling someone who had committed a crime, for not carrying a *cédula* (card of legal residence), for being physically strong, for marrying a white woman, for not speaking Spanish, or simply for speaking.[5]

These testimonies also reveal the sadistic nature of many of the "masters," overseers, and sailors, who would tell the Chinese, for example, that their lives were expendable, since others would gladly take their place. In this context, Chên Lung complains: "Near Malacca the vessels received injuries [were damaged], but though the water was entering the hold, the hatchways were not opened; and it was only when the water reached our necks and when more than ten were already drowned that they were raised" (46). Upon the coolies' arrival in Cuba, their situation would not improve significantly. Several Chinese men testified that they were humiliated, deprived of all dignity, and treated like animals.

To better grasp the concept of shame and dishonor in Chinese culture, and particularly in this situation, it would be useful to refer to one of Confucius's sayings, as recorded in the *Analects* (*Lun Yü*):[6] "If you would be employed by a just country, it is shameful to be employed by an unjust country" (Confucius 63). And "shame" is indeed the word most frequently used by these Chinese laborers to describe the moment when, before being sold, their queues were cut and they were physically examined by purchasers in a denigrating manner.

Approximately 90 percent of the workers were sent to sugar plantations, where life was even harder than in the city. Others of them were assigned to farms or tobacco or coffee estates. The overseers' job, as the petitioners point out, consisted of extracting the greatest possible amount of labor, regardless of the coolies' health or well-being. Concerned exclusively with their own economic profit, Cuban planters made them work twenty to twenty-one hours (twenty-two in one case) a day. According to the testimonies, when Chinese laborers slowed down because of lack of food and rest, dogs were set upon them or they were severely beaten. These abuses took place despite the fact that the emigration agreement signed by the Spanish and Chinese governments stipulated in one clause that the workday would last no more than twelve hours and that Sunday would be a day of rest. The deposition of Wang A-ching and twenty-two others provides an idea of a typical day for them: "the work is very hard. We get up at 3 a.m., and labour until noon; at 1 p.m. we resume work until 7 p.m., when we rest half an hour and are allowed a ration of maize, after which work continued till midnight. We are struck and flogged, and out of our party of more than 200 men, only over 80 remain" (63). While several sections give detailed descriptions of physical abuse, section 39 is invaluable in estimating the level of disdain for Chinese life that pervaded Cuban plantations: "Liang Pai-shêng, after being wounded on the head and body by the administrator, was attached by the latter to his horse's tail and dragged back to the quarters. He proved to be then dead, and his body was cast upon the dung-hill" (100).

Humiliation was one of the tactics used to debase these men and deprive them of their human dignity: "the Chinese in chains were beaten severely if they did not imitate the cries of sheep and dogs" (51), testifies Wu A-san. Another tactic, torture, was applied by both the administrators and the overseers (often described by the Chinese as wolves and tigers) in the numerous cells that existed throughout the island. Some claimants allege that those who attempted to run away had their fingers cut off and that immediately after receiving two hundred blows, they would be forced to continue their labor. As might be expected, the death rate was very high, in numerous cases because of suicide. If we are to trust the depositions, the Chinese received punishment even without giving provocation or committing an offense. The sadistic mindset of administrators and overseers, and their desire to intimidate the Chinese, sufficed. Despite possible exaggerations, the number of testimonies depicting gratuitous violence makes it clear that these were not isolated cases, but a distressing and consistent pattern of injustices.

Corroborated by some of the testimonies of Chinese coolies in Peru, one of the most revealing findings of this report is that after very many years of suffering, some black Africans had internalized a false consciousness and were reproducing colonial repression. Black overseers are often accused of beating or killing Chinese workers in the report: "I saw a man named A-chi so severely struck on the neck by the Negro overseer that he died in three days" (105). For the Chinese respondents, having slave foremen and overseers punish them was obviously a double source of shame and humiliation. Animosity, rivalry, and even jealousy between the two ethnic groups permeate many of the pages in the report. In fact, three different depositions and the conclusions of the imperial commission complain of the apparently preferential treatment received by blacks. While few claimants contrasted their own servitude to the complete freedom that other foreigners had in Cuba, blacks continued to be the main frame of reference: "We learn that friendly relations now exist between China and the greater powers of the West, and that it is by the efforts of the latter that the traffic in Negro slaves has been suppressed. Why do they not render to us a similar service?," Jên Shih-chên and two others queried (90). And even in cases where black and Chinese men joined forces to resist their mistreatment by cruel administrators, coolies complained about employers' favoritism toward blacks: "four Negroes in league with certain recently arrived Chinese killed the new administrator. By an outlay of money on the part of our employer, the participation of the Negroes was not mentioned, and the crime was imputed to us," stated Wu Yeh-ch'êng (88). Denise Helly, in her introduction to the report, speculates about the reasons for the excessive mistreatment of Chinese workers: "to treat these nonwhite people differently than the slaves were treated would have meant deviating from the racist code of slavery and thereby inciting the slaves to revolt" (22). She also conjectures about the underlying causes of the mutual jealousy between the two ethnic groups: "because they received salaries at all, and because some sought to establish relations with black women, the Chinese became potential objects of jealousy for some male slaves" (20).

Likewise, Hu-DeHart has studied the relations between slaves and coolies in Cuba: "Even if slaves could see that the daily treatment meted out to them and to the coolies was not substantially different, they also observed the somewhat greater facility with which coolies were able to free themselves from the plantations and open up small businesses nearby" ("Race" 89).

Along with all these repressive tactics, Cuban planters had created an elaborate net of fraudulent means to keep the Chinese laborers trapped in their desperate circumstances. For example, instead of paying them the money they had promised, they gave them tickets to buy food in the overpriced shops they owned on the plantations. If the Chinese dared to purchase products elsewhere, their masters accused them of running away. Evelyn Hu-DeHart has also exposed the use of opium in Cuba and Peru as a means of manipulating and controlling the coolies: "Plantation managers quickly caught on to this dependency and exploited it to discipline the coolies by threatening to withhold opium until the daily tasks were done" ("Opium" 176). Thus, the planters used opium to punish or reward the Chinese, to perpetuate debt peonage, and to recuperate the money they had paid them.

Adding to the humiliation, indentured workers enjoyed no legal redress because their employers often bribed authorities empowered to address their grievances. Nevertheless, the Chinese responded to these abuses in various ways besides suicide. While some admitted to committing crimes just because they preferred prison to working in the fields, others fled, burned the plantations, joined rebels, killed overseers, or refused to work, particularly at night. These historical data call into question the alleged docility of Chinese workers: "20 percent of the Chinese under contract had fled their plantations, that is, 8,380 men, of whom 1,344 were captured and sent to prison in 1873" (Helly 24).

Moreover, despite knowing from experience about the corruption of the Cuban judicial system, they persisted in appealing to the authorities. Huang Shih-jung, for example, declared that to protest the brutal mistreatment of a peer that had led to the latter's suicide, he and others refused to work: "Twenty of us preferred a complaint to the officials, declaring that we were unwilling to return to the plantation" (67). The employers, however, solved the problem by selling some of the workers to other plantations. Although these acts of resistance were frequently met with violence, Chinese workers tried repeatedly to appeal for justice and to fight for their freedom. Accustomed to having legal recourse in their homeland, they continued appealing to the Cuban justice system in hopes that some official would eventually listen.

Another nonviolent way of ending the abuse was setting money aside from their meager earnings in order to buy their freedom or return to China. However, only a few succeeded: "Between 1865 and 1874, only 2,000 Cantonese managed to return to China" (Helly 25). According to the deponents, whenever the authorities found out that a Chinese man was trying to return home, he was accused of being a deserter and was tortured, robbed, and sometimes killed. Of course, joining the insurrection was another popular way of avenging the oppression and the suffering that Chinese laborers endured for decades. Ultimately, there is little doubt that giving evidence to the commission constituted in itself another form of resistance. In some cases the deponents delivered their testimonies in the presence of their masters and overseers, while in others they had to send secret letters to the commission, as their masters did not allow them to be interviewed.

Despite their tenacity, life after the plantation was not easy for the Chinese in Cuba. Chuang A-I's arduous odyssey attests to this fact. After he completed his contract, he opened a butcher shop and a store that sold miscellaneous articles. When a white soldier refused to pay for the articles he took, Chuang A-I tried to accost him but was struck with a stick. In addition, one of his Chinese assistants was killed and two others were seriously injured. Yet officials did nothing to punish the offender. In the deponent's words, "The people here declare that the killing of a Chinese is no more than the killing of a dog" (83). Hu-DeHart has also revealed that, after their contracts expired, some Chinese made a living by selling opium on the plantations: "they stayed at or near their old plantations to own and run small shops (*tambo* in Peru, *bodega* or *puesto* in Cuba) and canteens (*fonda* in Peru)" ("Opium" 179).

The predictable marginalization of Chinese migrant workers took many different forms. For instance, they were often accused of conspiracy if four or five of them conversed in the street, and were charged with gambling if they met in a house and closed the door. In fact, in the report many Chinese men profess not to know the reason why they were beaten or arrested. Police extortion was another frequent grievance of these indentured workers. Many complained that corrupt guards and policemen constantly accused them of forging their *cédulas* or deprived them of their freedmen's papers in order to steal their money and property.

Beyond these corrupt methods of victimizing the Chinese, physical violence and torture were often employed openly. The imperial commission found many of the Chinese workers maimed, vomiting blood, and with severe health problems resulting from years of torture and mistreatment. As the deponents declared, when they became ill, they were rarely allowed to use the plantation infirmaries; instead, they were punished and forced to continue working. Others reported seeing some of their ill peers killed by overseers, knowing that others were dying of starvation in the infirmary with the complicity of surgeons, being aware that someone had committed suicide after being punished, or being forced to drink their own urine for reporting an illness.

Interestingly, Western perceptions of China, as Jonathan D. Spence has shown, were often informed by descriptions of Chinese tortures published by sixteenth- and seventeenth-century travelers, like the Portuguese soldier and trader Galeote Pereira and the Dominican friars Gaspar da Cruz (or Gaspar de la Cruz) and Domingo Navarrete. French philosopher Charles de Montesquieu also emphasized, in his book *The Spirit of Laws*, this aspect of Chinese and other Asian cultures: "what the people of Asia have called punishment those of Europe have deemed the most outrageous abuse" (124). Therefore, despite all the cruelties suffered by the coolies in Cuba and in other countries of the Americas, the stereotype about the unlimited capacity for cruelty of the Chinese has been one of the most persistent topoi throughout the centuries. Even today, in order to emphasize, in Spanish or in English, how terrible something is, it is common to say "it is a Chinese torture."

Furthermore, the coolies' anguish did not end with death. As may be concluded from this report, besides having their queues cut, being stripped naked, and being sold like animals, the worst indignity was that of not receiving proper burial. Thus, several claimants expressed anger that those who had not been baptized were not buried in the cemetery: "it is certain that for us," stated Jên Shih-chên and two others, "there will be neither coffin nor grave, and that our bones will be tossed into a pit, to be burnt with those of horses and oxen and to be afterwards used to refine sugar, and that neither our sons nor our sons' sons will ever know what we have endured" (110). Their indignation must be understood in the context of Confucian thought, which emphasizes the importance of a proper funeral and mourning: "Observe a man's aspirations while his father is still alive; observe his actions after his father passes away. If he does not change his father's way for three years, then he can be called filial" (Confucius 79). "According to Confucian belief," Helly reminds us, "the spirit of a person, detached from the body at death, carries on an autonomous and human existence, inasmuch as the spirit must continue to be nourished and honored.... If these honors are not conferred upon the ancestors, their spirits suffer an unfortunate fate and become malevolent" (19).

One of the most frequently recurring topics in the report is that of suicide.[7] Different sources mention that sailors, overseers, and plantation owners were shocked to discover how often the Chinese resorted to suicide. Dorothy Ko has studied the cult of suicide in China. She lists, for example, the public suicides of protesting women during the Ming-Qing transition, the morbid fascination in seventeenth-century Jiangnan with the death of teenage poets, and the suicide of prostitutes (81).[8] Evidently, at the time suicide was more widely accepted in China than in Western countries. Considering that in many cases it was the only way out of slavery, this historical precedent may explain why so many coolies committed suicide during the voyages and in Cuba.[9] In this light, Richard H. Dana echoes the dealers' rationale for buying Chinese laborers despite their proclivity to suicide: "The dealer did not deny their tendency to suicide, and the danger of attempting to chastise them, but alleged their superiority to the Negro in intelligence, and contended that their condition was good, and better than in China, having four dollars a month, and being free at the end of eight years" (80).

In fact, if one takes the rate of suicides per capita into account, this trafficking in human lives reached genocidal proportions. "Between 1850 and 1872," Helly estimates, "there were approximately five hundred suicides annually among the 100,000 Chinese on the island" (24). Likewise, Jesús Guanche Pérez has considered the coolie trade one of the biggest human catastrophes of the time: "While the working conditions had a profoundly negative cultural impact that led to the loss of the human condition and, therefore, to a type of mass suicide (the greatest in the world per million inhabitants in the decade of 1850–1860), it acquired its own voice as an eloquent social denunciation of what human trafficking means."[10] Indeed, not only for these Chinese workers but also for Amerindians and African slaves before them, suicide and self-mutilation were seen as brave forms of resistance and as a gallant escape from a life not worth living.

While several works studied here, including *Memorias de una cubanita que nació con el siglo* (Memoirs of a Little Cuban Who Was Born with the Century; Méndez Capote 1963), *Monkey Hunting*, and *Biography of a Runaway Slave*, present suicide as a distinctive cultural trait ascribed to the Chinese, nowhere is its presence more appalling than in the testimonials compiled in the report. There, we read about astounding numbers of suicides committed on the ships and in Cuba. At times coolies adopted this means of resistance to avoid being taken abroad against their will or when they could not withstand the humiliation of having their queues cut or other types of mistreatment. According to the report, the corpses were tossed overboard and on some occasions, men were thrown into the ocean while still alive. In addition, some of the petitioners told the commission they had been contemplating suicide for some time. Indentured workers in Cuba who found their treatment unbearable used different methods to end their misery. Numerous coolies hanged themselves, cast themselves under the wheels of carts, jumped into water wells or sugar caldrons, poisoned themselves with opium, or cut their own throats. Others drowned themselves or killed overseers knowing that they would be punished with death, and there was even a case of a man who killed "himself by a wound inflicted on his private parts" (103).

In all, despite its flaws, the report represents a long-overdue effort by the Chinese government to protect its subjects abroad. As stated earlier, however, not everything in the report should be accepted without question. Like most testimonials, *The Cuba Commission Report* does not include much reflective analysis and, when it does, it is certainly tendentious. A good example of the Chinese government's political agenda underlying the document is the outrageous diatribe against voluntary migration that appears in the introduction to section 32. There, the commission cynically accuses all those who migrated voluntarily (as Helly points out, of the 2,841 deponents, only 90 men said that they had migrated freely) of being bad characters who are trying either to escape their crimes or to avoid paying their gambling debts. The coolies who were not kidnapped or deceived are described as "stupid fellows," since "industrious men who work willingly and well, can support themselves at home, and do not emigrate voluntarily" (69). As a result, the understandable indignation over the ill-treatment of Chinese subjects is tainted by an unexpected shifting of guilt from the planters and administrators to the migrants. In the commission's view, the latter will inevitably adhere to their bad habits in the new country and will never be able to save money. In a way, this type of reproach was no more than a ploy to hide the inability of a weak government to protect its nationals from the greed of Western capitalist countries and from the corruption of the recruiters who abducted and swindled them in Chinese territory. If nothing else, the dismal list of abuses against the Chinese in Cuba that is contained in the report reveals that they were allowed to leave China with no guarantee of protection.

One reasonable criticism, however, deals with the participation of the Chinese in the Mambí insurrection. The report admits the possible distortion of facts due to the impossibility of interviewing coolies on the rebel side. Yet it does not take into account the potential for witnesses to exaggerate in the depositions, given their desperation and the fact that they had no legal recourse to escape the abuse.

Biography of a Runaway Slave is another testimonial that is useful in reconstructing the ways by which the coolies resisted abuse on the plantations. As William Luis points out, Montejo's answers did not always mesh with Barnet's initial goals for the book: "Although a committed ethnologist, Barnet was aware of the importance of blacks for the revolution and the historical and cultural significance of his subject matter. He may have stressed the independent and revolutionary aspects of Montejo's life as a way of overcoming bureaucratic censorship" (212). In the introduction, Barnet explains how Esteban Montejo, a former runaway slave who lived in the province of Las Villas, voiced an objection that he had not been asked anything about the Chinese community in Sagua la Grande. For Montejo, this was obviously an unacceptable omission. His cultural memory could not conceive the reconstruction of the last years of the colony without registering the presence and contributions of the Chinese community. As Barnet points out, during their conversations, Montejo would often choose topics that he considered crucial. A frequent one was his contact with Chinese workers in sugar plantations and in Sagua la Grande. In this light, Montejo defines the African cultural heritage on the island by contrasting it with the Chinese worldview. Therefore, by looking for his "Other" in the Chinese coolies rather than in the free Creole and Spanish citizenry (as might be expected), he subtly overturns the traditional white-black dichotomy.

The former runaway slave remembers in particular the rebelliousness that characterized the Chinese: "They killed their own overseers with sticks and knives. The Chinese didn't trust anybody. They were rebels from birth. Many times, the master put an overseer of their own race with them to gain their confidence. Him they didn't kill" (43).[11] Montejo also elaborates on the attitude of the Chinese toward death and suicide. He underscores, for example, how silent they were, even when committing suicide: "They sure did kill themselves. They did it silently. After several days passed, they appeared hanging from a tree or lying dead on the ground. Everything they did, they did silently" (43).[12] Later, contrasting the differing reactions to slavery of blacks and Chinese, he comes to the conclusion that the latter committed suicide more often because they thought excessively. He also emphasizes their strange beliefs about the afterlife. Montejo explains that whereas blacks believed that once the spirit had left the body, it would fly to Africa while still alive, "The Chinese didn't fly and didn't even want to go back to their homeland" (43).[13]

But Montejo does not want the reader to remember the Chinese only for their violent resistance on the plantations. He commends their perseverance, providing the example of old sugarcane cutters who, because of their advanced age, could no longer do agricultural labor and had turned to selling sesame seeds around the plantations. Likewise, he constantly praises their culture, their institutions, and their character to the point where he considers them the most refined people on the island. Even in the last paragraph of the text, in one last example of his high regard for everything Chinese, Montejo compares the elegant uniforms and weapons of the Spanish soldiers to Chinese letters.

Along with this glowing encomium, however, the former runaway voices his suspicion of the unfamiliar: "In Sagua la Grande they had their own clubs. They gathered there to speak their languages and read newspapers from China out loud. They probably did it to be annoying, but since nobody could understand them, they kept right on with their reading as if nothing else mattered" (89).[14] He also laments the cultural degeneration he felt they suffered once they began to own grocery stores.

The image of the indomitable Chinese that appears in some passages of *The Cuba Commission Report* and *Biography of a Runaway Slave* has survived to the present day in both testimonials, such as the documentary film *Nadie escuchaba*, and works of fiction like *Monkey Hunting* (2003), by the Cuban American Cristina García (1959–). In García's two previous novels, *Dreaming in Cuban* (1992; finalist for the U.S. National Book Award) and *The Agüero Sisters* (1997), the exploration of Cuban and Cuban American identities has been a recurrent leitmotif. It is probable that she also modeled *Monkey Hunting* on her own experience as a Cuban American born in Havana and raised in New York from the age of two years, in order to re-create the contradictions of living in the liminal space between two or more cultures. This novel also explains how coolies committed suicide after being punished or simply reprimanded by the crew, even if not in a particularly severe way. One of them jumps down into the ocean silently, others hang themselves, poison themselves with opium, or commit suicide by jabbing a sharpened stick into their ear. Consequently, the slavers, who saw them as a commodity, became concerned over the economic loss their actions entailed.

In fact, several passages in *Monkey Hunting* seem to have been inspired by *Biography of a Runaway Slave*. For example, García re-creates the same type of silent suicide: "A squat melon-grower from T— announced that he would throw himself into the ocean to end his torment. Chen Pan crept on deck with two others to watch him jump. The melon-grower didn't shout or linger but simply stepped into the breeze" (9). Among other scenes obviously modeled after *Biography*, there is one representing the obscene games men played to entertain themselves on the plantations, as well as those in which the Chinese runaway slave Chen Pan is persecuted, like Montejo, by a bird that seems to be the reincarnation of his deceased mother. Likewise, one of the scenes in García's novel was probably inspired by the passage where Montejo states that hypnotism is "the foundation of the Chinese religion" (90):[15] "Chen Pan overheard one criollo commenting on the Orientals' hypnotizing skills. It's part of their religion, more dangerous than the Haitians' voodoo. If you look them straight in the eyes, you're doomed" (243).

Despite the inevitable process of assimilation, the proclivity toward suicide on the "devil ships" and on the plantations persists throughout the decades. Saddened by an irrepressible feeling of melancholy upon noticing the disintegration of the once-dynamic Chinese community of Cuba, Chen Pan thinks about killing himself. Likewise, many years later Domingo Chen's father commits suicide by throwing himself on the rails of the subway in the Bronx, and the same way out is sought by some young wives brought from China by former coolies: they either commit suicide or poison their husbands. Yet Chinese cultural attitudes toward suicide do evolve throughout the years. Reiterating the denunciation of universal male chauvinism that is prominent in García's novels, all the veteran Chinese Cubans, except for the perhaps over-idealized Chen Pan, find it disrespectful that unfaithful wives no longer commit suicide by throwing themselves into wells. They also condemn the fact that widows remarry without even considering suicide, as they would have in the past.

To return to the testimonial genre (although this time going from the written medium to film), the French–North American documentary film *Nadie escuchaba* (Nobody listened; 1989) provides evidence of the unremitting perception of the Chinese as courageous and unyielding people.[16] Written, produced, and co-directed by Néstor Almendros and Jorge Ulla, it presents victim testimony of the human-rights abuses committed by Fidel Castro's regime. One abuse in particular is of interest to this study, as it deals with the assassination of a Chinese Cuban man named Julio Tan. According to Miguel Torres Calero, the narrator and a former fellow inmate of the victim, the incident took place at a hard-labor camp in Isla de Pinos, when a corporal ordered "Chino" (his nickname) to strike the ground harder with the hoe. After the latter refused, the guard took the hoe away from Chino and ordered him to pull grass by hand. Seeing that he was not going to comply, the corporal tried to hit him with the flat of his bayonet but Julio Tan fended off the blows with his arms. Then, another guard picked up the hoe and hit him on his lower back, causing him to fall to his knees. At that moment, the rest of the prisoners attempted to help him, but the guards began to shoot over their heads. Afterward, the sadistic guard jabbed the bayonet into Chino's thigh, opening his femoral artery. He later bled to death.

The story of Tan's death is corroborated in the documentary by a former inmate, Carlos Santana, who lamented the fact that the guard who bayoneted Chino was promoted days later to head of "the punishment block."[17] Apart from the human tragedy, what is more relevant to this study is the subconsciously essentialist way in which his sympathetic fellow inmate, Torres Calero, describes Tan´s stubbornness and defiance: "He was of Chinese origin and that was the way he was. He was not going to change and never did."[18]

In all, these testimonials, novels, and documentaries form a network of ideological discourses that display a wide range of sentiments, ranging from nostalgia to resignation and resentment. Marginalized, dispossessed, and sometimes vilified, Chinese subjects find in testimonials such as *The Cuba Commission Report* a vehicle for reconstructing their collective history. Simultaneously, these counter-narratives—albeit often mediated by the interviewers' political agenda—become sites for resistance and identity construction.

Likewise, behind purportedly autobiographical accounts such as Chuffat Latour's *Apunte histórico de los chinos en Cuba* and Seuc's *La colonia china de Cuba 1930–1960* lies a political struggle for representation and empowerment that responds to a collective project. At times marked by vacillation and contradiction, particularly when referring to political and ethnic affiliations, these texts ultimately represent an alternative way to narrate the nation. From the world of the sugar plantation, we move on, in the next chapter, to some analyses of Cuban Sinophobia in different cultural manifestations.

3

Cuban Sinophobia

> Pour forth this all-consuming activity onto countries which, like China, are crying aloud for foreign conquest. [...] Nature has made a race of workers, the Chinese race, with its marvelous manual dexterity and almost no sense of honor.
>
> Ernest Renan

At both official and popular levels, xenophobic anti-Chinese sentiments have been common in most countries with a significant Chinese minority. Cuban cultural production often reflects this irrational fear and hatred, which may originate from very different sources. In the tradition of the "Yellow Peril" complex, the hostility may be caused by the Chinese having emasculating jobs traditionally assigned to women, competition in the job market, jealousy of the Chinese immigrants' economic success, or fear of the unknown, among other factors. In other cases, the increasing number of Chinese gave rise to fears that the local culture would be tainted or, worse yet, that Western civilization itself would be undermined. As we will see, some texts even flirt with the notion of the Chinese as subhuman beings, and reject cultural differences, which are seen in negative and stereotypical ways, such as the proclivity to silence, the "sinister" secrecy of their societies, or even their peculiar smiles.

The politics of representation surrounding the Chinese Cuban subject has undergone a telling evolution throughout the decades. Whereas the texts published during the last decades of the nineteenth century silenced or erased the Chinese presence, those published during the first half of the twentieth century echoed the tacit and at times overt racism of their authors. From the 1950s to the 1980s, the texts evolved into Orientalist and strategically self-Orientalizing perspectives that eventually gave way in the 1990s and early twenty-first century to a more realistic and less homogenizing depiction of their presence and heritage on the island. When analyzing works published during the first half of the twentieth century, a period when the Chinese colony was thriving, it is important to take into account that they were produced during the U.S. military occupation (1899–1922) and the subsequent North American political control of the island (1923–1958).

This foreign presence exacerbated an animosity that had existed ever since the first Chinese indentured laborer arrived in Cuba. As several historians and critics (including Juan Jiménez Pastrana, Duvon Clough Corbitt, Napoleón Seuc, and Kathleen López) point out, the occupation brought with it North American anti-Chinese legislation and, in the 1950s, the complete prohibition of Chinese immigration:[1] "The legislation then in force in that country [Cuba], a Decree of January 13, 1939, revalidating Military Order No. 155 of May 15, 1902, issued by the North American Military Government to apply to Cuba the immigration laws of the United States at that time, went the limit in discrimination" (Corbitt i). After these laws were enacted, only Chinese merchants, tourists, and diplomats, along with their families, were allowed entry. However, on November 12, 1942, a new treaty that allowed Chinese citizens to enter Cuba and to have full legal protection improved diplomatic relations between Cuba and China (Corbitt ii).

Like testimonials, other manifestations of popular culture, such as jokes and humorous stories, reflect the collective attitude toward the Chinese and the all-too-common stereotypes about the Chinese mind. Notably, in the collection *Cuentos populares cubanos de humor* (Popular Cuban Humorous Tales; 1981), edited by Samuel Feijóo (1914–1992), an entire section is devoted to jokes about Chinese men, who share stereotypical traits: they are naive, easily scared and deceived, physically abused by others, and unable to pronounce the phoneme /r/. Of course, this common way of depicting Cantonese speakers' pronunciation of Spanish gives the false impression that all native speakers of Spanish pronounce the language the way it is written. As we know, this is not always the case for many native speakers, in either Spain or any of its former colonies.

Lack of linguistic competence has been a key factor in the marginalization of the Chinese community in Cuba, as we see in this cultural production. French sociologist Pierre Bourdieu has emphasized the social conditions of communication: "the efficacy of an utterance, the power of conviction which is granted to it, depends on the *pronunciation* (and secondarily the vocabulary) of the person who utters it; that is, through this particularly reliable measure of statutory competence, it depends on the authority of the speaker" (70). Indeed, in many of the dialogues included in *Cuentos populares cubanos de humor* one notices that the way Chinese characters speak is regarded as unacceptable by listeners, who seem predisposed to react in certain ways. On the other hand, the obsession with the racial Other's pidgin Spanish sheds light on the stereotyped racial identity and degrading image assigned to the Chinese by sectors of the population.[2]

Compounding the difficulty of learning a completely different language, coolies learned Spanish not from their masters but, as John M. Lipski has pointed out, "from their fellow workers, many of whom were not native speakers of Spanish."[3] In real life, Chinese Cubans are perfectly aware of the potential for marginalization posed by the lack of linguistic competence. Thus, when I asked Carlos Alay, an expert in the lion dance, what he thought about José Martí's erasure of Chinese Cubans from his literary imaginary, he answered that he found it normal because of the language barrier. Likewise, the journalist León Choy pointed out to me that he had been less marginalized than other native Chinese thanks to his competence in standard Spanish.

In this context, elaborating on style or "individual deviation from the linguistic norm," Bourdieu explains,

> What circulates in the linguistic market is not "language" as such, but rather discourses that are stylistically marked both in their production, in so far as each speaker fashions an idiolect from the common language, and in their reception, in so far as each recipient helps to *produce* the message which he perceives and appreciates by bringing to it everything that makes up his singular and collective experience. (39)

In this sense, the communicative situations in the humorous tales collected by Samuel Feijóo, which often transcribe the pidgin Spanish-Chinese used by Chinese characters, reproduce specific relations of power. As we will see in the exchanges between characters, the peculiar accent, intonation, vocabulary, and grammar used by the Chinese automatically position them at the lowest levels of the social hierarchy. Language becomes a tool for racial parody and racist stereotyping.

One of the jokes, "El discurso del chino reaccionario" (The Reactionary Chinaman's Speech), the only one dealing with the stereotype of the Chinese being dirty, bases part of its humor on the character's lack of linguistic capital. The Chinese man is unable to produce the appropriate language for a particular linguistic market or context, in this case a public speech at the inauguration ceremonies of the Chiang Kai-shek Society in Camajuaní:

> "Chinaman no wash lettuce whel [where] wash undelpants!"
> "Lies! Chinaman lecent pelson!"[4]

This joke also brings to mind Jorge Mañach's *Indagación del choteo* (An Examination of Choteo; 1928) and Gustavo Pérez Firmat's elaboration on the topic. Pérez Firmat has criticized Mañach for censoring, or "cleaning up," Cuban *choteo*: "Mañach attempts a 'purification' of *choteo*, a filtering out of its baseness and filth. Deliberately or not, he acts to cleanse or edulcorate his subject by glossing over its scatological subtexts, its bottom lines" (76). In Pérez Firmat's view, Mañach's definition of *choteo* brings it closer to the concept of *relajo*. Cuban historian and anthropologist Fernando Ortiz (1880–1969) defined *relajo* in the following way: "There is something else that aggravates our national unity. I refer to what we call *relajo*, that is, relaxation of discipline, lack of respect, mocking of authority, evasion of laws, admiration for vulgarity, flippancy, lack of restraint, impunity of crime, tolerance of baseness, avoidance of all forms of sacrifice" ("Relations" 28). Although authority goes unchallenged in "El discurso del chino reaccionario," scatological overtones are evident in the allegation of the Chinese washing produce in laundry water.

Along these lines, a Chinese man is the victim of gratuitous violence in "El chino y el guajiro de vendedores" (The Chinaman and the Peasant as Salesmen), contained in a collection titled *Cuentos populares cubanos* (Popular Cuban Tales; 1960), also edited by Feijóo. There, a Cuban peddler who is selling fish becomes irate with a Chinese peddler who is simultaneously hawking his wares. In anger, the Cuban dumps his fish on the Chinese man's head. This violent outcome again brings to mind the scatological, that is, the refuse and filth that Pérez Firmat assigns to *choteo*.

One can also understand Mañach's notion of a "benign" and healthy type of *choteo* (i.e., when it shows a selective disrespect for illegitimate authority) in four other humorous stories. First, the title of "El chino que no era bobo" (The Chinese Who Was Not Stupid) implies that Chinese are typically unintelligent. Set during one of Cuba's wars for independence, the story focuses on a Chinese man who is repeatedly beaten by forces on both sides because he erroneously yells "¡Viva Cuba!" (Long live Cuba!) when the Spaniards ask him to identify himself and "¡Viva España!" (Long live Spain!) when the Cubans ask him. As the title foretells, he is not stupid because, the next time he is asked, he answers in the stereotypical pidgin Spanish-Chinese: "What the hell, long live whoevel!"[5] Once again, the substitution of /l/ for /r/ is supposed to be humorous. In this case, however, the Chinese protagonist's use of the quintessentially Cuban *choteo* brings him closer to the perceived national psychology. His *choteo* is benign for two different reasons: it is sporadic rather than habitual (a characteristic trait of "toxic" *choteo*, according to Mañach), and it acknowledges authority, although he disrespects it and tries to subvert it.

Both *choteo* and linguistic mimicry reappear in "El cura y el chino fusilado" (The Priest and the Executed Chinaman). Also set during the wars of independence, this story features a Chinese man who, "like many Chinese who rose up in arms" is about to go before a firing squad.[6] After listening to a priest tell him about heaven's wonders, the Chinese *mambí* asks the priest whether he wants to take his place, "You want change?"[7] Although to some extent recognizing hierarchy (this time ecclesiastical), the Chinese character undermines it with his sarcastic question, thus ridiculing the priest's supposedly comforting words. Another object of laughter is, of course, the way in which he speaks, which indirectly stigmatizes his ethnic group and his racial identity as well.

In the third story, titled "Tin Malín," a Chinese boy undermines his teacher's authority by turning the latter's mockery into a sexual joke. Punning on the children's popular rhyme "Tin, marín, de dos pingüé, cúcara, mácara, títere fue" (Eenie, meenie, miney moe, catch a tiger by the toe), a teacher makes fun of his name, Tin Malín. When the teacher says "de dos pingüé" after the boy's name, the Chinese boy reinterprets the words as "two penises" (dos pingas):

> A teacher once asked a little Chinese boy who was attending school for the first time:
> "Little Chinese boy, what is your name?"
> And the little Chinese boy answered:
> "My name is Tin Malín."
> And the teacher added:
> "De dos pingüé."
> And the little Chinese boy answered:
> "No, just one pingüé."[8]

Of course, if the boy's answer stemmed from a lack of familiarity with Cuban popular culture, it would not be benign *choteo* because no challenge would be posed to the teacher's authority.

In another peculiar tale, "El chino cambia chucho" (The Chinaman in the Train Station), a Chinese man who is being interviewed for a job in a train station shows his wit. He is able to find solutions to different hypothetical problems that are presented, except to the last one, which is impossible to solve. Then, disregarding the gravity of the situation, he undermines the interviewer's authority by answering, in his stereotypical accent that, in the last situation, he would only be able to invite his wife, María, to see an amazing crash. As shown, perhaps all these jokes unconsciously "Cubanize" the unfortunate Chinese protagonists by making them creative participants in Cuban *choteo*.

Chinese presence in Cuban aesthetic practices reaches across literary genres and cultural fields without significantly compromising prevalent views about this ethnic group. Moving on to the manner Chinese are depicted throughout Cuban fiction, in Zoé Valdés's novel *La eternidad del instante* (The Eternity of the Instant; 2004) we find a curious display of linguistic double mimicry. Won Sin Fon, a Chinese acrobat, practices self-Orientalization by pretending to have a strong Cantonese accent: "'Yestelday you looked pletty in a man's outfit,' said Won Sin Fon in her Cantonese accent, *yestelday* for yesterday and *pletty* for pretty."[9] Later, however, when she needs to sound more severe, she drops her "comical" Cantonese accent and switches to a pronunciation more in keeping with standard Spanish. Therefore, this character, which was based on a real person, has learned to take advantage of people's expectations, moving in and out of an "Oriental" space according to her own interests. This play with pidginization represents a counter-mockery of the racist mocking that appears in the collection of humorous tales and other texts.

Similarly, in Alfonso Hernández Catá's "Los chinos" and "Cuarenta y nueve chinos" (Forty-nine Chinamen), we find valuable evidence of Cuban attitudes during the first half of the twentieth century.[10] Centuries after the notorious 1550 debate between two Spanish theologians, Bartolomé de las Casas (1474–1566) and Juan Ginés de Sepúlveda (1490–1573), regarding whether Amerindians were human, the humanity of the so-called yellow race was unofficially questioned, at least metaphorically. In fact, along with the aforementioned arguments, the Sinophobia displayed by these narrators and characters provides a meaningful insight into some of the reasons behind the dreadful mistreatment of the Chinese described in *The Cuba Commission Report*.

"Los chinos," from the collection *Piedras preciosas* (Precious Stones; 1924), explores a case of anti-Chinese hysteria arising from the Chinese competing for local jobs. Unfortunately, this adverse reaction was common throughout the Americas. In 1885, for example, three years after the U.S. Congress passed the Chinese Exclusion Act, twenty-eight Chinese workers were murdered by settlers in Wyoming. Historian Tomás Almaguer has also studied the use of Chinese laborers as strikebreakers in urban manufacturing centers in the United States, and the bitter resentment it created among the white working class.[11] Along these lines, the symbolic power of "docile" Chinese labor in the Cuban imaginary has been studied by Frank Scherer:

> For the Cuban oligarchy, then, the transition to wage-labor was only to be accomplished by means of a cheap and "docile" workforce. And it is precisely here, where the representation and perception of China and Chineseness, and ultimately the Orientalist production of knowl-

edge about "the Chinese," makes its entry into the Cuban imaginary. ("Culture" 37)

In "Los chinos," Hernández Catá provides an example of a class-specific conflict between Chinese and non-Chinese laborers. Following the advice of an agitator, a group of international workers striking for better wages poisoned the coffee of ninety Chinese men who were brought in as strikebreakers. Initially, when the striking workers see the thin and small men, they feel sorry for them, convinced that they will not endure the arduous work: "Poor yellow monkeys! They will not withstand that harsh work! [. . .] they were great for cooking in their small restaurants, or to wash and iron most skillfully. . . . Good for women's jobs! But to put up with the sun on their backs for eight hours, and to make holes in the iron, you needed very manly men!"[12] Despite the racist vocabulary, the first-person narrator expresses his admiration for the tireless diligence and resilience of these Chinese men, whom he compares to nervous yellow ants. He also notices that they do everything in silence, without sweating, and that they are satisfied at mealtime with small amounts of rice. Yet, even after the unjust murder of ninety human beings, he is unable to overcome his disgust for this ethnic group: "While a Chinaman always instills in us an insurmountable feeling of repugnance and remoteness in which there is also a bit of fear, a dead Chinaman is something dreadful. . . ."[13] Paradoxically, it is unclear whether the anti-Chinese sentiments of the narrator reflect those of Hernández Catá or whether, on the contrary, this short story continues his line of criticism of racist attitudes toward ethnic minorities, such as blacks and mulattos.[14] In any case, the story ends with a new group of Chinese strikebreakers arriving to replace their dead countrymen, and the narrator, bemused with their persistence and their identical appearance, continuing to animalize and dehumanize them in his descriptions.

This same attitude reappears in another of Hernández Catá's short stories, "Cuarenta y nueve chinos," included in the collection *Cuatro libras de felicidad* (Four Pounds of Happiness; 1933). There, the narrative voice reproduces the dialogue he had with a deck officer of a boat, who for years had not disembarked in Panama or New York, fearing the revenge of a Chinese man. As the mate tells the narrator, many years earlier they were shipping a cargo of Chinese men when one of them escaped while under his watch. Then, to avoid being fired, the deck officer and two other sailors kidnapped a Chinese man from a New York laundry who was bringing his clothes to the ship. Since that day, the mate had feared for his life.

As in "Los chinos," the reader cannot help but wonder whether any of the overtly racist ideas and terms used in the story represent Hernández Catá's point of view or whether, on the contrary, he is denouncing the abuses committed against this ethnic group. At any rate, the mate's disregard for Chinese life is evident in several of his statements and exclamations. In fact, he admits to previously having considered Chinese people on a par with animals and objects. Perhaps for this reason, he repeatedly describes them in animalistic terms, emphasizing their unpleasant and monstrous high-pitched screaming: "From the edge of the hatchway, one could see, down there, the group of pitiful skeletons tightly covered in yellow, with narrow eyes and mouths full of an ancient silence or a short and guttural screaming that had nothing in common with our voices."[15] In another passage the mate compares the Chinese to snakes: "For that piece of yellow meat that, after slithering across the deck, must have slid to the wharf along the length of a cable, I was not going to ruin my career. [. . .] Oh, no way, much less for a Chinese, for a damn Chinese!"[16] When the mate later confesses to a callous crew what he has done, they laugh and celebrate his dastardly deed. It is at this moment that we find the apex of his racist discourse:

> For me, as for all Westerners, a Chinaman was a bile-colored boy doll, viscose, stranger to our sensitivity than the lowest of domestic animals. He was not a fellow man: he was . . . *A Chinaman*, that is, a sort of mechanized meat, with no precise features, mass-produced by an immense country where men were not made in the likeness and image of God.[17]

However, the tone of the narration changes drastically in the last passages, where the mate confesses his remorse for having kidnapped the Chinese man and left him in Panama. Now, his only hope is that the two never meet.

In a more recent work, Miguel Barnet's *Gallego* (Spaniard; 1981), the criticism goes in a different direction.[18] Barnet based this testimonial novel on the real-life data provided by Ángel Pérez, a long-time neighbor of his. In this work Manuel Ruiz, a Galician emigrant who arrived in Havana in 1906 fleeing poverty and the war in Morocco, cannot conceive of framing Chinese behavior within the Cuban national character: "He who is born here lives with hot blood in his veins. This comes from the mixture of the African and the Spaniard. Because what runs through the veins of the Chinese is warm tea. The Chinese have always been very calm."[19] Then, he proceeds to prove the stereotypical docility of the Chinese by providing the real-life example of a Chinese man named Joaquín who, after being harassed by the local police, continued hawking as if nothing had happened. In the protagonist's view, Joaquín's lack of aggressiveness separates him from the ideal notion of *cubanía*. The other Chinese character in the novel, Chino Alfonso, does little to improve these immigrants' image. The protagonist describes him as an annoying, dirty, and vicious man who also smokes opium. Later we learn that Alfonso was imprisoned for life for killing his girlfriend Margarita. Although he was a known murderer, his countrymen refused to provide any information about the case, to the dismay of the police and the protagonist, who cannot understand this lack of cooperation: "It was useless. They wouldn't divulge a thing. Their lips were truly sealed."[20]

As we have seen, this type of passive opposition to Creole dominance, along with their refusal to adopt certain cultural norms from the hegemonic group, increases the antagonism against the Chinese. According to Néstor García Canclini, resistance to the acceptance of certain forms of hybridization takes place "because such phenomena generate insecurity among different cultural groups and conspire against their ethnocentric self-esteem" (xxxvii). In fact, in several of these texts one can observe what García Canclini calls "restricted hybridization": rather than accepting Creole cultural elements indiscriminately, there is a process of selection, which is at times marked by contradictions.

From Cuban fiction, testimonial novels, and popular jokes, let us move to a different genre, theater, where the Chinese in Cuba made their presence known. Napoleón Seuc has argued that the folkloric figures of *el chino* (the Chinaman), *el gallego* (the Spaniard), and *el negrito del batey* (the "darkie" of the sugar refinery) were among the most popular ones in early Cuban theater. In fact, El Chino Wong (Emilio Ruiz) was one of the most popular comic and dramatic actors in Cuba during the 1940s and 1950s, when he played the role of a Chinese in the famous Shangai Theater in Havana.[21]

Besides Chinese characters appearing in Cuban theater, Chinese theater itself was quite popular in Havana. Antonio Chuffat Latour has explained its impact on Cuban society: "Chinese theater was a great event for Cubans, because of its music, which the Creoles found so strange. The kids would sing in Chinese in the streets and would annoy their parents at home."[22] In contrast, the Cuban author Antonio Orlando Rodríguez (1956–) offers an unflattering depiction of Chinese theater in his novel *The Last Masquerade* (*Aprendices de brujo*; 2005).[23] When the Colombian protagonists, Lucho and Wen, attend a play in a Chinese Theater of Havana's Chinatown, they dislike it so much that they call it a "Chinese hell" and describe the music and singing as noise and screaming.

In the context of Chinese theater, Creole perception of the Chinese during the colony's heyday is reflected in the three-act play *El chino* (1947), by Carlos Felipe (his full name was Carlos Felipe Fernández y Santana; 1914–

1975).²⁴ This melodrama takes place in the Havana of this period, where Palma, a woman obsessed with the memory of a love affair she had twenty years earlier, refuses to move to Buenos Aires with her lover, Sergio. Her only hope is that Luis "El Chino" (who despite the title of the play is a secondary character) may remember the real name of her former suitor, a sailor known as José "El Mexicano," who supposedly was his friend. To help Luis remember, a theater play is staged. The mise-en-scène of this play includes an intercalated play set in a replica of the inside of Luis's hotel-brothel, where Palma had the tryst with "El Mexicano" before he left her, promising to return in seven days. Incidentally, the same night a violinist named Santizo committed suicide there, after realizing that his lover would never return to the hotel.

Although Palma claims that she will lose her will to live unless El Chino remembers that man's identity, her lover Sergio does not take her seriously and even jokes about the possibility of her being treated by a Chinese physician. Suddenly, "El Mexicano" shows up at the house. He does not remember having met either Luis or Palma, but tries to win Palma's heart nonetheless. She, on the other hand, recognizes him but wants to confirm his identity with Luis. In the end, the mystery remains unsolved. It is not clear whether that first love really was the newcomer or whether it was Santizo, the violinist who committed suicide. However, it is implied that Santizo was the man Palma had waited for all along and that El Chino is to blame for the suicide, since he never told Palma of the violinist's presence in the hotel.

Certainly, the character relevant to this study is Luis, "El Chino," who is not described in the most flattering way in the stage directions: "He exhibits curious traits: he is lively and talkative at times and depressed and quiet at others, always revealing some sort of mental deficiency, which at times may be interpreted as outright stupidity."²⁵ The other characters refer to him as either "El Chino" or "that thing." When Luis—his presence on stage foreshadowed by the sound of his nervous laughter in the wings—finally appears at the end of the first act, he always speaks in the third person, referring to himself as "Captain."²⁶ Luis's mental deficiency is also pointed out by Palma when she chastizes El Mexicano for not remembering her: "Jerk! Will I need to refresh your memory, like the Chinaman's? In his case, it is understandable; in yours, a healthy man. . . ."²⁷

Luis is portrayed as an annoying and unstable man who constantly complains about insignificant things, such as the shirt they want him to wear for the performance or that the stage does not resemble his hotel. Within the Orientalist trope of passivity Luis carries a fan throughout the performance and is always followed by a red spotlight as he waits indifferently for his turn to speak. Significantly, the stage directions also insist on presenting Luis behind a curtain, as a silhouette, in a manner reminiscent of Chinese shadow puppets. At times, his silhouette grows disproportionately large, perhaps to underscore the importance of his memory; in other scenes, the shadow is described as "phantasmagoric" (92). He becomes a threat, a distorted symbol of his community. Santizo's reaction to his expulsion adds to the grotesque stature of Luis's shadow behind the curtain: "I hate you, damn Chinaman! Abortion from hell! Oh, were you made of mud I would tear you to pieces, I would pulverize you. . . ."[28] In all, the Chinese character that appears in the title is reduced to a simpleton who is often described with denigrating epithets and is indirectly responsible for the violinist's death. Even his alter ego Renata, the Quiet One, is portrayed as a poor paranoid devil. His passivity and dullness make him responsible for the suicide as well as for Palma's despair.

The last work dealing with Cuban Sinophobia that will be analyzed in this chapter is Leonardo Padura Fuentes's detective story *La cola de la serpiente* (The Snake's Tail; 2001).[29] Like Severo Sarduy, Padura Fuentes (1955–) acknowledges Westerners' limitations in understanding the Far East and makes no attempt to understand the Chinese *Weltanschauung*. Instead, he resorts to setting a humorous tone, one somewhat attuned with Cuban *choteo* and maintained by all the characters. In this sense, his protagonist, Detective Mario Conde, repeatedly describes the Chinese in animalistic terms: "One dies and others come, don't they say that the Chinese are like ants?"[30] Juan Chion (whose Chinese name is Li Chion Tai), the police auxiliary that Detective Conde tries to use as an informant for his investigation of the murder of another Chinese man, feels offended by this remark and later reminds him about that comparison several times throughout the plot. To counter the stereotype (although he does so by using another one), Chion maintains that the Chinese "enjoy teasing and are mysterious."[31]

The most serious case of Sinophobia in this text involves Chion's cousin Sebastián (Fu Chion Tang). Years after Sebastián decided to move from Cuba to San Francisco, Juan Chion learned that Sebastián, his last relative, had died, along with thirty-one compatriots, in a cold storage locker where they had been purposely trapped in order to kill them and steal their possessions. Later, the sailors had disposed of the dead bodies by throwing them overboard off the coast of Honduras. Apart from this crime, the list of stereotypes and commonplaces about the Chinese in this short novel is different from those in others, in that both the narrator and the protagonist are aware that they usually have little to do with reality. In fact, they often mock their own ignorance immediately after enumerating their unwarranted assumptions: "Yes, that is precisely a Chinaman, he told himself after pondering the matter for a while; yet he concluded that, better put, that artificial character was hardly a *typical* Chinese, but the byproduct of a schematic Western understanding."[32]

Conde actually wonders why, although the Chinese have lived in the heart of Havana for more than a century, Creoles know virtually nothing about them. Then he contrasts his own prejudice with the historic achievements of the Chinese. By the same token, when the detective asks Chion whether he thinks that the assassination may have had something to do with the Chinese mafia, the old man answers scornfully: "You watch too many movies, Conde. There is no Chinese mafia in Chinatown any more."[33] Later, Chion again mocks the policeman's cultural assumptions and ignorance of Chinese cuisine (perhaps the main symbol of Chinese culture in this novella) by pretending to have cooked dog for him. Despite recognizing his stereotypical assumptions, however, the detective still feels that he needs to uphold them if he is to be a good investigator.

In sum, as we have seen in these texts, there is a darker side to the creative energy and the dynamic originality usually ascribed to the processes of transculturation and hybridization: they have certainly not been harmonious for the Chinese in Cuba. Consequently, this cultural production emphasizes the hostilities, the suffering, the hopelessness, and the feeling of loss produced by displacement.

From these first Sinophobic representations of the Chinese, which abounded in popular jokes, short stories, testimonial novels, and the theater, we will proceed to analyze Orientalist views of the Chinese culture in the next chapter.

2

Strategies for Entering and Leaving Chineseness

4

Orientalism

> I saw and knew that they [the Chinese] were a contemptible herd or crowd of ignorant, sordid slaves, subjected to a government qualified only to rule such a people.
>
> Daniel Defoe, *Robinson Crusoe*

In the introduction to his seminal work *Orientalism* (1978), Edward Said laments the manipulative appropriation that characterizes Orientalism, a hegemonic discourse that connects individual authors with the imperialistic projects of Western powers. In his words, the Romantic invention of the "Orient" mainly by British and French colonists, academics, travelers, artists, and writers, far from contributing to the understanding of this region, facilitated European hegemonic domination through its essentialist emphasis on the ontological inferiority of the colonial subject. In Said's view, misrepresenting the Orient through prejudicial historical generalizations that focused on despotism, splendor, cruelty, and sensuality served to strengthen European self-esteem. *Orientalism* has generated numerous debates between those who praise it and those who criticize it for numerous perceived flaws. Among other criticisms, Said has been accused of being Orientalist himself, creating a sort of Occidentalism, ignoring the voice of the "Orientals," disregarding the Far East, and ignoring gender issues. In any case, this work is still considered one of the key texts of postcolonial studies.

As to the application of Said's theories to Latin American cultural production, Julia A. Kushigian presents a shrewd explanation of the reasons Hispanic Orientalism is so different from its French and English counterparts (as did Juan Goytisolo in the preface to the Spanish translation of Said's book in 2002): "[it] does not present the Oriental society as static and reactionary" (109); rather, it stems from "a spirit of veneration even when it signifies an implied respect for the 'enemy'" (14). Concentrating on the "high" literature produced by Octavio Paz, Severo Sarduy, and Jorge Luis Borges, who were mostly interested in metaphysical aspects of Asian cultures rather than in their sociopolitical reality, Kushigian proposes three characteristics that distinguish Hispanic Orientalism from the Anglo-French version:

(1) its openendedness that promotes an unstable relationship between East and West, wherein its elements are in a constant state of flux and renovation linking the past to the present, reality to fantasy, and so on, thereby never presenting a complete and closed image, (2) its polyglot nature imbuing itself with a cultural and creative consciousness that actively arises from a history of cultural and military invasions, as much of the Iberian Peninsula as of Hispanic America, and (3) its persistent dialogue with the East and interanimation of images, reinforced by intertextuality or an exchange among works unfettered by genre boundaries, that seeks not to erase distinctions but to celebrate them, thereby bringing the Other closer. (14)

Indeed, the abundance of references to the Chinese community in different cultural manifestations is testimony to the importance of this ethnic group in the Cuban imaginary. However, as we saw in the previous chapter and will again in this one, there are also numerous examples of a less "respectful" and "venerating" approach to the Chinese and their culture.

O Mandarim (*The Mandarin*; 1880), a roman à clef by Portuguese author José María Eça de Queiroz (or Queirós; 1845–1900), is an example of this type of Orientalist representation of the Chinese.[1] In a letter to the editor of *La Revue Universelle*, in which Eça de Queiroz attacks Realism and Naturalism in literature, he describes his novella as "a fanciful and fantastic story [. . .] concerned with dreams and not with reality" (3). Yet there is ample evidence that he is indirectly condemning the abuses committed against the coolies in Cuba. In the prologue to *The Mandarin*, he presents a dialogue between two friends, supposedly part of an unpublished play, where one of them proposes to write "as in those wise and delightful Allegories of the Renaissance, let us be sure to include an unobtrusive Morality. . . ." (7). Here, the capitalized words "Allegories" and "Morality" are crucial to understanding the novella. In *Vida y obra de Eça de Queiroz* (Life and Works of Eça de Queiroz), João Gaspar Simoes, Eça de Queiroz's biographer, makes the connection between the plot of this story and the author's experience as Portuguese consul to Havana, a fact José Suárez points out (51).

When, on December 20, 1872, Eça de Queiroz began his diplomatic career in Cuba, he was shocked to discover the terrible working conditions of Chinese contract laborers.[2] According to Suárez, after Eça de Queiroz denounced these abuses, plantation owners tried to bribe him, but he rejected their offers and remained an outspoken critic. It seems plausible that this experience may have inspired him to write *The Mandarin*. In this fictional piece, Teodoro, a clerk in the Portuguese Royal Ministry, finds an ancient folio with a passage titled "The Sundering of Souls"; its contents are about to change his life. The passage indicates that by ringing a small bell in the room where he finds the document, the reader will inherit all the riches of Ti Chin Fu, a mandarin. The Devil appears and encourages Teodoro to do as the passage says if he wishes to obtain the promised wealth. Teodoro rings the bell and later learns that indeed he has inherited a fortune from a deceased mandarin. He goes on to lead a decadent and indolent life, thanks to his newly acquired wealth. Nonetheless he has to live with the guilt of having caused the demise of a man and with recurring visions of the dead mandarin. Concerned that the mandarin's family, now deprived of their rightful estate, may find itself destitute, he decides to go to China to help them. During his stay in China, Teodoro sees this country through an Orientalist lens; that is, as a place where rulers live in lavish luxury while their subjects starve. For this reason, a visiting Russian general, Camiloff, warns Teodoro that should he decide to give millions to the Chinese emperor, "They would be swallowed up in planting gardens, collecting porcelains, carpeting floors with furs, and providing silks for concubines. They would not relieve the hunger of a solitary Chinese or repair one stone of a public highway. They would go into orgies of Asiatic extravagance" (49). Evidently, this passage connects with a long-standing Western literary tradition that began with Marco Polo's accounts of Kublai Khan's luxury, excesses, and centralized power. This situation was hardly unique to Asia, however; it could be found in Europe, in pre-Colombian civilizations, and throughout the world.

Through several allegorical references, the tale equates the mandarin with the coolies in Cuba and Teodoro with their exploiters. For instance, mention of coolies in a fictional piece written by someone who lived in Cuba during those days naturally brings to mind Chinese indentured workers; the mandarin's family lives in Kwangtung province, the region where most coolies were recruited; moreover, condemnation of the Chinese slave trade is implied at the story's end through this observation: "And to you, Mankind, I leave only these words, without comment: 'Only that bread tastes good that we earn each day with our own hands. Do not kill the Mandarin!'" Suárez has interpreted other allegorical clues: the mandarin's riches represent the great fortunes amassed by slave drivers and landowners; the Devil's justifications must have been similar to those given by the bribers; killing the mandarin may be figuratively seen as the exploitation and abuse of Chinese workers by Creoles; and Teodoro's complaint that he was swindled "by all the Latin Republics bordering the Gulf of Mexico" (34) is an obvious swipe at those former Spanish colonies that Eça de Queiroz so despised (Suárez 55). Therefore, the Orientalist scenes depict not the indentured workers in Cuba, but Chinese in China.

Chinese in mainland China are also a source of inspiration for José Lezama Lima (1910–1976). In his short story "Juego de las decapitaciones" (The Beheading Illusion; 1944), included in *Cuentos Cubanos* (Cuban Short Stories; 1974), we again see the pervasive exoticism and cruelty attributed to Chinese emperors, whose orders were always followed by a gong sound.[3] Lezama Lima uses the stylized, perhaps idealized, world of the Chinese as an escapist device to criticize the intellectual elite during the rule of Fulgencio Batista in the 1940s. This topic is expanded in the strange adventures of a magician called Wang Lung, who is in love with the empress. After Wang Lung performs the simple tricks that the emperor enjoys, the latter capriciously decides to imprison him to show the superiority of his authority over magic (read "culture"). Later, the empress helps the magician escape and together they flee to the northern lands ruled by El Real, a bandit who is also a pretender to the throne. In El Real's headquarters, Wang Lung is able to perform true magic, far beyond the emperor's plebeian taste for entertainment; that is, the preferences of Cuban officials in charge of cultural programs.

Similarly, examples abound of Orientalist representations of Chinese in Cuba. Severo Sarduy (1937–1993) had not only Spanish and African roots, but also Chinese because of a distant ancestor from Macao (one of his surnames was "Macao"). He is one of various authors who have conceptualized the Chinese contributions to Cuban identity and cultural memory.[4] Julia A. Kushigian has studied his particular use of Orientalism, concentrating mostly on his views of Buddhism, Zen, and Tantrism, as well as on the Indian, Tibetan, and Mongolian cultures. For this study, however, his Orientalist elaboration of Chinese characters and topics is more relevant. Indeed, Sarduy's works propose a reinterpretation of Cuba's national identity through incorporating previously ignored Chinese cultural contributions into the acknowledged syncretism of the European and African cultures. This approach arises from his contempt for a similar long-standing search for what constitutes Latin American identity, a theme which has dominated fiction throughout that region. In his view, this search is "yet another ideological maneuver by essentially epic novelists who want to strengthen the hold of the mechanisms of authority" (González Echevarría; *Maitreya* viii).

Although both Judith A. Weiss and Roberto González Echevarría have emphasized Sarduy's criticism and mockery of Western Orientalism, his representation of Chineseness seems to coincide, paradoxically, with the stereotypes of "Oriental" cruelty and despotism that Edward Said condemns so vehemently. His novels evoke the merciless cruelty and perversity that supposedly pervade the Chinese realm. Thus, in *From Cuba with a Song* (*De donde son los cantantes*; 1967), an Asian tattoo artist pulls out the general's pinkie fingernail as punishment for his voyeurism. Soon afterward, a Chinese woman takes the general to a laundry where the same tattoo artist warns him that, if he does not stop following Lotus and María Eng, he will be eliminated after being horribly tortured. Extending the exotic visualization of the East, this Chinese woman claims to have been born with a jade stone in her mouth and to have been one of the emperor's concubines.

Chinese cruelty resurfaces in another of Sarduy's novels, *Cobra* (1972), where a Spanish deacon talks about "Leng T'che, the Chinese torture of one hundred pieces" (49).[5] In an interview with Emir Rodríguez Monegal, Sarduy explains that the axis of this novel is the counterpoint between East and West (Rodríguez Monegal, "Conversación" 319) and recalls the origins of his interest in this type of torture: "It deals with that photo taken during the carrying out of a Chinese torture known by the ideograms Leng and T'che, which mean 'one hundred pieces.' [...] The photo so traumatized me that I decided to follow its 'ramifications' or its repercussions in the West."[6] Paradoxically, as mentioned earlier, Chinese coolie testimonialists in *The Cuba Commission Report* complained about suffering the same types of torture in Cuba that were said to take place only in their country. Anyone who has visited a Holocaust museum or the Inquisition museums in Lima, Cartagena de Indias, or Santillana del Mar, Spain, understands that torture and cruelty are not unique to Chinese culture.

Other negative Chinese character traits besides cruelty appear to stem from the Orientalist perspective. In the context of the transculturation process that has taken place in Cuba, non-Chinese characters in *Cobra* adopt several Chinese traditions. Thus, both the protagonist and the madam practice footbinding (which may be considered a form of torture) and other customs: "The two of them, finally, gave in to *passive* resistance. They practiced nonintervention, the *wu-wei*. Like the ancient Chinese sovereigns, they adopted great hats from which hung a curtain of pearls, meant to cover their eyes. They wore earmuffs. Plugging these openings they closed themselves to desire" (17; emphasis added).[7] Here, Sarduy borrows the concepts of *wu-wei* (usually translated as "non-doing" or "inaction") and *wu-yu* (without desire) from Taoist philosophy. Because of the typically Orientalist conceptualization of "the Orient" as "passive" and "static" in both the quoted passage and the following answer provided in an interview, it seems that Sarduy misinterpreted *wu-wei*, in a reductionist way, as stagnancy, passivity, or inertia: "The Chinese world seems to me a world of perception or, rather, a static world, a world located in the dialectics of contemplation and extreme action."[8] Rather than being mere passivity or laziness, as it has been wrongly understood in the West, *wu-wei* is the result of listening within, of the intense alertness and watchfulness resulting from relaxation, of inner nonresistance, and of "going with the flow" of the Tao.[9] This exercise leads to a sense of connection with others as well as with one's environment, thereby reminding us that we are part of an interconnected whole. As Victor H. Mair puts it,

> *Wu-wei* does not imply absence of action. Rather, it indicates spontaneity and noninterference; that is, letting things follow their own natural course. For the ruler, this implies reliance on capable officials and the avoidance of an authoritarian posture. For the individual, it means accomplishing what is necessary without ulterior motive. (138)

Returning to *Cobra*'s strange plot, we find that after consuming drugs and herbs, the protagonist turns into a dwarf and undergoes a sex-change operation in Tangiers. Eventually, she ends up mutilated during a perverse religious ceremony performed in Amsterdam by a gang of bikers and a sect of exiled Tibetan lamas. Julia Kushigian has interpreted these grotesque and carnivalistic rituals in Sarduy's works as a tool for familiarization. In this light, Sarduy does not aim at the core of Eastern worldviews. Instead of attempting to interpret or represent their essence, he humbly limits himself to mimicking and exposing their repercussions in the West. In other words, he focuses on how Westerners have traditionally conceived of Asian cultures. "The Orient," Julia Kushigian points out, "will be recognized in Sarduy's novels for its apparent artificiality and superficiality as he confirms that the essence of his work is the surface" (78).

In the final analysis, although Sarduy does mock Western misrepresentations of the East, his attempt to unite East and West through a postmodern cultural dialogue marked by artifice ends up reducing Chineseness to the same stereotyping ethos of Western Orientalism that he supposedly condemns in *From Cuba with a Song*. Although Sarduy often uses a parodic tone in his works and ensures that the reader does not confuse characters and landscapes with reality, he is unable to escape the traditional perspective through which Westerners have misinterpreted Eastern cultures. Notwithstanding the symbolic and metaphoric levels of his prose, his identification of Chinese characters and culture with passivity and cruelty (violence, mutilation, castration, death, scatology) leads us to question whether Sarduy manages to evade the paradigm that he condemns.

A sort of benevolent Orientalism appears in Zoé Valdés's *La eternidad del instante* (The Eternity of the Instant; 2004), a novel where the Chinese world turns into an exoticized re-creation that often lacks verisimilitude.[10] Here, once again, a Western author interprets the Oriental mystique. However, the fact that Valdés dedicates the novel to her grandfather Maximiliano Megía/Mo Ying increases the verisimilitude of the story, perhaps "giving her permission" to explore Chinese culture. In any case, the author acknowledged that, in order to evoke a Chinese world with which she was not familiar, she found her inspiration and information in Chinese literature and art. As a result, the novel displays an impressive array of high and popular cultural manifestations that are typical of Chinese life in both China and Cuba. This inclusion places the text within the *costumbrista* tradition.[11] The author's implicit fondness for Chinese culture is manifested in her enthusiastic underscoring of Chinese achievements, including their invention of paper, the sailing compass, and gunpowder. These didactic passages appear throughout the plot, often included in narratives of the characters' dreams and reveries.

Valdés offers equal praise to the Chinese community in Cuba for its achievements and tenacity. Thus, despite the partial loss of his memories, the protagonist, Mo Ying/Maximiliano Megía (who was born in 1902 and left China in 1925) reminds his friends about the Sino-Cuban ice-cream parlors, laundries, hardware shops, and grocery stores. In some chapters he is one hundred years old (the plot does not follow a chronological line) and believes that Chinese laundries that have been closed down for decades are still in business. Other characters also mention landmarks of Sino-Cuban culture, including the Chinese saint Sanfancón, the Shangai Theater, the *chiffá* (Chinese charades), and Chinese festivals, as well as Cuban customs related to the Chinese presence on the island, like the *chinita de la suerte* (little Chinese good luck girl).[12] Perhaps Zoé Valdés tries to include too much of her research in the plot, a decision that occasionally detracts from the story line and brings the novel close to literary chinoiserie. Furthermore, the author's literary construction of a Chinese ambiance is often disrupted by her mention of French and other European authors and painters.[13] She makes occasional cultural mistakes, such as in the passage where Sueño Azul gives Mo Ying a white suit to wear to her sister's wedding, when in China white is the color for mourning and therefore inappropriate for a wedding. Also, Valdés apparently does not realize that in China the surname comes before the given name. It was only after their migration to Western countries that many Chinese changed the order of their names.

In spite of her mention in the novel of widespread male chauvinism, opium consumption, and an affinity for gambling and prostitution, Valdés generally romanticizes the sensuality, refinement, and exoticism of Chinese culture. For this reason, certain scenes in China seem overly wrought and melodramatic, with occasional stereotypical inclusions, such as the gong. Xue Ying, the protagonist's sister, who is able to fly from one roof to the next, is reminiscent of characters in recent films such as Ang Lee's *Ngo foo chong lung* (*Crouching Tiger, Hidden Dragon*; 2000) or Zhang Yimou's *Shi mian mai fu* (*The House of Flying Daggers*; 2004): "In the yard, Xue Ying performed dance movements, using an old saber, as she sang a beautiful melody;"[14] "and with a triple jump she rose and fell on the roof of the adjoining Harmony Room without making the slightest sound."[15]

However, unlike male authors writing about the Chinese in Cuba, Valdés adds her feminine perspective to the subject by also depicting the suffering of the wives and children the coolies left behind. Albeit lapsing occasionally into an affected sentimentalism, *La eternidad del instante* recalls these collateral victims of colonial exploitation. Thus, Li Ying's wife and daughters suffer due to his departure and the ensuing lack of contact. Consequently, the behavior of Li Ying's daughter Xue Ying becomes rather odd: she spends hours on the roof of the house with her eyes covered and takes to expressing herself in a babble that no one understands. When her brother Mo Ying tells her that their mother is worried about her, Xue Ying, with a kerchief over her eyes, criticizes their father's decision to abandon them, thereby causing his wife to forsake life. In the criticism of her father lies a woman's interpretation of the real motives behind male emigration: "Instead of digging in with Mom and us, the children, he chose simply to say that he was going far away in search of wealth. You may have bought that, but I consider his decision only a poor excuse. He chose the easy way out: he reneged on the family and left Mom with the weight of the world upon her shoulders."[16] This character's stance adds a new dimension to Chinese migration because, as she makes clear, men often saw immigration as a way to test their manliness, to prove themselves to themselves and to their families. Yet this interpretation is certainly questionable if we consider that four out of five indentured workers testified that they were deceived into emigrating or were abducted.

Xue Ying's younger sister, Irma Cuba Ying, is equally eccentric and also suffers the consequences of her father's decision to migrate: "I suffer from an ear ailment. Noises really worsen my condition. I guess since Daddy left I don't want to listen to anything but his voice."[17] In fact, the suffering of Li Ying's family is reminiscent of that of the families of the "disappeared," or missing citizens, during South American military dictatorships. Worried that her husband does not write, Xiao Ying suspects that something serious must have befallen him. She spends her days in deep depression, writing him poems, although she has no address where she can send them.

Within the context of this rhapsody about all things Chinese, the sage master Meng Ting, who is somewhat of a simplistic stock character, describes his protégé Mo Ying to the boy's parents as a wise man, a prophet, and an ascetic. The protagonist receives a wonderful education from both the monks in a nearby monastery and his parents. Under their auspices, Mo Ying discovers ancient Chinese poetry, becomes a very talented singer, and learns to play several instruments.[18] Similarly, Mei, his future wife, is introduced as an educated seventeen-year-old girl who spends her leisure time reading, copying old manuscripts, and composing poems that she records by wetting the tip of her queue in tea and writing them in a velvet-covered notebook.

This romanticization of Chinese refinement is accentuated through a contrast with the unrefined lovers' dialogues in scenes taking place in Cuba. In China, for example, Mei discovers sexuality by perusing one of her father's books, which is illustrated with erotic drawings bearing captions such as "Spring sensual ritual."[19] Likewise, love scenes between Mei and Mo Ying are depicted in a lyrical mode through references to jasmine fragrance, water lilies, and jade, and female body parts are evoked with exotic metaphors such as Clear Water Springs, Great Sea, Eternal Mountain, and Shady Door. By comparison, in Cuba, the sexual encounters between Maximiliano Megía and his Irish wife, and those between the widow Paulina Montes de Oca and her Chinese lovers (a female contortionist, dancer, and performer named Won Sin Fon, and a male performer named Lou Tang) are depicted in quite prosaic and light-hearted terms, often tinged with humor. The preponderance of graphic eroticism and vulgar language are indicative of Valdés's perception of her own country's worldview as opposed to that of the Chinese. In a way, by writing about the Chinese Other, she is constructing a national identity for all of Cuba.

Part of the "benevolent Orientalism" in the novel arises from the author's penchant for underscoring that culture's exoticism, to the extent that some characters drink hydromel with peach juice and powdered gold, and midwives are paid with coral pieces, and prostitutes with poems. In this context, Mo Ying discovers in his journey the coincidences between reality and the descriptions of his country in Marco Polo's *The Description of the World* (also known as *The Travels of Marco Polo*), a book that he always carries. Regardless of whether or not these passages lack verisimilitude, Mo Ying, before he sets out on his travels, has already "seen" China through the eyes of a thirteenth-century European who probably never reached China, an impression that corroborates the novel's Eurocentric or Orientalist views.[20]

To understand Valdés's position, it is worth noting comments that she made in an interview: "Something I was very interested in learning about was the history of the Chinese ideogram and erotic drawings."[21] Her expectations, like those of Flora Fong, Herrera Eng, and others, coincide with one of the exotic mysteries that has always kindled the imagination of Western travelers: the Chinese writing system, which is described several times in her novel.[22]

In spite of these flaws, Valdés is one of a few authors who incorporate the suffering of Chinese families who did not make the voyage into the coolie experience and who explore the causes of Chinese migration to Cuba. Thus, in May 1919, disillusioned with sociopolitical events and skeptical about artists' future in China, Li Ying, the protagonist's father, chooses to join his cousin Weng bu Tah in Cuba. The dialogues in chapters that take place in China before he makes that decision portray a country that is on the verge of collapse: peasants living in dire poverty, Chinese culture becoming extinct, a tragic dependency on foreign countries, and a society that had been disintegrating since the 1890s. In fact, Li Ying claims that his father became ill through witnessing the demise of his culture. Local corruption, greed, and constant harassment by the superpowers of the period account for Chinese poverty. Under these circumstances, Mo Ying's mother and his master, Meng Ting, advise him to leave China. Therefore, although the author does mention the recruiters' ploys, Mo Ying and his father, Li Ying, migrate voluntarily, unlike the indentured workers who stated in *The Cuba Commission Report* that they had been kidnapped or deceived.

Moving on to a different literary genre, we find the Chinese community often represented in Cuban poetry as well. A similar process of exoticization and libidination of the Chinese appears in a poem by Luis Rogelio Nogueras (1945–1986) entitled "Mirando un grabado erótico chino" (Looking at a Chinese Erotic Engraving), which is featured in his book *La forma de las cosas que vendrán* (The Shape of Things to Come; 1989).[23] In the poem, he envisions China as an impenetrable and arcane world: "Looking at a Chinese erotic engraving / You asked me / How was it possible to do it that way / We tried / Remember? / We tried / But it was a failure / China has its arcana / China has its secrets / China has its insurmountable walls."[24] Other Cuban poets, like Nicolás Guillén, Miguel Barnet, and Nicolás Cosio Sierra, have also found inspiration in their imagined versions of the Chinese world. Thus, in an untitled poem by Cosio Sierra, the poetic voice visualizes the stereotypical cruelty assigned to Chinese despots: he plans to visit "ancestral China" some day to admire its pagodas and to hear firsthand "the tale about the powerful and cruel Empress" (2–3). Similarly, Barnet conjures a sensual world of empresses, princesses, jade, lotus flowers, dragons, and great walls in the ten poems included in his collection *Poemas chinos* (Chinese Poems; 1993). In "En el barrio chino" (In Chinatown), written in 1940, he re-creates an imagined Chinese past while waiting for his loved one on Calle Zanja, in Havana's Chinatown. In this poem, after describing nostalgically the broken signs of a Cantonese movie theater, "the yellow smoke / of a broken lineage" (5–6), and the "black ideograms / that no longer say anything" (9–10), he envisions himself, from an Orientalist perspective, "in the company of a choir of eunuchs" (18).[25]

Some of the most obviously Orientalist passages in Cuban cultural production have to do with the representation of Chinese women, who, as will be demonstrated in the following chapter, are fetishized and turned into objects of desire.

5

Chinese Women as Exotica

> Free woman,
> be free
> as the moon is freed
> from the eclipse of the sun.
> With a free mind,
> in no debt,
> enjoy what has been given to you.
> Get rid of the tendency
> to judge yourself
> above, below, or
> equal to others.
>
> "Songs of the Nuns," *Therigatha*

Most Chinese who migrated to Cuba and other countries in the Americas, particularly in the early years, were men. "There were 56 Chinese females in Cuba in 1862, 32 in 1872, and 81 in 1877," according to Denise Helly (29).[1] As of December 8, 2005, only 30 native Chinese women remain on the island. For this reason, cultural products resulting from the Chinese presence in Cuba tend to pertain to men and their "bachelor societies." With time many of these men intermarried with black and Creole women; others brought Chinese wives from the homeland. It is the *mestizo*, or multiethnic, daughters resulting from mixed marriages who are often depicted as characters in Cuban and Cuban American literature.

The first European writers to travel to China often included in their works commentaries about the role of women in that society. For instance, in 1575, Miguel de Luarca, a Spanish soldier, exposed the intricacies of Chinese punishment for unfaithful wives.[2] Likewise, anthropologists have often stressed the subordinate situation of dependency and oppression that women suffer in the patriarchal and patrilineal societies of traditional, rural China. Chinese women were not even allowed to inherit property from their parents:

> When they married, they exchanged their dependence on fathers and brothers for absolute dependence on husbands, and later in life, sons. Without divorce as an option to protect themselves against ill treat-

ment, women went to great lengths to develop the strongest bond possible between themselves and their sons in order that the latter would rise to their mothers' defense when necessary. So single minded were many women in developing such relationships with their sons that they often made life miserable for their daughters-in-law, who were seen as competitors for their sons' affections. (Haviland 264–65)

These social practices have often been associated with a Confucian textual tradition. However, Alejandro Lee Chan and other critics have pointed out that, contrary to popular belief, one should not ascribe the origin of these misogynistic traditions to Confucius's writings, but to his translators and interpreters (Lee Chan 46).

Indeed, for centuries many Chinese women endured conditions of semi-slavery. Many were not allowed to leave the house except when absolutely necessary, and then only in the company of their father or husband. Arranged marriages usually took place when girls were between the ages of ten and fifteen. If the husband died, the eldest son became the head of the household. This traditional social exclusion of women was brought to Havana's Chinatown and is often echoed in their literary and cultural representation, as can be noticed in Chuffat Latour's *Apunte histórico de los chinos en Cuba*. In this sense, Lisa Yun states, "Chinese women mostly appear in Chuffat's text as social capital for the merchant male community. Repeatedly, successful merchants were described as being heads of family, as being married to either white 'cubana' or 'china' women, and as having produced educated children" (38).

Yet the works analyzed here contain exceptions to this general rule. In her study *Teachers of the Inner Chambers*, Dorothy Ko argues that literate gentrywomen in seventeenth-century Jiangnan, China, were neither silenced nor oppressed; rather, they exerted influence on family affairs and, consequently, on politics. In addition, in spite of mobility limitations resulting from the practice of footbinding, they traveled with their husbands as well as with other women. Ko reveals that, thanks to the socioeconomic improvements in the region, there existed a "growing availability and acceptance of women's education, which, by the seventeenth century, created a visible cohort of gentrywomen with a literary and classical education" (*Teachers* 11). Although it is true that in seventeenth-century China the percentage of women within the population of educated people was very small, the visibility of literate and erudite women, and their valorization in local histories, is proof that women were able to go beyond domestic confines and receive an education. As Ko explains, these women became published and anthologized poets, recognized painters, and teachers. Curiously, some of them were even known as "honorary men," and there were cases of transvestite girls being reared as boys.

A literary example of a girl who has been reared as a boy is the character Chen Fang in *Monkey Hunting* (2003), Cristina García's (1959–) third novel. She is unique among female Chinese characters in that she is not objectivized for her "exotic" physical appeal. The erotic scenes with Dauphine de Möet, the wife of a French former diplomat, are described from Chen Fang's point of view. In fact, she is the only character in the novel who narrates the story from a first-person perspective.

For years, Chen Fang's mother lied to her husband, Lorenzo Chen, a Chinese Cuban physician, so that he would keep sending the money to cover the costs of educating the person he thought was his son. Cross-dressing while receiving a formal education fosters Chen Fang's rebellious and independent spirit, in sharp contrast with her sisters' submissiveness. By narrating Chen Fang's trials and tribulations in China, Cristina García exposes the collective Cuban identity as well as her own. One chapter includes a seventy-two-year-old Chen Fang, who has been imprisoned for three years and is now the victim of China's political and sexual intolerance. Accused of having a foreign father, of being a spy for the Kuomintang and the French, and of "engaging in decadent behavior with the enemy" (229), she is constantly interrogated and tortured by Mao Zedong's Red Guard during the "Great Proletarian Cultural Revolution" (1966–1976). It may be inferred that the description of the Cultural Revolution reflects the author's dissatisfaction with modern Cuba. Later, the author abandons indirectness and makes her criticism of Fidel Castro's politics more explicit through the rumors Chen Fang has heard about her father's country: "I understand that everything in Cuba has changed since his time, that his country is experimenting with a similar madness. For what else can one call the subjugation of millions to the will of a troubled few?" asks Chen Fang (232).

In contrast to Chen Fang, other Chinese and Chinese Cuban female characters are libidinized and objectivized for their "exotic" physical appeal. Alejandro Lee Chan points out that the sensuous *china mulata* is one of the stereotypical characters in the portrayals of Chinese Cubans. Three of the most developed fictional Chinese mulattas appear in *The Messenger* (*Como un mensajero tuyo*; 1998), by Mayra Montero; *I Gave You All I Had* (*Te di la vida entera*; 1996), by Zoé Valdés; and *La cola de la serpiente* (2001), by Leonardo Padura Fuentes.[3] Aida Petrirena Cheng is the protagonist of Montero's *The Messenger* and one of the most well-rounded Sino-Cuban female characters.[4] At the same time that her mixed ethnic background is fetishized by men, it is also the basis for society's rejection and suspicion of her. Thus, Ester, Baldomero Socada's white wife, commits suicide upon realizing that her husband has had a daughter with "a mulatta seamstress, and, to make matters even worse, someone they called 'Chinita'" (15).[5] As a result, Aida assimilates these views and develops a double consciousness that is evidenced in several passages where she describes herself in racial terms: "I was a mulatta who had her father's Chinese eyes and a nose that came from the Lucumi part. I was a combination, as mixed as Neapolitan fever" (59).[6] Evidently, when the character compares the mixture of her blood to a fever, she is seeing herself through the eyes of the Creole Others. Along these lines, she tends to associate her African heritage with her sex life: "All I did was take him inside me, but it was his will, he sank into this Chinese flesh because he wanted to, this flesh that turned mulatta when we made love" (176).[7] In spite of the fact that she is of mixed blood and thus not fully accepted by either blacks or Chinese in Cuba, her mixed physical traits have made her an irresistible exotic beauty and the living proof of the legendary beauty of the *chinas mulatas*. Other characters in the novel so stress her combination of Chinese and African features that it is this combination, rather than her beauty, that becomes sexually charged. Just as the characters Vicente Pérez Navarro and Abadelio Trujillo had done, the cook Violeta Anido recalls Aida's voluptuous beauty, which resulted from the combination of her African body and her dark, straight Asian hair and delicate features.

Another *china mulata* who becomes an object of desire for male characters and an object of analysis for Zoé Valdés is Cuca Martínez, the protagonist of *I Gave You All I Had*.[8] As the author lightheartedly explains, her phenotype, which includes gently slanted golden eyes, makes her irresistible to men: "She had a way of sashaying down a street, with a swish to the left and a swish to the right, of bobbing back and forth between Irish passion and Oriental patience, that could bring even the most languid penis to attention" (36).[9] As the plot develops, however, readers realize that Valdés has chosen this Sino-Cuban character to allegorically depict the progressive physical decay of Old Havana since 1959. Therefore, whereas in *Monkey Hunting* Chen Fang's search for freedom symbolizes the sociopolitical struggle in Castro's Cuba, here Valdés voices her rage at the disappearance of a beloved past through satire: an exotic Chinese mulatta extracts her own teeth and destroys her beauty to protest her lover's abandonment.

Similarly, Padura Fuentes's detective story *La cola de la serpiente* reinforces this sexual objectification of Chinese mulattas.[10] The protagonist, Lieutenant Mario Conde, stifles his sexual desires for the *china mulata* Patricia Chion by convincing himself that she is a nymphomaniac and a prostitute, although the text does not support his assumptions. In contrast with other descriptions of Chinese mulattas, however, Patricia is not only sexualized but also described as an aggressive man-eater. Delving into the mythology of the *vagina dentata*, shared by both Asia and Europe and popularized by Sigmund Freud, Lieutenant Conde dreams that Patricia's vagina devours his entire body: "After the thick bush, Conde explored the furrow climbing up toward a deep, mossy and ravenous well, through which his hand entered, and then his arm, and finally the rest of his body, as if sucked in by a relentless whirlpool" (189).[11]

Like Chinese mulattas, Chinese women are also seen as sensual objects of desire by male characters. The notion that Chinese women are irresistibly exotic and erotic even appears in a 1976 lecture by Alejo Carpentier in Havana. María Elena Balán has noted that in describing the commercial vitality of Havana's Chinatown during the first three decades of the twentieth century, Carpentier made references to the Chinese theater and to Won-Sin-Fon, a beautiful Chinese actress. Carpentier confessed that he and his friends were jealous of a young Cuban who had had an affair with Won-Sin-Fong, to them "the embodiment of Chinese exoticism," about which they had read in poems by Rubén Darío, Julián del Casal, and José Manuel Poveda.[12] The contortionist Won Sin Fon (another spelling for Won-Sin-Fong) is also a sexualized character in another novel by Zoé Valdés, *La eternidad del instante*. In fact, her character is first introduced when Paulina Montes de Oca sees her having sex with a Chinese man named Lou Tang. Later that night, Won Sin Fon, who is stereotypically depicted as a Chinese porcelain doll, has sex with Paulina Montes de Oca in a graphically described erotic scene. While having sex, Won Sin Fon asks Bambú del Sur, a smiley Chinese female servant dressed in see-through tulle, to fan them. In addition, Won Sin Fon offers Paulina additional sex with her and Lou Tang, in a ménage à trois, if the latter helps Mo Ying.

Still within the realm of Chinese women's representation, *La eternidad del instante* briefly broaches the controversial custom of footbinding.[13] Along with Chinese writing, footbinding is a Chinese cultural practice that has intrigued Westerners since the sixteenth century. Historian Dorothy Ko has assigned the origins of this tradition to the Neo-Confucian philosopher Zhu Xi (1130–1200), who allegedly tried to teach locals the need to segregate women from men (*Teachers* 148). She also points out that Chinese women's refusal to show themselves to European travelers may be seen as an act of defiance against foreign intervention ("Bondage" 13).[14]

Through Mo Ying, Valdés questions the tradition. However, surprisingly for a novel by a contemporary woman writer, the dialogue does not evince strong objections to this oppressive and painful practice perpetrated against Chinese women. Rather than criticizing it, Valdés borrows from the aesthetic tenets of magical realism. Thus, Mo Ying meets women with almost invisible feet who, instead of walking, always dance on their tiptoes. Sueño Azul, one of them, explains that, although the custom was abolished in 1911, in her town they maintain it to preserve a regional dance that requires that its dancers have such feet. She also claims that footbinding is a source of pride for the local women and glorifies the custom by attributing magical powers to it: "'It is not just a tradition. For us it is the outcome of centuries of aesthetic respect for all that is nature. Here, we women are considered flowers or clouds as well as shamans. We bring rain with our endless dancing to ensure a successful rice harvest.'"[15]

While this character's ideas do not necessarily reflect those of the author, the dialogue brings to mind one aspect of multiculturalism criticized by Susan Moller Okin and other political theorists; namely, that "culture" and the concern for preserving cultural diversity should never be an excuse for oppressing women or ignoring gender discrimination in minority cultures:

> In the case of a more patriarchal minority culture in the context of a less patriarchal majority culture, no argument can be made on the basis of self-respect or freedom that the female members of the culture have a clear interest in its preservation. Indeed, they *might* be much better off if the culture into which they were born were either to become extinct (so that its members would become integrated into the less sexist surrounding culture) or, preferably, to be encouraged to alter itself so as to reinforce the equality of women—at least to the degree to which this value is upheld in the majority culture. (Okin 22–23)

Continuing with the exotic idealization of Chinese culture, Valdés validates and counterbalances Sueño Azul's stance by presenting her as a sexually liberated woman who, in spite of her respect for footbinding, refuses to follow social conventions. In fact, she feels free to give Mo Ying a strong aphrodisiac before having sex with him, and when the latter promises to come back to marry her, she reminds him that he is not obligated; she prefers to be a free woman. To strengthen her position, Sueño Azul gives accounts of rebellious Chinese women who dared to defy their parents' authority.[16]

As an extension of last chapter's discussion of Orientalism in Severo Sarduy's opus, it is worth noting his tendency toward the libidination of Chineseness, a flaw that fills his writing with the stereotypes of "Oriental sensuality" that Said criticized. In this sense, Donald Ray Johndrow has noticed the correlation between Cuban Chineseness and sexual desire in his works:

"The distillation of this *collage* yields its central theme and, for Sarduy, the essence of *lo chino en lo cubano*: desire" (451). From a different viewpoint, Julia Kushigian has linked the presence of eroticism in Sarduy's novels to his interest in Buddhist philosophy and his recurrent fusion of binaries (East/West, male/female, self/other): "In the West that which is sacred is separated rigorously from the erotic or the illicit, while in the East, and specifically in Buddhist philosophy, the differences between the profane and the sacred are dissolved" (87).

However, it could also be argued that Sarduy's depiction of Chinese characters falls within a Western Orientalist fascination with Chinese women as exotica. Thus, in his novel *Maitreya* (1977), eroticism suddenly turns into pornography in the description of a ménage à trois that includes the Chinese Luis Leng and two Chinese lesbians in a New York Chinese restaurant called El Jardín de los Song (Garden of the Song Dynasty): "Carefully closing the screen, Louis Leng entered the room. He opened the curtain. Cautiously he kneeled between the thighs of the women caressing each other. When they were about to come, he separated their pussies with his hands, sticking his prick between them" (94).[17] Chinese characters, particularly female ones, are sexualized time and again. This is also evident in the scene of Cobra where we read about "two Indonesian girls, newly arrived, who sprayed their beds with jasmine water, masturbated with their fingertips, soaked in privet powder, and who attained dilations of the rear thanks to a breathing method of scanning with samsaric sighs" (121).[18]

Commenting on the centrality and symbolic complexity of Chinese cuisine, Fredric Jameson points out "that the very rich Chinese vocabulary for sexual matters is extraordinarily intertwined with the language of eating" (74). In this light, Chinese characters in *Maitreya* are also eroticized through culinary metaphors. As Alicia E. Vadillo points out, the references to Chinese food hide implicit meanings related to the analogy between food and sex (n.p.).

A similar identification of Chineseness with sexual desire and exoticism takes place in the novel *From Cuba with a Song* (*De donde son los cantantes*). Its five sections focus on the main ethnic groups that, according to Sarduy, have contributed to Cuban culture: the Chinese, the Spanish, and the African.[19] The three chapters of the second section, which is devoted to Chinese contributions to Cuban identity, take place at the Shangai, the legendary theater for burlesque opera located, before the Cuban Revolution, in Havana's Chinatown. There, Mortal Pérez, a lecherous Spanish general, woos a Chinese transvestite called Lotus Flower, whom he confuses with a beautiful

Chinese soprano and vedette. Chineseness is here reduced to the fantasy or obsession of a perverted Western military man.

In his anti-Orientalist interpretation of Sarduy's writings, González Echevarría maintains that the deformations of the characters "result from the West's desire for the East (Mortal for Lotus), an East that is really a projection of the West's own mystification" (Maitreya ix). In like fashion, Judith A. Weiss, in her analysis of Sarduy's novel *Cobra* (1972), explains that relations between East and West go beyond the sexual conversion and the parody of Asian religions as a Western fad, to include a "final conversion of West to East, paradoxically through the passageways of North Africa and the dives of Amsterdam (with its parodies of Orientalism)" (63).[20] While both interpretations are astute, evidence abounds that Sarduy's attempt to mock and debunk Orientalism by adopting an Orientalist standpoint turns into an example of Orientalist fetishism itself, since most if not all images of boundless cruelty and erotic exoticism ultimately remain in the reader's mind.

Along with Lotus Flower, other Chinese characters, such as María Eng and the ubiquitous prostitutes Help Chong and Mercy Si-Yuen, are also sexualized in the novel. Although Help and Mercy assure the blond general that Lotus Flower is a mirage and a trompe l'oeil, he cannot fathom that his muse is a simulacrum.[21] In line with the principles of Orientalism itself, the general's vivid imagination has created its own expectations and nothing will change his mind. Unable to visit Lotus Flower, he stifles his fetishism by sighing with desire upon finding "her" underwear. He also participates in sadomasochist sessions with the other Chinese characters, Help and Mercy, whipping them while asking them whether they have seen Lotus. Later, he tries to requite his longing for Lotus by observing María Eng having sex with a character called Johnny. Eventually, the general concedes that Lotus Flower will never reciprocate his love and, frustrated, decides to kill her.

In spite of his allegedly good intentions, Sarduy limits his views of Chinese contributions to Cuban culture to desire, sensuality, and exotic splendor, thus imbuing his novels with Orientalist overtones. In fact, Sarduy himself stated that the Chinese world is "both fixed and spinning with desire. It's a world of desire."[22]

Moving away from the views of Chinese and Chinese Cuban women as exotica, the next chapter will analyze how writers and artists have been Orientalized not only by critics, but also by their own biases.

6

Self-Orientalization

> If I am inescapably Chinese by *descent*, I am only sometimes Chinese by *consent*. When and how is a matter of politics.
>
> Ien Ang

When critics use the term "Western Orientalism," it is because of the synchronous existence of Eastern Orientalism. This type of self-perception coexists with Eastern Occidentalism, an approach that resorts to similar patterns of essentialization, stereotyping, and dehumanization and that can be often traced in Islamic and Asian studies of the so-called Western world.[1] This chapter, however, will focus on a related occurrence: the processes of self-Orientalization displayed in the works of Chinese mulatto poet Regino Pedroso and in the paintings of Sino-Cuban artists Flora Fong, Pedro Eng Herrera, and María Lau.

The very title of the collection of poems *Nosotros* (We; 1933) by Regino Pedroso (1898–1983), indicates a redirection of his poetry from Modernist individualism to avant-garde social commitment.[2] At the same time, in this collection he asserts his ethnic pride through a process of Sinicization of his own poetry. Writing during the heyday of the Negrista poetic movement in Cuba (whose most famous representative was his friend Nicolás Guillén), Pedroso follows the ethnic trend and chooses to rediscover his Chinese heritage through his poems and essays.[3] And here I emphasize the verb "choose," as being Chinese is clearly an option in the cases of Pedroso, Flora Fong, and others. This power of selection opens our eyes to the strategies artists and authors use for entering and leaving Chineseness depending on the circumstances. In effect, Pedroso's situation is more a case of social affiliation (in Said's sense) than of instinctual filiation to Chinese culture; that is, although he does not inherit much of this culture, he consciously chooses to adopt it.

Pedroso could claim African ancestry, as Guillén did, because he was the son of a black mother and a Chinese father whom he hardly knew. When the poet was still a young boy, his father abandoned his mother and five siblings to return to Canton, where he died a short time later. Debbie Lee has interpreted as follows the segment of the "auto-bio-prólogo" (auto-bio-prologue) to *Nosotros* where Pedroso states that he belongs to "the human race" and that his pigmentation is "black-yellow. (With no other mixture)":[4]

> Not only does Pedroso affirm his ethnicity, he calmly rejects any claim to European ancestry. The "(Sin otra mezcla)," seeming to refer to the European blood mix that is a part of so many Cubans, reveals that it plays no part in the Afro-Chinese man who is Regino Pedroso. His self-alienation from the body that originally alienated him frees him from the restraints, thus placing the power of self-definition in his own hands. (75)

The prologue, which resembles an application form, describes Pedroso's profession as "Exploited." A few lines later, the poet elaborates on the origins of such exploitation: he belongs to the proletariat, considers himself a victim of Yankee imperialism, and is a member of the "Ethiopic-Asian" race, conceived of as inferior in "bourgeois ideology."

As part of his avowed goal of writing socially committed poetry, Pedroso mentions both his personal Chinese heritage and the injustice of the coolie trade in several poems in *Nosotros*. In "Los Conquistadores," for example, he briefly mentions the coolie trade in a line where the Spaniards go to the "old land of Li Tai-pe."[5] Likewise, his political commitment and his Chinese ethnic background are alluded to in the title of another poem, "Salutación a un Camarada Culí" (Salutation to a Coolie Comrade), which includes the following lines: "We are doubly joined / by ties of lineage and by new ideological concerns."[6] The poetic "I" honors the perseverance of all coolies who, despite long years of debasement and exploitation in Cuba, never ceased to fight for their freedom and for that of their adopted country. Simultaneously, he tries to persuade his Sino-Cuban comrade and sympathetic readers to fight a pan-American revolution. According to the poetic voice, meeting the coolie comrade has awakened in him an awareness of his Asian heritage, which had been dormant because of his yearning to bring together all Hispanic peoples in the Americas. He realizes that, since his background is Chinese and black African, he is the product of two colonial oppressions. Furthermore, these oppressions are now joined by new threats that hide behind the mask of civilization: Yankee imperialism and "the hateful threat posed by the barbarian Nippon."[7]

Intertwined within these lines that overflow with social commitment (a new edition of this book was published for the twenty-fifth anniversary of the Cuban Revolution) is the view that the Chinese past is a negative set of oppressive and passive traditions. Besides mentioning the "corrupt and sickly mandarins" and repeating the notion of the "black night of the past," the poet condemns opium consumption in three different lines.[8] Likewise, in spite of the line "I am of your race, yellow man," a double consciousness makes Pedroso perceive his own ethnic group through the eyes of his Creole countrymen.[9] At the same time as he embraces his ethnic roots, he has obviously internalized the colonial discourse to the point where he tries by every means to distance himself from China and from the "embarrassing" past of his ancestors. Thus, he finds the Chinese language "exotic" (17) and considers Chinese philosophy passive: "and from the useless quietism of your philosophy / may the clamor of war rise."[10] On the other hand, the present becomes the threshold to a bright future of freedom and hope offered, from the poet's perspective, by Cuba. Sheng-mei Ma, in his analysis of Chinese American literature, has linked this type of stance to self-hatred: "a large number of texts in Chinese American discourse Orientalize China, its immigrants to the United States, and ultimately American-born Chinese. This divorcing of oneself from one's ethnicity bespeaks a disguised self-hatred" (25).

In the prologue to *Nosotros*, Pedroso apologizes for including poems that respond to what he considers an out-of-date sensitivity, although he admits to having written them only five or six years earlier. Indeed, after fourteen poems marked by revolutionary ideology, Pedroso adds two other sections at the end of the book, as if he is now ashamed of these poems: "Traducciones de un poeta chino de hoy" (Translations of a Contemporary Chinese Poet) and "Diez poemas de ayer y una canción de amor" (Ten Poems of Yesteryear and a Love Song).[11] Whereas in the last section the Modernista influence is easily noticeable, the preceding one consists of two poems inspired by his Chinese lineage: "Conceptos del nuevo estudiante" (Concepts of the New Student) and "El heredero" (The Heir). Lacking firsthand experience of Chinese culture (Debbie Lee has pointed out that Pedroso had few memories of his Chinese father), he finds a basis for the re-creation of the Chinese world in the hackneyed and idealized Western stereotypes of Chinese exoticism. Consequently, in "Conceptos del nuevo estudiante" he portrays the Chinese as peaceful, ceremonious, and wise. Lao-tzu; Confucius (Kung-Fu-Tao); the Confucian philosopher Mencius (Mengzi); and, again, Li Tai-pe are listed as representatives of Chinese millenary wisdom. By providing a spelling close to the original pronunciation (Pedroso calls them Lao-Tseu, Kung-fu-Yseu, and Meng-seu), he tries to present these sages from a Chinese perspective, to which he lays claim. The poem closes with the poetic voice yearning to leap over the Great Wall, a symbol of a shunned past: "A curious restlessness has wide awakened with insomnia / my slanted eyes / and to scan the horizon more deeply, / I leap over the old wall of the past . . . / until yesterday I was ceremonious and peaceful. . . ."[12] In this poem, the stereotypical image of the passive Chinese is no more: the poetic voice is now a "new student" who has learned from past mistakes. His fingers are prepared to pull the trigger if necessary.

The "I" that opens "Conceptos del nuevo estudiante" embodies not only the Chinese that were forcibly taken to Cuba (in the first three stanzas), but also the author and his new political consciousness (in the last three). Pedroso, therefore, becomes one with the coolies in a poetic voice that unifies past and present beyond nostalgia, while the "you" lumps together the Spaniards and Creoles who enslaved the coolies and the imperialist North Americans who colonized Cuba yet again. Predictably, in the last two stanzas the positive stereotypes and the idealized past of China turn into his perceived reality of an obsolete, passive culture: "The sunrise of the West / has undressed before my eyes. / Between my pale hands, the long pipe of the centuries / no longer offers me the opium of barbarism; / and today I march toward the culture of the people of the world / exercising my fingers on the trigger of the / rifle."[13] Here, the West represents a new beginning, a sunrise: the culture of the people of the world (read Western) has raised his awareness of the double oppression he has endured as a colonized person of color. In this sense, whereas the coolie of the first three stanzas is portrayed as a victim, the "I" of the last three is ready for armed resistance, having traded the opium pipe for a weapon.

In contrast with "Conceptos del nuevo estudiante," "El heredero" adopts not the coolie's viewpoint but the heir's. Despite all of its idealized exoticism, the poetic voice conceives of the new Cuba as a "new sun" and emphasizes even more the negative commonplaces and stereotypes of the Chinese society of the past and its "archaic ideology."[14] He also declares his intention to reject all the bourgeois opulence that his moribund and sage uncle, Wey-tchung-tseu, is planning to will to him, and to accept only the wisdom of his culture. He refuses to accept gold that he regards as "the transmutation of blood and sweat from coolies."[15] This line seems to imply that Pedroso's (or the poetic voice's) uncle became wealthy by exploiting his own people during the coolie trade. In this sense, the Marxist notion of class struggle (the economic inequalities of Chinese society in China and in Cuba) prevails over ethnic differences. Yet the lines that open and close the poem hardly conceal his pride in having noble ancestry (his uncle has a ring with the gem of a Ming prince): "although I am a son of the Revolution, / my ancestors are illustrious."[16]

In contrast with the socially committed direction of previous works, in his collection of "Chinese poems" *El ciruelo de Yuan Pei Fu* (Yuan Pei Fu's Plum Tree; 1955), Pedroso concentrates on the re-creation of the exotic world of his ancestors from a philosophical and nostalgic perspective. In fact, the exoticism of his imagined China is reminiscent of the Modernismo that characterizes his first poetry. The same is true of the recurrent use of images such as jewels and "marble swans," adjectives like "divine" (so frequently used by Rubén Darío), and the eroticism of poems like "El pabellón de los secretos" (The Pavilion of Secrets) or "Las tres doncellas de Kang Nan" (The Three Maidens of Kang Nan). In the prologue, he justifies this new stance by asserting that socioeconomic difficulties "have hardly found an echo in the poetics of Confucius's children."[17]

The poet's prologue states that the book was inspired by his contemplation of the portrait of a "Mandarin with red buttons,"[18] presumably his paternal grandfather, who lived during the Qing dynasty. Allegedly, this portrait is, along with a bundle of yellow papers, the only inheritance left by his "yellow ancestor" with "slanted eyes, elongated like sabers."[19] As in "El heredero," Pedroso here insists that he is proud of having a noble ancestor. Unsure of the origin of this painting, the poet decides to Sinicize his identity by "inventing" a Chinese ancestor: the multifaceted Yuan Pei Fu lived as a wandering apostle, preaching to his disciples and performing miracles; however, he ended up becoming a rich mandarin in the court and leading a life of "Asian luxury." Pedroso, like so many of his contemporaries, resorts to the Orientalist envisioning of China as a place where the subjects starve while the emperors squander riches and time on jewels, feasts, and orgies. This is precisely the China that appears in the poem "Mi amigo Liu Po Cheng" (My Friend Liu Po Cheng): "Above, gold, silks, obscene orgies, and below, poor people enduring a sad infamy!"[20] In this case, Orientalism may well respond to the poet's attempt to incorporate the empowerment of his ethnic group into the socioeconomic notion of the class struggle.

In "El maestro" (The Master), Yuan Pei Fu's disciple openly criticizes his former master, the same mystical man who pledged to stop eating rice as long as there was injustice in the world, for apostatizing: now he shows the button of high rank on his hat, dresses in silk, and is carried by slaves. In response, Yuan Pei Fu seemingly quotes the Taoist philosopher Chuang-tzu (or Zhuangzi; 370?–301 BCE), stating: "Do not judge the absolute, / as nothing is eternal and everything flows eternally / so nothing remains the same forever."[21]

In the prologue, Pedroso questions the true existence of Yuan Pei Fu and his disciple, and even the authenticity of the poems: "sometimes we doubt whether they are really Chinese."[22] Apparently, though Pedroso was Chinese Cuban, he questions the Chineseness of his own poems. Despite this presumed disadvantage, he later challenges the innovations of contemporary avant-garde poets by claiming the central position of poetry in the culture of his ancestors: "for the man of this millenary race, poetry is not a simple game of the intellect [...] but an emotional way of feeling and seeing life [...] it is born out of a profound contemplative state before nature, or rather, of his cosmic immersion in it, and it is in his stellar soul rather than in the simple game of producing literature."[23] In fact, here Pedroso is resorting to what Gayatri Spivak has termed "strategic essentialism," or rather, "strategic self-Orientalization" (to use Scherer's term) in order to defend his own poetry as a more authentic discourse than that of his avant-garde peers. He claims, through a sort of affected exoticism, a Chinese space that is impenetrable for Westerners but not for him, because his Chinese ancestry provides him with an epistemological privilege denied to Westerners: "the only thing is that, for Westerners, it will always be difficult to penetrate the depth of his smile."[24] Yet he continues to fall into occasionally essentialist views of the Chinese: "For the yellow man, although he is materialist and a persistent defender of his daily ration of rice [...]"[25]

In this process of Sinicization of his own writing, the poet re-creates an imagined Chinese ambiance by enumerating toponyms; names of people; and social figures such as mandarins, lamas, and the old sage; along with buildings, weather conditions, and objects associated with the Chinese: pagodas, monsoons, jade, old porcelains, lanterns, fans, ivory pipe, bamboo, plum wine, and pheasants. With respect to this process of imagining the culture of one's ancestors, the sociologist Martin Bulmer has defined the term "ethnicity" as "a collectivity within a larger society having real or *putative* common ancestry, *memories* of a shared past, and cultural focus on one or more symbolic elements which define the group's identity, such as kinship, religion, language, shared territory, nationality or physical appearance" (54; emphasis added). The words "putative" and "memories" are crucial here. Memories can be transformed by the passing of time. By the same token, if a "putative" ancestry is valid, then it is licit to re-create or imagine a collective past, which is, perhaps, Pedroso's endeavor in this book. For instance, in the poem that closes the collection, "Yuan Pei Fu despide a su discípulo" (Yuan Pei Fu Says Farewell to His Disciple), the poet imagines a nostalgic view of the stock character of the old master who, before dying, wishes to give a last word of advice to his disciple.

Curiously, Yuan Pei Fu's aphorisms are sometimes more reminiscent of Socrates than of Chinese philosophy: "Although one day you will know that you know nothing."[26] In other cases, however, Pedroso does attempt to imitate the discourse of Eastern philosophers. Thus, Yuan Pei Fu assures his disciple that wisdom comes with age, that asking questions is useless, and that people are richest when they have no money. Likewise, following notions expressed in the *Tao Te Ching* (a book that Pedroso quotes several times), the master advises his disciple to be humble, prudent with words, cautious with conduct, and to adapt externally to different surroundings without ever changing internally.[27] In fact, when the sage states that happiness and sorrow are inseparable, one can easily trace his teachings not only to those of Lao-tzu, but also to Buddha's philosophy, which taught that joy is inseparable from the *dukkha* (unsatisfactoriness, suffering).

Like Orientalism, self-Orientalization crosses literary genres and artistic expressions. Moving on from poetry to the fine arts, the rest of this chapter will concentrate on Flora Fong's and Pedro Eng Herrera's paintings and María Lau's photographs. A more recent case of voluntary Sinicization and deliberate self-Orientalization appears with the publication of *Nube de otoño* (Autumn Cloud; 1997), a collection of reproductions of paintings by the Chinese Cuban Flora Fong García (1949–), containing essays by the artist as well as her critics.[28] To leave no doubt as to the "genuine" Chineseness of her art, one of the pictures in the book shows the painter with a framed photograph on her lap, in which both her Chinese father and her Creole mother may be seen. Although at first sight many of her paintings do not show evident signs of her professed Chinese roots, she claims that her work has been inseparable from her father's ethnic roots since the early 1980s (her artistic debut was in 1970, and she visited China for the first time in 1989). In fact, almost her entire preface constitutes an effort to guarantee the genuinely Chinese connotations and background of her works. It begins with an explanation of the origin of Chinese pictographic characters and their relevance to her work: "Chinese characters are an essential part of my art since the early 1980s. An example is the character FOREST, whose meaning and appearance served as the bases of my representation of tropical forests. [. . .] Other compositions utilize squared-off Chinese characters, in an intentional manipulation" (6).[29] Surprisingly, only in the last paragraph of the preface does she make a brief reference to the influence of tropical flora and fauna in her art, though they seem in truth to be the main source of her inspiration.

Fong's conscientious effort to link her paintings to Chinese pictographs is noticeable if we compare the Chinese character that represents the word "forest" to her paintings "Bosque tropical" (Tropical Forest; 1990), "Palmas barrigonas" (Big-bellied Palm Trees; 1991), "Hoja amarilla" (Yellow Leaf; 1994), and "Bosque" (Forest; 1996), among others. In fact, to convince readers of this connection, the last page of *Nube de otoño* provides a list of Chinese characters that Fong uses in her painting along with their translations: autumn cloud (which is the meaning of the artist's name), great wind, sun, rain, cloud, person, mouth, way out, one, forest, mountain, and garden. The titles of some of her works and series since the 1980s also evoke her Chinese background: "Serie ancestros" (Ancestors Series), "Ideograma," "Vista aérea" (Aerial View),[30] "Esperando el año del gallo" (Waiting for the Year of the Rooster), "Girasol en jarrón chino" (Sunflower in Chinese Vase), those representing Chinese kites, and the more recent "De China al Caribe" (From China to the Caribbean) and "Caligrafeando" (Calligraphying). However, most of her paintings depict Cuban landscapes (palm trees, banana leaves, plants, forests, the ocean), with a particular emphasis on the wind (tornados, cyclones, and hurricanes). Incidentally, Cuban coffee rather than tea, the traditional Chinese drink, inspires many of Fong's paintings.

In her critique of Fong's art, Adelaida de Juan points out the same social affiliation that was earlier used to describe Pedroso's poetry. She states that the influence of Chinese art and culture was "actively assimilated by the artist through her own initiative" (120).[31] In contrast to Miguel Barnet, who fails to recognize these deliberate strategies for entering and leaving Chineseness and conceives of Fong's and Lam's ethnicity as a necessary and almost ineluctable factor in the alleged Asian traits of their art, de Juan points out that Fong, at a certain point in her career, made a conscious choice to include Oriental motifs. Similarly, Graziella Pogolotti sees Chinese culture as an essential part of Cubanness: "Thus, in a *conscious* process she has recovered her Chinese past, one of the indisputable presences in the common good of our culture" (123; emphasis added).[32] Both critics underscore the painter's "affiliation" with her father's roots, and her deliberate decision to embrace a Chinese culture that did not inform her art until the early 1980s.

As mentioned earlier, Barnet takes a different approach. From a blatantly essentialist perspective, he sees Fong's work through the prism of her Chinese ancestry: "The blood running through Flora Fong's veins marked her painting before she made the voyage that took her to the land of her grandparents" ("Flora Fong's Painting" 124).[33] Later, he compares Fong to Wifredo Lam, a Chinese mulatto painter who, according to Barnet, could feel his Chinese cultural heritage through his blood. Frank Scherer has interpreted this review of Fong's work as an example of self-Orientalization ("Culture" 107). Indeed, according to Barnet, Fong's paintings reflect a long tradition of artworks that bridge Asian and Western cultures. Tellingly, in his essay he persistently resorts to Chinese clichés: Chinese ink, bonsai gardens, the yin and the yang, the Tao . . . and like a Taoist sage, he states, Fong does not need to use her eyes to see the world.

Like Barnet, other critics seem unable to see beyond Fong's phenotype. In 1985, when Chinese influences were not yet as pronounced a feature of

Fong's painting as they have been since the 1990s, Ele Nussa, in her critique of Fong's drawings on rice paper, stated, "Even the emperor would be trapped in the spell, as demanding as he is" (126). Likewise, Jorge de la Fuente posited in 1989, "I have come to think, while contemplating them, of a philosophy of genesis which could change the well-known Biblical verse into an aphorism with Eastern resonance: in the beginning, before the word there came drawings and symbols, from which all sensible forms emerge. . . ." (126). Even Cuban Minister of Culture Abel Prieto points out, in the brief video clip available on Flora Fong's personal web page, "the Asiatic wisdom" that permeates the painter's works. In light of these critiques, it may fairly be argued that her critics' interpretation of her art as Chinese, even those that were made before she declared this influence, may have informed the choice to Sinicize her painting.[34]

Pedro Eng Herrera (1935–) is a lesser-known Sino-Cuban painter who is also determined to establish intricate connections between his Chinese ancestry and his country's culture. His Chinese name, Tai Chao (The Emperor's Shield), was given to him by his father, a Chinese businessman who went to Cuba in the nineteenth century and once there, married a woman from the Canary Islands. Since Eng Herrera's mother died shortly after his birth, he grew up with a Chinese nanny and did not learn Spanish until the age of five. For years, he earned a living selling groceries. His artistic career began when, in 1956, he exhibited in the Octavo Salón Nacional de Pintura y Escultura del Museo de Bellas Artes (Eighth National Exhibition of Painting and Sculpture of the Fine Arts Museum) his work "Danza del león" (Lion Dance). Since then, as he himself explains, he has devoted his work to making connections between the cultures of China and Cuba: "In the House of Art and Traditions of the Havana Chinatown Promotion Group there is one of my works where I wanted to express the essence between both cultures: The Morro Castle and the Chinese Wall, intercalated."[35] To this end, Eng Herrera combines, in his murals and drawings, the gods of Chinese traditional religion with Abakuá devils, and images of Chinese warriors with those of José Martí, Ernesto "Che" Guevara, and Fidel Castro, all of them decorated with poems written in Chinese. Like Flora Fong, Eng Herrera also incorporates Chinese characters and sunflowers into his paintings: "Sunflowers are flowers of life because they follow the sun, and sunshine engendered An Dong, the goddess of fertility, mother of Yan Di," he explains.[36]

Another artist of Sino-Cuban descent is María Lau, a photographer who currently resides in New Jersey. Lau's parents left the island in 1961, and she was born in the United States. In yet another case of self-Orientalization, the artist has recently reconnected with her Chinese heritage. This is noticeable in her photograph "Dad Divination," where Lau presents "a passport-type photo of her father as a young man, with images of slim wooden strips bearing Chinese characters superimposed over his face. The wooden strips are divination sticks that Lau used at a family altar in Havana, and in the photograph they become both barriers and keys to memory" (Turner n.p.).[37] In another photograph, Chinese pictographs partially cover an official document containing biographical information about her father, Santiago Lau. As the artist states on her own web page, cultural preservation, exploration of identity, and multicultural heritage have become the main topics of her artwork. Likewise, in her documentary photographs, Lau superimposes Chinese symbols and letters, as well as plaques and signs of Chinese societies (social clubs or associations) on otherwise nondescript images of old North American cars and decrepit façades in Cuba. In this way, she evokes a process of transculturation that needs to be preserved or revitalized. The ghostly, blurred marks of Chinese Cuban culture do not include people, thus hinting at the gradual disappearance of this ethnic group. In contrast, in other double-exposure photographs, the intercultural palimpsest is formed with images of Creole urban daily life (including numerous pedestrians), which are superimposed on images of Chinese Cuban newspapers, memorial halls, and societies.

The next chapter focuses on the representation of Chinese religious and philosophical thought, with an emphasis on its interaction and fusion with Catholicism and African-rooted religions.

3

Cross-Cultural Heterogeneity and Hybridization

7

Religious Syncretism

> Cultivated people harmonize without imitating.
> Immature people imitate without harmonizing.
>
> Confucius

It would be a mistake to assume that there was only one religion in China. Along with Buddhism, a major world religion, Taoism (both a philosophy and a system of religion) and Confucianism (which has never been an established religion with a church and priesthood) complete what is known as the "Three Ways." Of the three, Confucianism has been the most influential movement in Chinese thought, followed by Taoism and then Buddhism. Despite decades of antagonism from the Chinese government, Chinese traditional religion (a syncretic expression of all three religious systems together), with more than 400 million followers, is the fourth largest in the world, after Christianity, Islam, and Hinduism.

Most works dealing with Chinese religiosity in Cuba reflect the new developments that took place as a result of the contacts among Chinese, Creole, and black African creeds. The West African Yorubas who were transported as slaves began to practice a blend of Yoruba and Catholic beliefs that was called, initially as a derogatory term, Santería.[1] In order to have their religious practices accepted by their Catholic Creole masters, the Lucumí disguised the orishas (spirits that reflect God's various manifestations) as Catholic saints and worshipped them on saint's days (hence the name "Santería").[2] Because of this identification of orishas with saints, today the terms are often interchangeable.

A similar analysis may be applied to Chinese religion in Cuba. Referring to its syncretism with Catholic beliefs, Frank F. Scherer claims that, while none of the main religions in China were monotheistic, the invention of Sanfancón was used at the time and is still being used today by the Sino-Cuban community as a strategic alternative: "the making of a syncretic Chinese-Cuban 'saint,' Sanfancón, remains inextricably linked to bringing 'Chinese religion' into an orderly Hispanic pantheon, or at least into a mentality, occupied by 'Christian' gods so as to become intelligible even to the non-Chinese mind" ("Sanfancón" 164). In this sense, the recent Sino-Cuban reinvention of "Chinese religion" and of Sanfancón, a "saint" that is not recognized in China, is, according to Scherer, an illustration of the strategic self-Orientalization carried out by this community: "'Chinese religion' in Cuba today has less to do with long-standing 'Chinese' traditions, or even a return to 'religion' per se, but everything to do with the subaltern employment of strategies that allow for the opening of alternative spaces in which the construction of identities other than those prescribed by the State takes place" ("Sanfancón" 166). During the interviews I conducted in Havana's Chinatown in the summer of 2006, however, several Chinese and Chinese Cubans pointed out that, although they do refer to Sanfancón as a saint, the syllable "San" at the beginning of the name has nothing to do with the notion of sainthood; rather, it is a phonetic adaptation of the Chinese word for "alive," which explains the fact that the "saint" is based on a real-life person. Another of these strategies, Scherer adds, is the adoption of monotheistic values to represent supposedly Confucian precepts.

In contrast, following the tradition from Southern China, the Chinese in California have always built altars to honor Kwang Kung (or Kuan Kong)—the same god of literature and war from which the name Sanfancón derives—but they have never called him a saint. If we consider that Kwang Kung was also worshipped in China, the Chinese Cuban innovation resides mainly in considering him a saint. On the other hand, in her essay "The Great Bonanza of the Antilles" Mayra Montero seems to interpret the figure of Sanfancón as a Chinese version of the orishas of African origin, rather than as an example of syncretism with Catholic religion or an attempt to comply with Christian monotheism: "I was exposed to phenomena of syncretism as singular as that of Chinese Santería, and I visited, in the legendary Calle de Zanja, crucial heart of the Chinese barrio of Havana, altars in which the African Orishas blended with the improvised Orishas of Asian origin, such as the very miraculous San Fan Con" (199; qtd. Alejandro Lee Chan). In either case, the existence of the Chinese "saint" Sanfancón is a clear example of religious syncretism with other ethnic groups in Cuba.[3]

Another example of religious syncretism in Cuba may be found in the Church of the Caridad, located in Havana's Calle Salud, which was under the control of Chinese Franciscan monks before the Cuban Revolution. To the left of the main altar, one may see a syncretistic image of a Chinese Virgin sewn in silk that was brought from China and donated by the Chinese consul in 1950. In reality, this image represents the Buddhist deity Kwan Ying and includes the traditional images of a boy and a girl serving her. However, some Chinese in Cuba see this Virgin as the Chinese version of Oshún (the Yoruba orisha of the rivers, who also wears a yellow dress) and of the

Catholic Virgin of Caridad del Cobre, the patron of Cuba. There is also an icon of this goddess of love in the altar devoted to Sanfancón in the Chung Wah Casino. Likewise, Li Xuan is the Chinese version of the Catholic Saint Lazarus, whose equivalent in Santería is Babalú Ayé.

Zoé Valdés's *La eternidad del instante* displays an interesting fusion of the Three Ways, which is further syncretized once it comes in contact with African and European faiths. From the onset of the narrative, it appears in the conversations between Mr. Ying (Mo Ying's father) and Mr. Xuang (Mei's father). Thus, in keeping with one of the central precepts of both Taoism and Buddhism, Mr. Ying hopes that his son's marriage to Mei will not be driven by passion. Similarly, at the monks' request, Mr. Xuang, who claims to be a devotee of Taoism, writes a long essay on patience and solitude, inspired by the flight of birds. Later, building on the Confucian concept of the balance of opposites in the world, Mr. Ying talks about the yin, the symbol of passion and integrity. The next generation follows in his footsteps: while Mei compares her love for Mo Ying with the yin and the yang, Mo Ying, in order to improve his "inner vision," talks with turtles about slowness and patience. Mo Ying also learns to control his mind through meditation and breathing techniques, and is able to prevent his memories and desires from disturbing his life.[4]

Years later, Mo Ying, now known in Cuba as Maximiliano Megía, will blend these Asian religious beliefs with European and African ones. He keeps a Buddhist altar with burning incense at the same time that he prays to Catholic saints, practices spiritism, makes offerings to Eleggua, and even studies the Kabbalah.[5]

Up to this point, the novel follows the traditional characteristics studied by Alejandro Lee Chan in his study on the fiction of Isabel Allende, Mayra Montero, and Cristina García; that is, that wisdom is always attributed to men or male characters in Chinese culture. A deviation from the norm, however, takes place when Mo Ying's mother, Xiao Ying, teaches him the value of compassion and silence, two concepts that seem taken from Buddhism and Taoism. At times, she counsels him on spiritual matters and even dares to criticize the practice of fasting in traditional Buddhism: "I see no merit in a wise man's fasting. You must live in your time, accept nature and above all, respect it. Keep your independence, get rid of material things only when you are ready to carry on; but getting rid of material things does not mean that a wise man becomes indifferent to feelings, freedom, and happiness."[6] Valdés, therefore, subverts Chinese culture's traditional emphasis on male wisdom by allowing a female voice to compete with the stereotypical elderly male sage.

Like so many historical novels, *La eternidad del instante* uses the escapist pretext of re-creating the past of a foreign culture to examine the present sociopolitical situation of the author's country. Thus, in the last pages of the novel, which become somewhat propagandistic, Valdés seemingly uses Confucianism to criticize Castro's government as well as her fellow countrymen: "I learned, Confucius asserted, that when the country is lost and one does not realize it, it is because one is not intelligent; if one understands it and does not fight to defend it, then there is no loyalty; if one considers oneself faithful without sacrificing oneself for one's country, then there is no integrity."[7] Two early texts by Chinese mulattos, *Apunte histórico de los chinos en Cuba* (1927), by Antonio Chuffat Latour (1860–?), and the collection of poems *El ciruelo de Yuan Pei Fu* (Yuan Pei Fu's Plum Tree, 1955), by Regino Pedroso are marked by a deliberate process of Christianization of the Chinese ethnic discourse. In his treatise, a blend of autobiographical, biographical, testimonial, and historical study, Chuffat develops different strategies to incorporate the notions of patriotism and Cubanness in the Chinese diasporic identity. However, as Lisa Li-Shen Yun points out, this text is characterized by its recurrent contradictions: "If his work is taken as a narrative of political consequence, written by a man employing language that reflects education and awareness of literature and social history, Chuffat's text would call for an accounting for the tactics of contradiction and the formation of narrative strategy" (34). One of these strategies of identity formation is the Christianization of the Chinese community's image. To this end, he presents the legend of Kuan Kong (as he heard it in Cimarrones) in a manner reminiscent of the biblical Ten Commandments. Indeed, the coincidences are such that the commandments that Chung Si received were even engraved on stone tablets. As Scherer puts it,

> These Confucian values show, indeed, a great concern with "God Almighty." Although "Chinese religion" consists not only of Confucianism but also of Taoism and Buddhism, forming what is known as the "Three Ways," it is difficult to find in any of these doctrines the monotheistic prevalence so characteristic for Christianity. [. . .] Thus, it is this "Western" reading (and writing) of Sanfancón that may explain Chuffat Latour's "Ten Commandment" version of Confucian values. ("Sanfancón" 166)

However, there may be another reason for the Christianization of his discourse: the similarities with Christian dogma recall Hung Hsiu-ch'üan's particular variation of Taoism. Referring to Martí's intriguing description of "the Tao" (path) as a bearded man or creator deity in his 1888 article "A Chinese Funeral" ("Un funeral chino"), the article's editor and translator, Esther Allen, comments on these coincidences,

> Martí's description of a peculiarly anthropomorphic Tao may be attributable to the nature of the information he was given by former Taiping rebels. Hung Hsiu-ch'üan, the visionary leader of the Taiping (Great Peace) Rebellion, in which Li-In-Du apparently took part, had studied Christianity for two months with an American Protestant missionary named Roberts and believed himself to be the younger brother of Jesus Christ. He subsequently evolved a syncretistic Taoism influenced by Christian theology, which even included a Taoist version of the Ten Commandments. (José Martí, *Selected* 432)

Religious syncretism also permeates Cuban poetry. In *El ciruelo de Yuan Pei Fu* one of the main strategies Regino Pedroso uses to bring the Sino-Cuban community closer to the Cuban national identity is again the Christianization of Chinese philosophical discourse. First, Pedroso tries to make his writing sound "genuinely Chinese." To that end, poems like "Los caballitos de Tai Ping" (The Carousel of Tai Ping) represent a curious imitation of Chinese poetry and philosophy through epigrammatic paradoxes: "that which is uncertain, certain is, and that which is certain is uncertain."[8] Pedroso Christianizes the "collection of Chinese poems," as he describes it, by mentioning in this same poem apostles, martyrs, saints, and prophets. To leave no doubt about the implicit Christian quality of his writing, the poetic voice further states, "I think about the bleeding cross of a cruel martyrology."[9] Aware that this line may seem surprisingly out of context, Pedroso justifies it in this endnote: "Although written in a Taoist-Confucian spirit, Yuan Pei Fu's reasoning provides evident signs that his mind was not unaware of the seraphic essence of the most pure Christianity."[10]

The references to Christian thought do not end there. In the poem "Retorno de mandarines" (Mandarins' Return), Pedroso dwells on the concepts of sin, penance, and repentance, which are closer to the tenets of the Judeo-Christian tradition than to those of Taoism or Confucianism. In similar vein, in "El lama de Tu Fan" (The Lama of Tu Fan) the poetic voice mentions "the Son of Heaven,"[11] another notion closer to the Christian concept of Jesus Christ or the Jewish Messiah than to Lao-tzu, Confucius, or Buddha. These Judeo-Christian echoes resurface in the only short story included in the book, "Yuan Pei Fu hace el milagro de las jorobas de los camellos" (Yuan Pei Fu Works the Miracle of the Camel Humps): "You will suffer hunger, thirst, the rod of punishment; but you will have a heaven to enter, like all beings on Earth."[12] Likewise, in the poem "Yuan Pei Fu entra en la áurea pagoda" (Yuan

Pei Fu Enters the Golden Pagoda), Pedroso again mentions martyrologies and heresy, two concepts more reminiscent of the Roman Empire and medieval and early modern Christian Europe than of Chinese philosophy and religion. Later, Yuan Pei Fu's disciple, reflecting the biblical episode where Jesus Christ drove the greedy merchants from the temple, declares that if one day his master enters the temple, the vile commerce of ornamentation and carriages will cease. Curiously, like Martí in his chronicle "A Chinese Funeral," here Pedroso considers "Tao" a religious figure, analogous to Jesus Christ.[13]

As might be expected, the interaction and fusion between the creeds of different ethnic groups are often incorporated into Cuban narrative fiction as well. We now shift from the verses of a Chinese mulatto poet who lived in Cuba to two recent novels that portray witchcraft as the threshold to the world of the Chinese in Cuba. Whereas the first work, *The Messenger* (*Como un mensajero tuyo*; 1998), was written by Mayra Montero (1952–), a Cuban expatriate who has written her entire opus in Puerto Rico, the second, *Cold Havana Ground* (2003), was written by Arnaldo Correa (1935–), a Cuban residing in Havana.[14] Chinese religion is even more pivotal in *The Messenger* than in *El ciruelo de Yuan Pei Fu*. Yazmín Pérez Torres has argued that "the equalizing of African religion and history" is essential to interpreting Montero's works.[15] Indeed, just as Haitian voodoo provides cohesion for the black African cultures in her novels *La trenza de la hermosa luna* (The Braid of the Beautiful Moon; 1987) and *Del rojo de su sombra* (The Red in Her Shadow; 1992), in *The Messenger* Chinese Cuban witchcraft and religious practices serve the same function. Montero does not attach any of the usual derogatory or diabolical connotations to the term "witchcraft." In fact, in this novel, it works as the axis of representation of the Chinese in Cuba, as well as being an alternative narrative of the history of the Chinese diaspora in the Caribbean.[16] For fictional characters of Chinese, African, and Afro-Chinese descent, it is an effective weapon for resistance and protection against Creole domination.[17]

Although Haitian voodoo had been a crucial theme in several of Montero's previous works, here most of her characters practice Afro-Cuban Santería or Chinese witchcraft or both. Whereas these religious practices are frequently interpreted as superstitious acts of witchcraft, the narrator of the novel presents them in a respectful manner. However, as José Luis de la Fuente indicates, "a thin line exists between superstition and reason, although we look at superstition from the realm of reason."[18]

The love story between the *china mulata* Aida Petrirena Cheng and the nonfictional character Enrico Caruso (1873–1921) provides coherence to the plot. At the same time, it becomes a narrative device for exploring the interaction between the black African and Chinese cultures and religions, thus rewriting history and rescuing some fundamental components of Cuban identity. Their adventures evolve around two parallel love stories: the plot of the opera *Aida* (1871), by Giuseppe Verdi (1813–1901), and the relationship between the orishas Yemayá and Changó.[19] Thus, Yoruba religion is introduced into the plot and contrasted with European (high) culture.

The Spanish title of the novel is taken from the line "Come un tuo messagero," by Italian poet Giuseppe Ungaretti (1888–1970), founder of the Hermetic movement. Here, however, it refers to the messenger of death, whose presentation splits into two different versions, one Chinese and the other Yoruba. While in the Chinese version we learn that "'The Messenger of Death, whose name is Chui Chi Lon, is always the messenger of our own hearts'" (163), in the West African one we are told that "when somebody dies with unfinished business, a messenger from his soul leaves the place of his death and flies to the place of his destiny" (203–4).[20] This dual interpretation of the word "messenger" puzzles the reader and challenges the assumption that witchcraft is an African cultural trait. As the novel explains, Creoles and Chinese also practiced witchcraft/Santería and still do in Cuba. In fact, the effectiveness of Chinese witchcraft (and of Yuan Pei Fu, its main practitioner in the novel) is understood mainly through its prevalence over African-rooted Santería, whose leader is the protagonist's godfather, José de Calazán "Cheché" Bangoché.[21] Thus, when Afro-Cuban witchcraft proves to be ineffective, Aida resorts to the more powerful witchcraft of the Chinese: "And what the black *nganga* can't do, the Chinese *nganga* always can" (21).[22] Likewise, when María Vigil, a friend of the protagonist's grandmother, discovered that Cheché had fallen in love with her and was trying to bewitch her with some powders called *afoché*, she asked Yuan Pei Fu, the Chinese *babalawo*, to prepare a *resguardo* (protection).[23] After ingesting it, she was protected from any sort of witchcraft. Years later, María Vigil mocks her old suitor: "Old man, can't you see that I took a Chinese 'protection,' and that all are powerless against Chinese witchcraft?" (185).[24]

It is worth noting that *The Messenger*, like *Monkey Hunting*, fluctuates between the exploration of an arcane world unknown to most readers and the presentation of Chinese culture as a part of the Hispanic world and, therefore, not really exotic. In this regard, magical powers and witchcraft are not unfamiliar to white characters: a deceased white woman casts a curse, Caruso's magnificent voice has supernatural powers, and readers become aware of white witches from the Canary Islands who used to live in the Cuban town of Trinidad.[25] In this way, Montero eliminates the potentially Orientalist figuration of Chinese witchcraft as an exotic cultural element that is exclusive to the mysterious and "cruel" world of the Chinese.

Colonial discourses have often conceived of witchcraft and fetishism as marks of otherness that justify the conquest and oppression of Third World peoples. In contrast, although Montero does use the oft-maligned term "witchcraft," none of the three types of witchcraft that appear in her works (Santería, voodoo, and Chinese witchcraft) is presented as an ignorant or primitive practice; instead, they are introduced as alternative religions. In this light, although both *babalawos* display an ambiguous morality (Yuan Pei Fu owns an opium den, and Cheché uses his powers to make women fall in love with him), their main objective in the novel is to preserve Aida's life. They are benevolent men who cooperate to help a woman they love for different reasons: Yuan Pei Fu is Aida's real father and Cheché, her godfather. Therefore, they distance themselves from the familiar stereotype of the evil sorcerer who manipulates common people's irrational fears and superstitions. The author refuses to pass moral judgment, mythify, or describe in pejorative or essentialist ways the doctrine of either ethnic group.

After the two *babalawos*, Cheché and Yuan Pei Fu, agree to a meeting arranged by Aida's mother, they come to the conclusion that "saints are the same everywhere, they're the same in China and in Guinea" (22).[26] Indeed, Yuan Pei Fu adheres to a syncretic form of witchcraft that incorporates African elements. As a *babalawo*, he has the power to bewitch dolls, foretell the future through the use of mirrors, create *resguardos* against witchcraft, and communicate with the spirits of Chinese ancestors. Several characters confess their fear of his witchcraft and of his Chinese henchmen. For instance, Tata Sandoval, the *babalawo* of a *cabildo* of Congos in Cienfuegos, knows that the Chinese "kill with paper, they do their work with crickets and dragonflies" (151).[27] Likewise, the pharmacist believes that Caruso has fallen victim to the Chinese witch's snares: "Chinese witchcraft tied him up in knots they say not even God could untie. He died not long afterward in New York: they say he rotted away inside" (80).[28]

Although Aida also has magical powers, she resorts to Yuan Pei Fu's teachings only to carry out benevolent acts, such as caressing the terrorized tenor's feet to appease his soul. She represents the embodiment of syncretism of the Catholic, Yoruba, and Chinese religions: "On the way to Pueblo Grifo I put myself in the hands of God, I prayed to Father Olofi to send away his messenger—I said my prayer in a whisper and then I held my tongue—and finally I had a thought for Sanfancón, the Changó of the Chinamen" (149).[29] In addition, she never forgets her mixed heritage: one day she simultaneously sees the ghosts of Chinese coolies from the brigantine *Oquendo* and those of black Africans who arrived with her Lucumí grandmother, Petrona. Yet, although Aida and her mother, Domitila, are treated as family in Yuan Pei Fu's opium den, Domitila always makes the sign of the cross to protect herself when she visits it. In keeping with the abundance of religious syncretism in the plot, before returning home Aida goes to the Catholic Church of La Merced to leave an offering to Saint Flora who, like Sanfancón, was beheaded.

Therefore, among the numerous aspects of Sino-Cuban culture described in *The Messenger*, Montero chooses religion and witchcraft as the most representative. They become physical and psychological defense mechanisms through which a good part of Cuba's history is rewritten, this time from the perspective of two of the ethnic groups (other than Amerindians) that most suffered the consequences of Spain's colonialism. Montero tries to provide a voice for the disenfranchised Chinese and blacks while exemplifying how Europe's economic and political expansion transformed distant cultures into new, hybrid expressions.

Witchcraft is again the most emblematic Chinese Cuban cultural trait in Arnaldo Correa's *Cold Havana Ground*. In its pages, he presents the arcane worlds of African and Chinese witchcraft as integral to Cuban identity and as useful tools for understanding the Cuban character. In fact, some passages with didactic overtones seem to be lessons on *cubanía* and an explanation of these beliefs. In spite of intense efforts, first by Spanish colonists wishing to eradicate non-Catholic creeds and later by a Cuban government trying to abolish religion, these beliefs have remained. However, in contrast with *The Messenger*, *Cold Havana Ground* displays an ambivalent stance toward Chinese-{#}and African-rooted religions. In certain dialogues, the author conveys skeptical respect for these beliefs while, in others, he openly discredits them.

Correa has explained in several interviews that he received death threats from members of the Abakuá secret society who were offended by the plot of his novel (Deznermio n.p.). Perhaps for this reason, he has Jacinto assure the protagonist twice that the Abakuá are not thieves, but "essentially a mutual-aid group with a history of terrible internal violence" (169). The author asserts that the description of Afro-Cuban rituals presented in his novel is true to life and discourages readers from practicing them on their own. Yet two different characters deride these creeds. First, Adrián Arrinda, the associate of Lorenzo Bantú, secretly rejects them as mere "stupidity": "How could anyone, at the door of the twenty-first century, still believe in such crap—especially in Cuba, where so much effort had been devoted to combating all types of religious beliefs?" (145). Some pages later, Major Fonseca states that they are "extremely primitive" and dangerous, and should therefore be prohibited: "These religions—not always, but many times—are merely instruments for delinquents and other antisocial characters. It's incredible that they have so much influence with all that the revolutionary government has invested in schools and in educating the people" (200).

Interestingly, the depiction of the Chinese and their magic is, for the most part, rendered through the eyes of followers of three African-rooted religions practiced in Cuba: Regla de Osha, popularly known as Santería; Regla Mayombe, also called Palo Monte; and the Abakuá secret society, an Afro-Cuban initiatory fraternity for men. A character named Jacinto speculates that Afro-Cuban perceptions of Chinese witchcraft as more powerful than its African counterpart must have originated during the first contacts between African and Chinese witchdoctors on the island. As he explains, these Afro-Cuban religions consider the corpse of a Chinese man to be an infallible magic shield: "No one can undo a Chinese curse, not even the person who made it. The old *Paleros* used to say that the cadaver of a Chinaman protects against anything; it's infallible" (133).[30] The *paleros'* reverence for the magical powers of Chinese corpses is such that, according to the gravedigger, when they are unable to steal a corpse, they take dirt from the four corners of the Chinese cemetery in Havana's Plaza District for their ceremonies.[31] However, as one *palero* puts it, these Chinese must be "legitimate," that is, "real ones, not one crossed with a black" (15).[32] The gravedigger adds to the atmosphere of mystery by revealing the popular belief that the tormented souls of the Chinese buried there have possessed the bodies of the bats in the cemetery and use them to move about.

In this context, a *santera* (Santería priest) who undertakes an investigation paralleling that of the police discovers that the spirit of the Chinese Rafael Cuan has taken possession of her brother Lorenzo Bantú, a *nasakó* (Abakuá priest). After having the spirit exorcised from her brother's body, she scolds him for risking his life by stealing the corpse and believing, naively, that his own magic "could prevail over the spirit of a Chinaman!" (220).[33] Lorenzo, on the other hand, is convinced that recent events are intimately related to the powers of the Chinese corpse he stole and stored in a *nganga*.[34] When his plans begin to fail, he tries to determine what is interfering with Cuan's work by decoding the signals he believes the *chino*'s spirit is sending him. Trying to please the spirit, Lorenzo offers him different objects, such as food and flowers, until he comes to the conclusion that what it wants is a cross.

The superiority of Chinese witchcraft is also underscored in nonfictional texts. Thus, in the essay *El Monte* (1954), by Lydia Cabrera (1899–1991),[35] we read that only another Chinese man is able to undo a curse cast by one of his compatriots, and that they never do it:

> That which a shaman does another one undoes: "a cane that kills a white dog also kills a black dog." The exception is "damage" done by a Chinese shaman, since Chinese magic has the reputation of being the worst and the strongest of all, and as our blacks say, only another Chinese man is capable of undoing it. And here we learn something terrible: no Chinese man ever undoes the curse, the "morubba," that a compatriot has cast! As in the case of the unfortunate E., daughter of a mulatta and a Chinese man, who died not many years ago in her prime. The doctor, also from Canton and whom her father took to her deathbed as her last hope, was unable, or rather did not want to remove the tremendous curse on this innocent victim.[36]

The impenetrability and mysteriousness of Chinese religious practices are emphasized again a few paragraphs later:

> Chinese witchcraft is so hermetic that Calazán Herrera [. . .], who "in order to learn has walked throughout the entire island," could never penetrate any of their secrets or learn anything from them. He only knows that they often eat a paste made of bat meat (eyes and brains are ground into it), and it is excellent for improving failing eyesight; that they make a very strong poison from lettuce; that the lamp they light for Sanfancón gives light but does not burn; that they always have, behind the door, a container full of magic water that they throw on the back of the person they wish to hurt; and that they feed their dead very well.[37]

In contrast with the story line in *Cold Havana Ground*, in *El Monte* it is an anonymous Chinese man referred to as S. who is saved from a Mayombe curse by two *palero* friends. In this rare case, we learn that the *resguardo* (protection) prescribed for the Chinese man was blowing in his ears and shaking his bed and mattress to such an extent that it was driving him out of his mind. When his *palero* friends arrive, they find the Chinese man shaking on the floor of his house "with his eyes out of their sockets," [38] and they save him by throwing the protection in a cesspool: "We did what we had to do, and as soon as the cesspool swallowed the protection, the *monte* became quiet, and our good Chinese S. was free from a force that was too violent for him."[39] When, on the way to the cesspool the four men hear the crying of children who are calling them, they avoid them by praying in Congo (Bantu).

This story, therefore, represents another case of transculturation, where a Chinese man practices a religion of African origin and prays in an African language.

To return to narrative fiction, in Leonardo Padura Fuentes's novella *La cola de la serpiente* the figure of Sanfancón and Chinese religious practices are approached in a more lighthearted way. Rather than providing answers, the author lets the dialogues unearth the secrets of the Chinese "saint." As mentioned, this detective story takes place in Havana's Chinatown, where lieutenant Mario Conde requests the help of the Chinese police auxiliary Juan Chion (Li Chion Tai) to solve the mystery of the death of another Chinese man. When Chion learns about the assassination, he immediately sees Sanfancón's signature in it, even though, as he explains, "Sanfancón does not kill in this manner, he uses a knife."[40] Suddenly, Sanfancón acquires evil traits that were absent in other texts. Conde, the protagonist, assumes that he is a "bad saint," particularly considering that all he knows about him is that when his "grandfather said that someone was worse than Sanfancón, it was because he was really bad."[41]

Within the premises of what seems to be the Lung Kong (Dragon Hill) Society, Juan Chion and Francisco Chiu, two old Chinese *compadres* who consider themselves direct descendents of the warriors who fought alongside Cuang Con (or Kwang Kung), show the protagonist and Sergeant Manuel Palacios the altar devoted to this Chinese "saint." They also inform them about the saint's history:

> "But he wasn't a saint, was he?" asked Conde. [. . .] I mean, they didn't canonize him as they do with Catholic saints. . . . Why San Fan Con?" [. . .]
>
> "That took place here. He came as Cuang Con, but he was Cubanized as San Fan Con, and since he is a led [red] saint, blacks say that he is Changó, see, Captain."[42]

Later, Francisco Chiu states that, although he does not believe in Sanfancón, he knows that this saint is the result of a process of transculturation, since this is the outcome of "Chinese who plactice black witchclaft and of blacks who plactice Chinese witchclaft."[43] Indeed, in the story's denouement, we learn that the murderer was Panchito Chiu, a Chinese *palero*. This proliferation of faiths in Cuba is later mocked by Lieutenant Conde who, before drinking from a bottle of rum, dedicates the spilling of a few drops to several "saints" of different religions.

Cuban author Daína Chaviano (1957–) has hinted, in *El hombre, la hembra y el hambre* (Man, Woman, and Hunger; 1998), at the possible reasons for this renewed interest in spirituality:[44]

> Spiritual hunger is worse, particularly when one begins to wonder how it is possible to dream or to have paranormal experiences if only what is palpable, visible, measurable, photographable exists. That is how my generation's profound devotion began. We needed orishas and miracles. And now we have become polyphagi. We eat it up like wild people. We are eager to devour God. These are the consequences of mixing European and African blood, and boiling it slowly in atheism for forty years: we are the biggest devourers of gods in the Western Hemisphere.[45]

As the protagonist, Claudia, posits, the clandestine thirst for spirituality has never vanished from the island, in spite of the Cuban government's early efforts: Santería, yoga, spiritualism, astrology, and even automatic writing and the study of the Chinese book *I Ching* were alternative ways to find answers.[46] Furthermore, *El hombre, la hembra y el hambre* exposes how the government-sponsored tourist industry has trivialized and commodified African religions and folklore: "This island is for sale. It is not even being auctioned off: it is being wholesaled. Not only its labor, but also its soul, every belief, every versicle, every religious song, every artistic brushstroke of those who painted it for centuries."[47] According to the narrator, tourists are being deceived by fake *babalawos* who have been hired by the government: "They don't even respect the orishas any more, and that really is worrisome. Nothing good can await a people who allow their saints to be stolen."[48]

As evidenced by the numerous works analyzed in this chapter, Cuban and Cuban American writers and artists have in recent years shown a renewed interest in religions of African and Chinese origins. Paradoxically, despite the fact that most of these authors (with the exception of Regino Pedroso and Arnaldo Correa) have voiced their criticism of Fidel Castro's policies, their interest coincides with the Cuban government's promotion of these practices for the purpose of attracting tourism. Let us examine, in the following chapter, how the processes of transculturation, hybridization, and assimilation influence the literary and cultural re-creation of the Sino-Cuban world.

8

Painful Transculturations

> Nothing and no one can destroy the Chinese people. They are relentless survivors. They are the oldest civilized people on earth. Their civilization passes through phases but its basic characteristics remain the same. They yield, they bend to the wind, but they never break.
>
> Pearl S. Buck, *China, Past and Present* (1972)

According to Antonio Cornejo Polar, "the category of *mestizaje* is the most powerful and widespread conceptual device with which Latin America has interpreted itself" ("Mestizaje" 116). However, as Juan de Castro elucidates, it was also demagogically used by Creoles during the wars of independence against Spain: "This discursive tradition originated in the attempt by the Latin American colonial Criollo (Euro-American) elites to rhetorically ground their struggle for independence from Spain and Portugal in the history of Amerindian resistance" (xiii). Since this sort of identity flag continues to be used by many Caribbean and Latin American writers, artists, and politicians today, perhaps the term should be used cautiously, as we shall see in the analysis of Zoé Valdés's *I Gave You All I Had*. In any event, the optimistic rhetoric of some of the writings analyzed in this study is somehow reminiscent of that found in *La raza cósmica* (*The Cosmic Race*; 1925), where Mexican thinker José Vasconcelos (1882–1959) asserted that a new, superior race would emerge from the best attributes of all races in Latin America.

In a similar vein, in his foundational work *Cuban Counterpoint: Tobacco and Sugar* (*Contrapunteo cubano del tabaco y el azúcar*; 1940), Fernando Ortiz rejected the English term "acculturation" (acquiring another culture) and proposed instead the word "transculturation." This term changed the emphasis from the result to the transitional blending process (occurring in different phases) that is characteristic of race mixing. In Ortiz's view, transculturation was more accurate because it made reference to both *deculturation* (or uprooting of a previous culture) and *neoculturation* (or creation of a new, synthetic, and original hybrid culture). Yet, despite his intention to redress historical injustices by celebrating the hybrid nature of the Cuban population, his choice of vocabulary to describe Chinese immigrants, "yellow mongoloids from Macao, Canton," is surprisingly uncomplimentary in comparison with his description of other social groups (Yun 43; Scherer, "Culture" 27).

The Uruguayan critic Ángel Rama has praised the term "transculturation" because it reinforces both the idiosyncratic and the creative values of Latin American culture: "It reveals resistance to the consideration of one's own traditional culture, which receives the external impact destined to modify it, as a merely passive, or even inferior entity, destined to be lost without any kind of creative response" (136). In this sense, Rama argues that, along with partial deculturation, incorporation of elements from an outside culture, and recomposition (using elements of both) of a new hybrid culture, one must also consider the receiving culture's selectivity and creativity: "The task of selection is, in fact, a search for resistant values, those capable of confronting the spoils of transculturation. Through the prism of transculturation one can also perceive a creative task [. . .] a neoculturation operating simultaneously on both cultural sources in contact with each other" (140). Yet Cornejo Polar emphasizes the factor of social asymmetry, since this cultural synthesis takes place "in the space of hegemonic culture and literature" ("Mestizaje" 117). He also warns against borrowing these terms from other disciplines, since hybridity connotes sterility and words such as *mestizaje*, transculturation, and Fernando Ortiz's *ajiaco* (Cuban stew) evoke a false sense of harmony in a process that was actually belligerent. Néstor García Canclini, in the introduction to the 1995 edition of *Hybrid Cultures* (*Culturas híbridas*), answers this criticism and provides a new definition: "I understand for hybridization socio-cultural processes in which discrete structures or practices, previously existing in separate form, are combined to generate new structures, objects, and practices" (xxv). Then, he proceeds to point out that the so-called discrete structures are not pure sources, but the result of prior hybridizations.

Indeed, although the Chinese in Cuba have made obvious efforts to be accepted by mainstream society, they have simultaneously struggled to maintain their cultural traits and heritage. Traditionally, they have not sought assimilation or blending into a "melting pot" (to use the North American concept) at the risk of losing their particular national character. In any case, some of these processes (of deculturation, incorporation, neoculturation, selectivity, and creativity, and even the false idea of a harmonic and nonviolent process that the term transculturation may evoke) emerge in the references to Sino-Cuban culture that abound in this cultural production. Thus, challenging stereotypes about Chinese insularity and non-assimilation, Richard Henry Dana, in his travel narrative "The Trade in Chinese Laborers," proves that Chinese adaptation and assimilation into mainstream Cuban society took place during the years shortly after their arrival: "after being separated and employed in work, they let their hair grow, and adopt the habits and dress of the country. The newly arrived indentured workers wear tufts, and blue and yellow, loose, Chinese clothes. Those who have been here long are distinguishable from the whites only by the peculiar tinge of the cheek, and the form of the eye." (80)

Another document that contradicts the stereotype of Chinese insularity is a 1950s photograph of the Masonic Lodge Mártires de la Libertad (Martyrs of Freedom), included in Napoleón Seuc's study *La colonia china de Cuba 1930–1960* (The Chinese Community of Cuba 1930–1960; 1998). In it one can observe the presence of Chinese members, along with Creoles and blacks.[1]

Yet other texts point in different directions. In the testimonial *Biography of a Runaway Slave* (Barnet and Montejo), Esteban Montejo expresses both his attraction toward this millenarian and mysterious (at least for him) culture and his rejection of what he considers an inexplicable separatism. Talking about his daily life as a slave, he observes that everyone would participate in games and dances except for the Chinese, who preferred to be isolated because they were "separatists." He even conjectures about the reasons for this attitude: "I noticed that the ones who were least involved were the Chinese. Those bastards didn't have an ear for the drums. They were standoffish. It was that they thought a lot. In my opinion they thought more than the blacks. Nobody paid them any mind. And folks just went on with their dances" (30).[2] Ironically, some pages later Montejo contradicts these statements about Chinese seclusion by recalling how, on certain festive occasions, they gambled and played *charada china, monte*, button, and other games with blacks and creoles in Sagua la Grande. In fact, Chuffat Latour reveals that the *charada china* itself, which he considers a dishonest and corrupt game, is the product of a process of transculturation that began with the Chinese gambling game chi-ffá (letter-flowers), brought to Cuba in 1873: "The real Chi-ffá was played by the Chinese for high stakes. We are unfamiliar with this game today because of the Chinese classical signs. The semi-Creole charade of the boa constrictor (*majá*), mouse, cat, fine stone, etc. is a simulated charade, full of pillaging."[3] What is important, however, is the fact that the *charada china* is a cultural borrowing: a Chinese game that became Cuban. This type of cultural appropriation, of course, went in the opposite direction much more frequently.

The depiction of cross-cultural heterogeneity and a criticism of the false idea of harmony conveyed by the term *mestizaje* are pivotal in Zoé Valdés's

I Gave You All I Had. The Sino-Cuban protagonist, Cuca Martínez, who has inherited the author's mixed ethnic background, is unlike any other studied in previous works.[4] Representing what Ien Ang has termed "post-Chinese identities" ("Can One Say No" 297), she is completely assimilated to the cultural practices of the island and her Chineseness remains at a merely anecdotal level.[5] While the novel replicates the patterns of *mestizaje* seen in other works, Cuca shows signs of assimilation to mainstream culture that were absent in previous characters. Besides her love for sentimental boleros, this *china mulata* never expresses nostalgia for the rapidly disappearing Chinese heritage in Cuba, and neither does she have any thoughts about returning (or, in her case, going for the first time) to the homeland.

Her Irish mother had married, "more for the exotic than for the Asian" (4), an unsuccessful Chinese man who had traveled from Canton to Mexico and then to Cuba, in hopes of becoming wealthy.[6] After they separated, the protagonist moved in with her *madrina de santo* (Santería godmother), a black woman named María Andrea.[7] Henceforth, Cuca will combine Catholic prayers and her devotion to the Virgin of Cobre with visits to *brujeros* (Santería priests) and *paleros*. Yet she never invokes Sanfancón, the Chinese Changó, as a character does, for example, in another of Valdés's novels, *Querido primer novio* (Dear First Boyfriend; 1999). It is obvious, therefore, that she identifies more deeply with the African component of the Cuban culture than with her Chinese and Irish backgrounds: "But I don't need to be an African specialist to know that my culture and religion come in large part from those parts. Because around here, if you're not Congo then you must be Mandinka!" (67).[8] In fact, in *I Gave You All I Had* the Chinese are conceived of as a remote chapter of Cuban history, rather than as a disappearing community: even old Chinese theaters have become cheap substitutes for old motels.[9] Other than these passages, we have to trace the Chinese heritage indirectly when men call their loved ones "mi china" (32, 173, 358) or when we read that it is almost a crime for a woman to have big feet in Havana.

In accord with the sarcasm that dominates the prose, the narrator condemns the official appropriation of *mestizaje* as a symbol of national pride, which, in her view, is part of a demagogical rhetoric typical of nationalism and nation building. This is notable in the passage after Cuca's description of her brother's Chinese features, which was surprisingly eliminated in the English version by the translator Nadia Benabid: "With that Asiatic karma that works so well, when it is convenient, on this little island—the queen of *mestizaje*. *Mestizaje*: our salvation. At any rate, it is sometimes manipulated, like a national banner in any folklorist minister's little speech" (my translation).[10] Scherer agrees with this stance when he argues, after one of his informants claims that the revolution brought equality to the formerly classist Chinese community, that "the concept of *mestizaje* is, therefore, not only critical, but vital for the ongoing dominance of the Cuban 'revolutionary' elite" ("Culture" 91).

As we learn in the last chapter of *I Gave You All I Had*, the story (which takes place from the 1950s to the mid-1990s) is being dictated to the implicit author by a dead woman named María Regla Pérez Martínez (Cuca Martínez's daughter). Mocking the governmental indoctrination of Cuban youth, from time to time María Regla is interrupted by her revolutionary consciousness, referred to as Pepita Grillo (Lady J. in the English translation), whose comments are written within parentheses. Once she meets her father, however, María Regla, who had been a firm supporter of the revolution, begins to question her reality. In this sense, the fact that she is already dead when she begins to dictate the story to the author hints at the fact that the revolutionary dream and consciousness are dead as well.

Although nostalgia for the formerly dynamic Chinatowns is nowhere to be found, melancholy dominates the entire plot. Thus, Cuca's daughter, María Regla, regrets not having lived in Old Havana, which, as she explains, used to be considered the most beautiful of Latin American capitals. One of the main topics in Valdés's novel is precisely the deplorable state of contemporary Old Havana and the intolerable living conditions of its inhabitants. In fact, perhaps the true protagonist of the novel is none other than the city of Havana itself, whose ongoing decay is implicitly compared to that of the *china mulata*'s physical appearance: "He was dying of love—for her and for his city. As if a city and a woman were one and the same, as if cities had a uterus" (54).[11] Ultimately, the sixty years of Cuca Martínez's life described in the novel become inseparable from the years that have witnessed the physical decay of Old Havana and, by extension, of Cuba. The character's hopelessness and disillusionment in the last pages of the novel are intended to reflect the country's mood at the end of the twentieth century.[12]

Another example of hybridity, transculturation, and supranational (or post-national) identity is Domingo Chen, the Chinese-Afro-Cuban-American great-grandson of Chen Pan in Cristina García's *Monkey Hunting*. Domingo has absorbed the African component of Cuban culture and now he prays to Ochún, speaks Spanish with words from Abakuá, and dreams about becoming a conga musician one day.[13] Andrew Meyer has underscored his significance as a symbol of Sino-Cuban identity in the diaspora, particularly in the scene where he is working at a New York restaurant and cannot identify with the Chinese Cuban waiters who order him to wash everything by hand when the dishwasher breaks. The generation gap is also highlighted by the fact that his father, accustomed to saving as much as he can, does not understand Domingo's spending so much money on clothes and concerts.

Even more telling is the scene where Domingo is nostalgically enjoying Cuban rumba rhythms in a nightclub when, suddenly, a nurse asks him a simple question, "Hey, where you from?" (47), which triggers a dilemma typical of migrant subjects: "Domingo wanted to answer her, to say that his blood was a mix of this and that. So how was he supposed to choose who he wanted to be? 'Cuba,' he said. 'I'm from Cuba'" (García, *Monkey Hunting* 47). Although he can choose from among several places (Cuba, China, Africa, the United States, a blend of them), Cuba ultimately wins his heart as his symbolic homeland. "In his food, music, and sexual flirtations," Meyer elucidates, "he exemplifies the materialism, sensuality, and exoticism which were so much a part of the reputed Cuban character. [. . .] Under García's pen, Domingo's assertion 'I am from Cuba' can be read as a kind of manifesto" (154–55). To his surprise, just when he has proudly constructed his own identity and place of origin, someone else (the nurse) reminds him of the uncertainty and ambivalence that characterize hybridity: "The nurse told him that she usually dated only white men but she'd make an exception in his case. Domingo knew then that he couldn't love the little nurse, but he still felt tenderly toward her" (47). Therefore, although Domingo decides to answer the question by naming his country of origin, she still sees him in racial terms. He has no alternative but to accept that externally imposed identity. Like his great-grandfather Chen Pan before him, Domingo Chen realizes that personal identities are inevitably informed by the way one is perceived by others.

In a way, the socially assigned identity imposed by the nurse positions this multiethnic character beyond chosen homelands and into that liminal gray area that Homi Bhabha calls "the third space" of ambivalence between sameness and otherness, equality and difference, inclusion and exclusion: "It is in the emergence of the interstices—the overlap and displacement of domains of difference—that the intersubjective and collective experiences of *nationness*, community interest, or cultural value are negotiated. How are subjects formed 'in-between,' or in excess of, the sum of the 'parts' of difference (usually intoned as race/class/gender, etc.)?" (*Location* 2). Moreover, Domingo Chen, a living palimpsest of the long process of transculturation that has affected not only Chinese Cubans but also the rest of his compatriots, finds himself located between an ethnic limbo and the perimeter of the Chinese diaspora. Indeed, as Ien Ang argues, both collective identities and the imagined community of the Chinese diaspora are limited by how bounded they are, a peculiarity that may even become a sort of prison house: "In the case of diaspora, there is a transgression of the boundaries of the nation-state on behalf of a globally dispersed 'people,' for example, 'the Chinese,' but paradoxically this transgression can only be achieved through the drawing of a boundary around the diaspora, 'the Chinese people' themselves" (*On Not Speaking Chinese* 16).

Another character from *Monkey Hunting* that falls within similar boundaries is Lucrecia, the mulatta slave whom Chen Pan liberates. Although she has no Chinese blood, Lucrecia represents the opposite of Domingo Chen: she cooks Chinese food, considers Havana's Chinatown her home, and even feels that her heart is Chinese. Likewise, she prays to both Buddha and Yemayá, and ends up being buried in the Chinese cemetery. In fact, Lucrecia's worldview has become so Sinicized that she is able to figure out the riddles of the *charada china* better than her Chinese common-law husband, Chen Pan. In contrast with Domingo Chen, in Lucrecia's case identitarian sedimentations are independent from biological miscegenation processes and remain at a purely sociocultural level. Although Peter Gordon, editor of the *Asian Review of Books*, considers the union between Chen Pan and Lucrecia "an improbable yet touching love story" (n.p.), there are several examples from real life that prove him wrong. For instance, Kathleen López mentions the case of Pastor Pelayo (Tung Kun Sen), who "purchased the freedom of a black slave who worked as a domestic on Rosario Estate named Wenceslaa Sarría, as well as that of two of her brothers, and together he and she had nine children" (124).[14]

The rest of the cast also contributes to making *Monkey Hunting* a work where the process of assimilation, the identity crises, and the psychological evolution of Chinese characters can be appreciated in unusual depth. In fact, the numerous analepses and prolepses in a plot that covers five generations of Chinese and Chinese Cubans throughout two centuries and four countries seem to mirror the physical and cultural dislocations suffered by the characters. While Lorenzo Chen, the Chinese mulatto herbalist and physician, devotes his life to learning the culture of his ancestors and even moves to China for some years, others cut their queues, adopt Spanish names, and adapt their taste to the local food.[15] Furthermore, some characters, brainwashed by the assumptions of the mainstream cultural discourse, are unable to perceive the nature, instruments, and sources of their own marginalization. Their false consciousness becomes evident when they subconsciously assimilate the views of their own oppressors. That is the case, for example, of the alienated Desiderio Chen, another of the protagonist's sons, who decides to de-ethnify himself and reject everything Chinese.

Cristina García chooses not to delve into the etiology or the psychological reasons for his demeanor. Yet, despite these narrative silences, readers can easily assume that the racialization of the Chinese in Cuba is the origin of Desiderio's negative cultural self-construction of his own ethnicity. Undoubtedly, the traumatic experience of the coolie trade, the years of virtual slavery, and popular and institutional ethnic prejudice must have damaged the personal self-esteem and collective self-image of Chinese Cubans. This fictional character, Desiderio Chen, embodies the "process of revolutionary de-ethnicization" during the 1960s when, according to one of Scherer's informants, "nobody wanted to be Chinese" (Scherer, "Culture" 84).

Perhaps Chen Pan is the character that follows most closely the transculturation phases postulated by Fernando Ortiz in *Counterpoint: Tobacco and Sugar*. Initially, he suffers partial deculturation or de-Sinicization and becomes a *chino aplatanado* ("banana-ized Chinese"; that is, a Chinese man adapted to Cuban culture, Creolized): he adopts local customs and attire and even wonders whether he is still authentically Chinese. Yet, as in the case of his descendant Domingo Chen, Chen Pan gets immediate feedback on his own choice of personal identity in the way he is perceived by society. Thus, minutes after Chen Pan buys Lucrecia and her son from Don Joaquín Alomá, the latter, who had hitherto been polite, now feels that he no longer needs to be so with a Chinese man, no matter how well dressed he is: "Now get out of here, you dirty *chino!*" (García, *Monkey Hunting* 68). Eventually, there is also an "effort at recomposition" and a defiant assertion of his ethnic pride. Although Chen Pan progressively loses the capacity to express himself in his native tongue, at the end of his life he reverts to wearing traditional Chinese clothing, grows back his queue, and even finds "Chinese explanations" for everything.

The assimilated Chen Pan speaks in Spanish but, as García puts it, his thinking becomes more and more Chinese. In contrast with the poet Regino Pedroso and the painter Flora Fong, who choose to enter or leave Chineseness according to the circumstances, this fictional character finds it is too late to resist Creolization and hybridity. Chen Pan is now one step closer to Ángel Rama's notion of neoculturation: he is unable to reshape his habits back to the way they were in China and suffers from the same identity crisis as Domingo Chen and some of his other descendents, who struggle to find a place among the fissures and borders of nationality. Chen Pan's adventures and those of his family ultimately become a synecdoche of the arduous history of the Chinese in Cuba and of the Chinese diaspora at a global level.

As Xiomara Campilongo points out, however, transculturation in *Monkey Hunting* does not work as a magic formula for the happiness of Chinese Cuban characters:

> it is true that by showing the transformation of the main character, the author destroys the stereotype of the "Oriental," giving him/her a place and a voice in the Western world. Nevertheless, there is no satisfactory solution. García portrays this process as painful, one with gains and losses. Chen Pan becomes a "chino aplatanado," he marries a Cuban and has children, but sometimes wonders "why old sadnesses were coming now to flood and rot in his chest" (62). The same happens with the other members of this family: they do not feel complete. (122)

Indeed, transculturation is no cure for the painful deracination of the protagonists. Ultimately, to use Sheng-mei Ma's term, Chen Pan becomes an example of the "schizophrenic immigrant" (or schizophrenic coolie in this case). Ill-adapted to the new land and torn between defensive Sinocentrism and assimilation, he loses touch with the reality of his adopted country and, as a result, the two halves (Cuban and Chinese) of his split personality are never reconciled. Even the tendency to suicide, pointed out by Ma, appears in the last pages of the novel.

The concept of transculturation is also useful for understanding the psychological evolution of Mo Ying/Maximiliano Megía, the protagonist of Zoé Valdés's *La eternidad del instante*. Despite initially rejecting it, he progressively becomes assimilated to Cuban culture. First, he learns about the differences between Chinese and Sino-Cuban cultures when his father's new wife tries to convince him to sign a contract by using what she thinks is a Chinese expression: "Little paper pulls tongue."[16] Then, Maximiliano rejects Cubans' behavior: he finds them too fickle and opinionated, and thinks that they touch others too much and that their conversations are insubstantial. Yet, with the passing of time, he avowedly adopts not only their positive traits, but also the negative ones: "he even became contaminated by their defects and assimilated their virtues. For an infinite number of years, Mo Ying had felt Chinese-Cuban, pronounced that way as just one word. Cuba was his second homeland. He would not return to China, he was too old, too poor, and too Cuban to die so far away."[17] As Rama suggests, colonized peoples often confront assimilation by keeping resistant values from their own culture. In this context, although Maximiliano adopts Cuban customs, he never completely abandons his own traditions and culture. He loves white *guayaberas* but also Chinese felt slippers, and wants to be wearing them, along with a henequen hat, on the day when he is buried upright in the Chinese cemetery, his head pointing to the East and with a "lightning stone" in his mouth.[18]

Finally, a chapter about transculturation in Cuban cultural production would be incomplete if Severo Sarduy were not mentioned. In contrast with most authors included in this study, Sarduy's explorations of Sino-Cuban culture and transculturation tend to have parodic overtones. In this sense, Cuban critic Enrico Mario Santí has pointed out that the omnipresence of parody in Sarduy's works in itself defines Cubanness: "[Cuban parody or *choteo*] dismantles all critical gestures at the very moment when they are posed. What if, one might ask, the very act of denying Cuban specificity through parody turns out to be the most peculiarly Cuban gesture of all?" (160).

In Sarduy's second novel, *From Cuba with a Song*, it is evident that, of the three ethnic groups integrated in Cuba, the first one to appear, the Chinese, is the most visible and the one that the implicit author finds most fascinating. Even in the section entitled "Dolores Rondón," which concentrates on the African component, Chinese motifs are recurrent, as we see in the passage in which the mulatta singer who lends her name to the chapter misses Chinese food. Without losing the parodic perspective, Sarduy tries to integrate the different ethnic groups that populate the island into a sort of gestalt where traits of one overflow into or blend with those of the others. Thus, one sees Chinese men in *guayaberas* dancing the "Canton mambo" and two black musicians playing in a Cantonese band.[19] Later, the narrator sardonically justifies this depiction of Chinese culture on the island: "A little disorder with the order, I always say. You're not going to ask me to arrange a full-feathered Chinese 'ensemble' for you right here on Zanja Street, next to the Pacífico (yes, where Hemingway eats), in a city where there's a distillery, pool hall, whore, and sailor on every corner" (26).[20] Eventually, Western landscapes become Eastern ones and the Orient and the West merge into a utopian unity: "The Forest of Havana is the Summer Palace's forest, and the waters of the Almendares, the Yangtze. . . ." (26)[21]

The same parodic exploration of *mestizaje* continues in *Maitreya* (1977), where people of Chinese descent lose their modesty and become coarser as they adapt to Cuban life: "The chubby Chinese mulattas stripped naked in the summer and sipped sugarcane juice with crushed ice" (68);[22] "Then, as he had seasoned his Cantonese dynastic modesty with crude Cuban caprices, he scratched his balls in irritation and dedicated to Lady Tremendous a Taoist grimace of offended disgust" (91).[23] Paradoxically, at times *Maitreya* leaves readers wondering about the extent of the identification between Sarduy and his narrator. Thus, in the following passage it is not clear whether the author is resorting to free indirect style or unconsciously using racial slurs when he talks about "half-breeds" (in the original Spanish version "guachinangos" [Chinese mulattos] and "jabaos" [people with black African features, fair skin, and blond hair]):[24] "Thus he [Luis Leng] regressed to his Santiago life as a bon vivant when in the company of Chinese mulattos and other half-breeds he deciphered his insomnias in Lebanese port brothels, provoked by the lashes of the Leibnizian crown of Bacardi" (95).[25]

Still within the realm of parody, in *Maitreya* transculturation is often represented by fusion cuisine, which combines elements of various culinary traditions. In this context, Luis Leng, a Sino-Cuban chef who happens to be Buddha's reincarnation, teaches his culinary art to a student who will blend what he learns with influences from other ethnic cuisines:

> To his ancient and refined cooking, he added the mastery of confection while he loafed around the Cuban Embassy in Paris. Later he worked in North Carolina, with lots of pastry and young turkey breast. Back in Cuba he trained the mulatto Juan Izquierdo, who added to the tradition an arrogant dash of Spanish cooking and the rich surprises of Cuban cuisine, which may seem Spanish but declared its independence in 1868. (90)[26]

In all, it seems evident that these authors and artists see syncretism, hybridity, and liminality as the concepts that best describe the Chinese experience in Cuba. Following this approach to the Sino-Cuban world through the prism of transculturation and *mestizaje*, the next chapter brings into focus the few texts in which one can explore Chinese Cuban self-perception. A particular emphasis will be placed on the image of the Chinese as patriotic freedom fighters.

4

Beyond Identity:
Ongoing Identitarian Sedimentations

9
Self-Definition and the *Chinos Mambises*

> [Colonialism] turns to the past of oppressed people,
> and distorts, disfigures, and destroys it.
> Frantz Fanon

> No one has related in prose, nor sung in verse, the deeds of
> the sons of the Celestial Empire in the epic Cuban war![1]
> Gonzalo de Quesada

For the purpose of promoting assimilation and presenting a positive image of immigrant Jews, some Jewish Argentine authors envisioned Argentina as the land of the future and used their Sephardic heritage as a link to their adopted country (despite their Ashkenazi origin).[2] In the same way, Chinese Cubans like Antonio Chuffat Latour and Regino Pedroso devote their efforts to a representation of difference based on the premise that the Chinese community "belongs" within the realm of the Cuban nation. In their zealous attempt to assimilate themselves and their community to mainstream society, however, they depict Cuba as the land of Western progress and freedom, while relegating China to the usual images of backwardness, oppression, and passivity; that is, the same images created by Western powers to justify their intervention and subsequent colonization. In *Apunte histórico de los chinos en Cuba* (1927), Chuffat Latour adopts a questionable stance: while emphasizing the Cubanness of the Chinese colony (and his own), he recalls Chinese celebrations of royal weddings in Spain, which he conciliatorily calls "la madre patria" (motherland).

Chuffat Latour challenges Creole dominance and demands the acceptance of Chinese culture in Cuba by using all available rhetorical devices to separate his ethnic group as far as possible from the image of the strange Other. His text constitutes a sort of symbolic victory over oblivion: a Chinese mulatto subject, refusing to become a passive object of a non-Chinese anthropological study, writes in the language of the former oppressors (he admits to having studied Spanish in order to formulate a manifesto of Chinese diasporic thought). *Apunte histórico* is, therefore, an invaluable document of self-representation and self-empowerment by an Afro-Chinese author. Oddly, Chuffat Latour positions himself both as a representative of the Chinese community in Cuba (a native informant) and as someone who distances himself from them and speaks about them from "the outside." He refers to the Chinese in the third person plural and often compares them with "us," the Cubans. While Chuffat Latour speaks for the disenfranchised Chinese colony and is proud of his Chinese descent, he considers himself fully integrated into Cuban society and allies himself with the Creoles at whom he targets his study. In a sense, he represents the colonial "mimic man" who reinforces colonial authority while he "talks back" (or writes back) to it.

Frantz Fanon has studied this psychological predisposition among "native" writers in the colonies: "While at the beginning the native intellectual used to produce his work to be read exclusively by the oppressor, whether with the intention of charming him or of denouncing him through ethnic or subjectivist means, now the native writer progressively takes on the habit of addressing his own people" (155). Chuffat Latour's conciliatory tone responds to a strategic positioning with a twofold goal: to "charm the oppressor," as Fanon puts it, and to express his disappointment in Cuba's failure to recognize the key role of the Chinese in the building of the nation. In this context, Lisa Yun reminds us that "Chuffat openly expressed his indignation at the easy forgetting of coolie labour and their pivotal role in Cuban independence wars" (33). As to his objective of gaining Creole support and pleasing his potential readers, he argues that the foreign usurpers were not exclusively Spanish, given that the coolie trade was carried out with international cooperation, that is, with recruiters and ships of various nationalities. He also perceives Western culture as embodying "civilization" and progress, while Chinese customs represent the past and need updating: China "needed to be injected and illuminated with the enlightenment of human progress. [. . .] The advancement of civilized peoples."[3] In other words, Chuffat Latour depicts China as an "uncivilized" space, thus showing how he has internalized a double consciousness in which he sees his own ethnic group through Eurocentric, hegemonic ideas of cultural supremacy. Later, however, he contradicts himself—as he does numerous times throughout the text—by stating that Western usurpers were "wrongly called civilized men."[4]

The introduction begins with a brief review of the Chinese political system at the time: the emperors, the mandarins, and other ranks of "the rancid Chinese aristocracy."[5] Following self-Orientalizing patterns, Chuffat Latour reveals his colonial mindset when he concentrates on the exotic sensuality conjured up by Emperor Tu Kong's harems. Essentialism increases when he describes the common Chinese man: "The subjugation, the slavery, the abjection in which the Chinese man lived made him shy, obedient, cowardly; being worthy of consideration for his intelligence and love of work."[6] A few paragraphs later, Chuffat Latour refers to the Chinese again as "a submissive and obedient race."[7] However, he negates traditional views of Chinese isolationism by arguing that part of their admirable progress and success is owing to their effort to assimilate into the local culture.

Chuffat Latour displays a wide range of attributes commonly associated with the colonized mind and the sub-oppressor (to use Paulo Freire's term). Despite the fact that he was of African as well as Chinese extraction, he often contrasts the assimilation of the Chinese to "the refinement of the white race" and their efforts to "civilize themselves" (16) with what he sees as the failures of black Africans in Cuba.[8] In her analysis of *Apunte histórico*, Lisa Yun claims that "the Chinese coolie and African slave constituted an interlocked social class, spoken of in joint terms." She goes on to say, "Chuffat's consistent conjoinment (rather than adjoinment) of coolie and slave sociopolitics is a departure from descriptive analyses of coolie history as a political economy of transition and post-slavery" (32). Yet Chuffat Latour's prejudicial views are evident, despite his efforts to camouflage color by referring to blacks as "the other race": "While the other race pitifully wasted time in silly things and stupidity, without any aspirations or pretensions to anything."[9] In the author's view, their intellectual superiority and their white skin are the main reasons the Chinese, unlike blacks, have acquired wealth and have been more accepted by mainstream Creole society: "The intellectualism acquired by the Chinese is the main reason they have surpassed other races [that is, blacks] in every social order. The Chinese considers himself white, period. His level of intelligence is superior."[10]

As a member of an ethnic subgroup (the *chinos mulatos*, or Afro-Chinese Cubans) within the larger ethnic group of the native Chinese and the Chinese Cubans, Chuffat Latour situates his discourse as a struggle for empowerment and representation between marginalized ethnic groups. Thus, on several occasions, he exemplifies Sino-Cuban achievements and Cubanness by contrasting them with the perceived failures of the black community. Later, he tries to compensate for this racist articulation of social difference by claiming paternalistically that blacks are not responsible for their own mistakes, as they have not been educated; coolies, by contrast, were much better prepared when they came from China. In the same way, the *chinos mambises*' heroism is contrasted with the attitude of the unarmed blacks who, according to Chuffat Latour, became more of a nuisance than anything else (63). Still trying to balance his stance, he laments the marginalization of blacks and even quotes a poem by Kan Shin Kon, the first editor of the Chinese newspaper *La voz del pueblo*, in which the enslavement of Africans is condemned.[11]

Therefore, this struggle for the right to signify Chinese Cuban Identity is carried out at the expense of blacks who, paradoxically, are also part of Chuffat Latour's ethnic extraction. Indeed, these racist views toward blacks are particularly disturbing considering that the author's mother was African and that in several passages he includes himself among the members of the Afro-Cuban community. Lisa Yun has pointed out Chuffat Latour's unique position:

> Chuffat's position as an Afro-Chinese Cubano, who officially represented the Chinese merchant community on local and national levels, is a unique historic occasion for the early 19th century and perhaps this could still be said of today. While this causes some reflection on Chuffat Latour's role and his importance historically, it equally causes reflection on the Chinese community that endorsed his role, participated in his biographical project, and sponsored its publication. Contrary to politics of Chinese diasporas, it is a rare occasion that a black man has been appointed a representation role for the Chinese people, though it is also one contextualized by Cuba's social history of interraciality. (36)

It is worth noting here that North American perceptions of persons of mixed Chinese and black origin as blacks may not coincide with Chinese Cuban perceptions. As a Chinese mulatto, Chuffat Latour was probably considered not black but a second-generation Chinese, like so many others. On the other hand, in spite of these Chinese merchants' willingness to have a Chinese mulatto represent them, one cannot help but wonder whether they also influenced Chuffat Latour's negative views on blacks.

Chuffat Latour's main rationale why the Chinese community should be accepted as an inextricable part of the Cuban nation and its essential Cubanness should be validated is the disinterested patriotism of the Chinese combatants and the "peaceful Chinese" who helped *mambí* troops free the island from Spanish occupation. In the fourth paragraph of his prologue, immediately after affirming the veracity of everything that follows, he declares his intention to record the testimonies of Chinese men who fought for Cuba's freedom: "I have traveled through the provinces of Santa Clara, Camagüey, and Oriente in search of data, among those Chinese men who belonged to the Liberating Army, and other peaceful Chinese who worked for the cause of the independence of Cuba."[12] At the same time, in a veiled attempt at self-aggrandizement, Chuffat Latour compares their patriotism to his own when he states his goals at the end of the prologue: "this book is the fruit of long years of diligence fulfilling a sacred duty for the benefit of my country [. . .] for the benefit of Cuba, our Homeland."[13]

Chuffat Latour elaborates on the heroism of the four or five thousand Chinese troops who participated in the October 10, 1868, insurrection led by Carlos Manuel de Céspedes, and quotes the impressions of their commander Jesús Crespo:

> I have never seen braver soldiers than the Chinese; they fought with abnegation and were faithful to their commitments. They never betrayed the cause of Cuban independence. They were sincere men, good friends, and obedient. They always occupied the extreme vanguard, smiling and happy; dying without lamentation, like the heroes they were. When the fire was over, after the combat, they made mockeries and hair-raising jokes about the danger.[14]

In keeping with the testimonial approach of the book, Chuffat Latour quotes Chinese war veterans such as Captain Bartolo Fernández, who fought alongside five hundred Chinese men, and Sergeant Crispín Rico, who insists that the four hundred Chinese men in his unit were guided by patriotism: "we honored our sacred duty to the Cuban homeland."[15] However, the author contradicts himself again when, after having emphasized the altruistic and unselfish nature of their participation in the wars, he admits that the Chinese saw in this insurrection a great opportunity to regain their lost dignity: "The Chinese were perfectly aware of their pathetic situation. They had to think about something patriotic that would provide them with a dignified position as free men, so that their shameful situation would end."[16] Likewise, whereas in some passages he proudly asserts that not a single Chinese accepted the dishonor of fighting on the Spanish side or becoming a guerrilla fighter, in others he explains that the reason Spaniards never recruited Chinese was because of their poor knowledge of the Spanish language.

Adding to the testimonies collected in Chuffat Latour's *Apunte histórico*, we have a contemporary version of Sino-Cuban self-definition in the interviews included in *Our History Is Still Being Written*. Like Chuffat Latour, the three generals of the Revolutionary Armed Forces interviewed, Armando Choy Rodríguez (1934–), Gustavo Chui Beltrán (1938–) and Moisés Sío Wong (1938–), contrast the different levels of disfranchisement suffered by the Chinese and black communities.[17] However, they also provide examples of discrimination by Chinese against blacks as well as of oppression by wealthy Chinese against less prosperous members of their own community.

Thus, General Armando Choy, the son of a Chinese merchant and a Creole mother, recalls how in his hometown of Fomento, in what was then Las Villas Province, one of his Chinese friends was not allowed to enter a dance club because it was for whites only. Reflecting his privileged position in Cuban society, General Choy also relates, in an impassive manner, how the Cuban Revolution adversely affected wealthy members of his community, including members of his own family, who ended up moving to the United States. As to his personal identity and national affiliation, when the interviewer, Mary-Alice Waters, asked him whether the fact that he is of Chinese descent had any impact on the development of his revolutionary conscience, he denied it: "I thought like a Cuban, not like someone from China. [. . .] The leading Cubans from the other high schools accepted me as any other Cuban. Within the movement there was no discrimination" (33).

General Gustavo Chui, although he points out the places where Chinese were not allowed to go and the racial slurs people made against them, admits that racism against blacks was harsher. In Santa Clara, he remembers, there was one promenade for whites and another for blacks, but the Chinese were allowed to use the one for whites. He also criticizes the anti-black sentiment within the Chinese community. It so happened that his father's compatriots convinced him to hire a lawyer to take away his black wife's parental rights. As a result, Gustavo Chui grew up with his father and never saw his mother again. In fact, it was one of his foster mothers, Lidia Wanton, who took him (at Chui's insistence) to the Sierra Maestra to join the rebels.

One of the strongest memories of the third Sino-Cuban general interviewed in the book, Moisés Sío Wong, is how his Chinese brother-in-law exploited his entire family by making them work in one of his restaurants for very low wages. He also points out that his mother was only fifteen when she arrived in Cuba to become the stepmother of four children (fourteen, thirteen, twelve, and eleven years old) and she later bore her husband nine more children. Since both of his parents were born in China, he spoke only Cantonese at home but later, like General Chui, he forgot the language.

The impact of the Cuban Revolution on the Chinese colony is at the core of *Our History*. Whereas Frank Scherer and others maintain that Castro's rise to power gave this community the coup de grâce that virtually finished it off, the three Sino-Cuban generals hold the opposite view. Considering their political background, their position is not surprising. As they state in their interviews, in their youth they participated in the clandestine struggle and later in the revolution that deposed Fulgencio Batista (1901–1973; dictator 1933–1940; president 1940–1944, 1952–1959).[18] Besides having leadership roles in the Communist Party of Cuba (of which they are founding members) and having participated in Cuba's internationalist missions in Angola, Mozambique, and Ethiopia, they were assigned prominent positions in the Revolutionary Armed Forces and in the government, including ambassadorships. Moreover, as *Our History* makes clear, these avowed Fidelistas continue to support a revolution in which, as members (and former members) of the military elite, they still believe.[19]

The three generals put forth their own achievements as officers in the Cuban Armed Forces, as high government officials, and as prominent members of Cuban society to prove that the revolution had a positive effect on the Chinese community. This is particularly relevant, Sío Wong argues, considering that "nothing similar happened in any other country where Chinese indentured workers were taken" (75).[20] As mentioned, General Sío Wong (the only one still on active duty) maintains that, while wealthy merchants and some smaller merchants did leave Cuba after 1959, most Chinese Cubans stayed on the island and joined the revolution. The question here is how to interpret the word "some," particularly since the number of Chinese Cubans on the island has dropped dramatically since Castro's takeover.[21]

In General Sío Wong's view, the revolution was beneficial for the Chinese in that it eliminated different types of discrimination that had prevailed until that time (in hiring and in denial of access to certain beaches, for example) and facilitated Chinese integration into all levels of Cuban society. It also erased, he contends, class divisions between rich and poor within the Chinese community. He remembers that while there were Chinese millionaires and even a Chinese-owned bank, there were also numerous destitute Chinese, like the street vendors. In fact, he believes that although the Chinese were discriminated against racially, "the economic discrimination by the rich against the poor was greater" (69). These claims are supported by two photographs contrasting an elderly and overburdened Chinese vendor in Havana in the late 1940s with a group of wealthy Chinese Cubans at a reception for a Chinese minister visiting Cuba.

Today, the Chinese community in Cuba is, according to General Sío Wong, very different from those of other countries of the Americas, precisely as a result of the socialist revolution: "The revolution eliminated discrimination based on the color of a person's skin. Above all, it eliminated the property relations that create not only economic but also social inequality between rich and poor. That's what made it possible for the son of Chinese immigrants to become a government representative, or anything else" (75). However, one can also conclude from his comments that the Cuban Revolution's success in integrating the remaining Chinese into mainstream society has also hastened the demise of Chinese identity on the island: "Chinese societies like the Chung Wah Casino have tried to rescue the cultural traditions of the Chinese community. But it's been difficult, since nearly all the children of Chinese are fully integrated into Cuban society. We've tried to bring them together, but undoubtedly it's not the same as in other countries" (73).

Our History also includes several photographs that attest to the support of a segment of the Sino-Cuban colony for the Cuban Revolution. To emphasize their long tradition of patriotic service, there are reproductions of drawings taken from the José Martí National Library that feature portraits of Chinese fighters during the 1868–1878 war of independence. These early efforts are linked to the twentieth century with a portrait of José Woong (or José Wong, Huan Tao Pai; c. 1898–1930), a communist revolutionary assassinated in 1930 by agents of the Machado dictatorship.[22] Another photograph, the one on the cover, brings Chinese participation in revolutionary struggles all the way to the Cuban Revolution. It features members of the Chinese New Democracy Alliance (Alianza Nueva Democracia China), an organization of revolutionary Chinese Cubans, at a Havana rally on September 2, 1960, carrying a banner that reads "Resident Chinese support the Cuban Revolution and its leader, Fidel Castro!"[23] This rally was organized in response to the U.S. government's efforts to unite Latin American governments against Fidel Castro. The same organization is shown in another photograph where they hold a banner that reads, in both Spanish and Chinese, "Homeland or Death," at a rally in support of the nationalization of U.S. holdings on July 10, 1962.[24] Also significant is the photograph showing General Armando Choy as a member of one of the revolutionary tribunals that tried members of the Batista regime accused of being war criminals. The inversion of the power hierarchy is notable if one thinks of the coolies' numerous complaints about the corruption of the Cuban judicial system, which systematically ignored their appeals.

As with the wars of independence, it is very difficult to calculate how many descendants of Chinese immigrants fought alongside Fidel Castro during the Cuban Revolution. General Sío Wong remembers that when Fidel Castro asked him about the approximate number, he answered that it was impossible to provide it because "unless the person's surname comes from the father, the next generation loses it" (60). By way of example, he proceeded to enumerate prominent Cuban leaders of Chinese descent whose surnames were not Chinese.[25] However, we have the testimony of the amateur historian and naive (in the artistic sense of the term) painter Pedro Eng Herrera (Tai Chao; 1935–), one of the most visible Chinese Cuban supporters of the revolution. He was a member of a brigade of fifty Chinese soldiers (most of them immigrants) who supported Fidel Castro during the first years of the new regime. Soon after joining the Revolutionary National Militia (Milicia Nacional Revolucionaria, MNR), Eng Herrera came up with the idea of organizing an all-Chinese platoon. As Ángel T. González explains, they used Mauser rifles, spoke in Cantonese, and wore sky blue shirts, olive green pants, and black berets (n.p.).

On February 17, 1960, the military command ordered the three platoons of the José Wong Brigade, commanded by Eng Herrera, to enter Havana's Chinatown and crack down on prostitution, gambling, and opium dens. They also helped carry out the nationalization of large capitalist holdings. Later, on October 10, 1960, they hoisted the flag of the People's Republic of China at the Chung Wah Casino, a symbol of the Chinese community in Cuba.[26] The José Wong Brigade also expropriated the building that hosted the headquarters of the Chinese Nationalist Party. The following year, Eng Herrera recalls, the José Wong Brigade was deployed to Isle of Pines (now Isla de la Juventud), where Cubans believed the U.S. invasion (which actually occurred at the Bay of Pigs) was to take place. After the invasion was thwarted, the Chinese soldiers were sent to study in a military school and most joined the Revolutionary National Police. Others went back to their jobs as waiters and shop clerks. However, these early contributions of the Chinese community to the Cuban Revolution would prove to be insufficient when two antagonistic economic systems (one communist, the other, capitalist) collided.

On the other side of the political spectrum is the blend of autobiography, testimonial, and historical study entitled *La colonia china de Cuba 1930–1960* (The Chinese Community of Cuba 1930–1960; 1998), by a Chinese Cuban lawyer and former member of the Kuomintang (Chinese Nationalist Party) Napoleón Seuc (1924–). Currently retired and living in Miami, Seuc expresses in this study his disappointment with a revolution that he initially supported. As he recalls, after refusing to attend a reception honoring diplomats from the PRC, he was fired from his job as a lawyer in the Ministry of Labor. Soon thereafter, Seuc continues, he joined the clandestine anticommunist struggle of the People's Revolutionary Movement (Movimiento Revolucionario del Pueblo; MRP). Subsequently, he was arrested twice. The second time he was interned for eight days in the G-2 headquarters in Miramar (headquarters of the Cuban Secret Police), in Havana's Marianao district. On September 14, 1961, he finally managed to go into exile in Puerto Rico and later in Miami. In San Juan he became a member of the anti-Castro Cuban Revolutionary Junta (Junta Revolucionaria Cubana; JURE), which failed in an attempt to infiltrate its members into Cuba. During the 1970s, this group reorganized in Costa Rica, founding the People's Revolutionary

Party (Partido Revolucionario del Pueblo, PRP). Seuc expresses his feelings toward the Cuban Revolution in the last lines of chapter 21: "Insofar as I am concerned, the struggle against communism and on behalf of the rule of law has not yet ended. Yet in that decade I renounced it as I found it useless for any worthwhile militant revolutionary activity. I am now a combatant only in the field of ideas, with the pen and the word."[27] Among many other criticisms, Seuc denounces the illegality of the so-called revolutionary tribunals and their misuse of the ambiguous term "counterrevolutionary crimes" after Castro's advent to power.

A darker side of the effects of the Cuban Revolution on the Chinese colony is discussed in an essay by Agustín Blázquez and Jaums Sutton titled "Barlovento: The Massacre of Cuban-Chinese" published on an anti-Castro web page.[28] It describes the assassination by Castro's forces of three Chinese Cubans from the town of Bauta—Lee Suey Chuy, Guan Xi Lui, and Yak Yim Pan—along with two other Cubans from the Marianao district (now Hemingway Marina). The accusations are based on various sources, including Alberto Fibla's book *Barbarie* (Barbarism; 1996) and Armando Lago's manuscript *Cuba: The Human Cost of Social Revolutions*, as well as the 1962 report by the Revolutionary Tribunal of the Revolutionary District of Havana, headed by Judge Vicente Álvarez Crespo. According to Blázquez and Sutton, on January 15, 1962, the Cuban Coast Guard machine-gunned twenty-nine unarmed civilians trying to flee Cuba in the rented boat *Pretexto*. The twenty-four survivors were sentenced to twenty years in prison by the Revolutionary Tribunal of La Cabaña Fortress (n.p.).

As we have seen in Chuffat Latour's *Apunte histórico* and in *Our History Is Still Being Written*, the ideologeme of the *chino mambí* is one of the Sino-Cuban community's most useful conceptual tools for self-definition.[29] This venerated image of the Chinese as patriotic freedom fighters also figures prominently in Cuban and Cuban American cultural production. In 1869, Carlos Manuel de Céspedes, the first president of the Republic in Arms (created by the Cuban revolutionary army at the Guáimaro Assembly, whose purpose was to end Spain's colonialism), issued a decree that abolished both slavery and indentured servitude. The Chinese community's integration into mainstream Cuban society was accelerated by the fact that, during the wars of independence against Spain, approximately six thousand of its members joined Cuban troops. "The coolie traders," Leonardo Padura Fuentes states, "had made, among other errors, a fatal mistake: along with desperate peasants from the south of China, they accepted, at a low price, a large number of political prisoners from the great Taiping Rebellion."[30] Many of these men would soon join rebel troops in the fight for Cuban independence. While the exact number of Chinese combatants during the wars of independence is unknown, General Choy reminds his interviewer in *Our History* that "in the battle of Las Guásimas alone, in 1874, there was a battalion of 500 native-born Chinese who fought under the command of General Máximo Gómez. An entire battalion" (61).[31] Indeed, the Chinese were organized into separate battalions, often with officers of their own ethnic group, because of their difficulties with the Spanish language. As part of the collective effort, other members of the Chinese colony contributed logistical support by donating money and food or by providing information about Spanish troops. As General Sío Wong explains, they took advantage of the fact that, allegedly, they all "looked the same" to the colonial forces; whenever they were questioned, they pretended not to speak Spanish (61).

Considering that, according to Roberto Fernández Retamar, *mambí* is "the most venerated word in Cuba" ("Caliban" 97), it is not surprising that the participation of *chinos mambises* in the war opened the door to a fuller acceptance of this racialized group.[32] Juan Jiménez Pastrana has seen the involvement of the Chinese in the struggle for liberation as a logical consequence of the exploitation they suffered: "They fought against the flag that had enslaved them; they would be the comrades and brothers in arms of those who suffered, like them, the colonial yoke."[33] Yet, in light of the testimonials published in *The Cuba Commission Report*, perhaps the participation and heroism of the Chinese during the wars of independence could be revisited. *The Report* is an invaluable document for evaluating Chinese self-representation in Cuba, because it is one of the very few surviving texts where it is the subaltern coolie, rather than the educated middle class (Pedroso, the three generals in *Our History*), who constructs his own image. In this context, in section 34 of *The Report* the imperial commission led by Ch'en Lan Pin, who mediated the subaltern testimonies, denies Chinese participation in the insurgency and even quotes many coolies who rejected it. Whatever the reasons underlying these statements, *The Report* certainly presents a very different picture from the one that appears in the other works about the Chinese in Cuba:

> The petition of Chang Luan and 30 others states, "The rebellion in Cuba is one of Spanish subjects against the Spanish Government; many instances have occurred of planters, when joining the rebels, endeavouring to induce the Chinese labourers to do likewise, and of the latter, even at the risk of death, refusing, or of, if constrained to go, at once returning." The number of those who have acted thus is not considerable, as is proved by the inquiry. (93)

While it is true that no Chinese are known to have aided the Spaniards during the wars of independence, one must keep in mind that, according to Chuffat Latour, they were not recruited by the colonial forces because of their unfamiliarity with the Spanish language. Moreover, in this section of *The Report*, many indentured laborers claim to have run away when their masters joined the insurgency: "when my master joined the insurgents I went away to another plantation," states Wang A-jui. Others affirm that they escaped after being abducted by the *mambí* army: "I was carried away by the insurgents, but in a few days I succeeded in escaping, and was subsequently conducted to a depot," declares Wu A-jung (94). In any case, although the report postulates that it is probable that the Chinese were unwilling to take part in the insurrection, it leaves some room for doubt in the conclusion: "minute details could only be ascertained by reference to sources of information—the camps of the insurgents—which could not be reached" (94). Therefore, despite the commission's efforts to minimize Chinese involvement in the insurgency, it reluctantly admits that it was unable to conduct interviews in areas controlled by insurgents. Furthermore, the following section acknowledges that in 1870 Cuban authorities had to halt the introduction of Chinese labor for a year as it hampered the pacification of the island. Indeed, alarmed by the high rate of Chinese participation in the struggle for independence, a royal decree was issued in Spain to prevent more Chinese laborers from arriving in Cuba.

Interestingly, these testimonies of coolies who refused to join the *mambí* troops, some of them even after being abducted, are not echoed in the cultural production by and about the Chinese in Cuba. To my knowledge, no Chinese or Sino-Cuban character in Cuban literature refuses to fight against the Spaniards or escapes after being forced to join the insurgents. Instead, we find Chinese rebels joining *mambí* troops out of love for Cuba and a desire for freedom. Neither the extent of nor the motivation for Chinese participation in the conflicts has been questioned in depth nor have they been the subject of speculation. This lacuna may originate from the authors' unfamiliarity with the findings of *The Report* or from their affinity to the Sino-Cuban community, which may have led them to avoid tampering with the figure of the Chinese *mambí*, an unquestionable source of ethnic pride for Chinese Cubans on the island and abroad. Yet there are reasons to believe that, rather than joining the rebellion for the patriotic motivations mentioned in so many historical and literary texts, Chinese in Cuba were just seeking revenge against the Spaniards or perhaps following their instinct to improve their individual and collective social status. In fact, when Chuffat Latour states that the Chinese had to "think about something patriotic" that would allow them to regain their dignity, one may easily infer that this patriotism (for a land that, after all, was not theirs and had not treated them well) was not necessarily sincere, but merely a tool for emancipation.

This observation is even more apparent if one compares the Chinese community in Cuba with that of Peru, which was in a similar predicament: during the War of the Pacific (1879–1883), when Chile fought Bolivia and Peru over the nitrate-rich Atacama Region, a battalion of approximately 1,500 Chinese coolies in Peru decided to side with Chile as revenge for the mistreatment they had suffered.[34] In any case, aside from the discrepancies between *The Report* and the cultural production about Chinese participation in the wars of independence, the Chinese in Cuba have also been misrepresented in texts dealing with the effects of the Cuban Revolution on the colony and the latter's stance toward it. In fact, none of these fictional works mentions the support that, as we have seen, some Chinese provided the Cuban Revolution.

This self-representation as heroic and patriotic combatants in texts by Chinese and Chinese Cubans is shared by non-Chinese peers like Renée Méndez Capote and Zoé Valdés.[35] Méndez Capote (1901–1989), in her *Memorias de una cubanita que nació con el siglo* (Memoirs of a Little Cuban Girl Who Was Born with the Century; 1963), shows the extent to which the sacrifice of the Chinese during the wars of independence was crucial in their being accepted and integrated into mainstream society: "I don't know whether the immense attraction that I feel toward everything Chinese comes from hearing people call my father Chinese [. . .], or whether it is because of the contact with the Chinese I experienced in my childhood or the stories about their heroic and honorable conduct during the Cuban wars."[36] Indeed, after fighting under the command of officers from their own ethnic group, the Chinese combatants' bravery was rewarded in the third article of the Pacto de Zanjón (Zanjón Agreement; February 10, 1877), which demanded "Freedom for the slaves or Chinese colonists who are now members of the insurrection."[37] The axiom, "In Cuba there was never a Chinese who was a traitor or a guerrilla," which appears in Méndez Capote's work, is reminiscent of a well-known adage uttered by the Cuban General Gonzalo de Quesada (1868–1915): "There was not a single Chinese Cuban deserter. There was not a single Chinese Cuban traitor."[38] Like the Chinese themselves, Méndez Capote, the daughter of an officer in the liberating army, sees the *chino mambí* as the quintessential Chinese Cuban.[39]

Chinese heroism is also emphasized in Zoé Valdés's *La eternidad del instante*. Like previous works, this novel never mentions the Chinese men who refused to fight or those who were abducted by *mambí* troops and forced to fight. Neither does it question whether or not those who actually fought alongside the rebels did so out of patriotism or revenge for long years of mistreatment. Yet Valdés dares to include characters whose opinions demythify the exploits of the *chinos mambises*, deflating this episode of Sino-Cuban history, a source of pride to the Chinese community. For example, Zhu Bu Tah, one of Li Ying's relatives, criticizes his brother Weng Bu Tah's decision to migrate to Cuba and join the insurrection, despite the fact that the latter's heroism as a *mambí* commander has turned him into a national hero. In fact, Zhu Bu Tah is ashamed that his brother has adopted a new name, José Bo, thus creating a false Creole lineage. He also condemns him for leaving China and not sending money to his family there: "I don't think migrating is the solution to our problems, no matter how much money you can send your family. In fact, not only have we not become rich from Weng Bu Tah's heroism in Cuba, but we don't even expect to make a living from it."[40]

In contrast, among the many other Chinese contributions to Cuban society, Maximiliano Megía again reminds us of their heroism: "Not to mention the war. Don't forget the great *mambí* José Butah, a relative of mine by the way, and another *mambí* of a renowned trajectory, José Tolón; there's a reason they built the monument to the Chinese combatant."[41] Likewise, another character, the Chinese female performer Won Sin Fon, praises José Bo's heroism and even claims that Máximo Gómez almost named him president of Cuba.[42] She also laments that, ignored by Cuban society, José Bo had to work for some time as a doorman at the Shangai Theater. Despite her expressed concerns for José Bo's present whereabouts and well-being, she is having oral sex with Paulina Montes de Oca at the time she recalls his heroism, which logically diminishes the gravity of the passage.[43]

Overall, it is evident that Chinese participation in the wars of independence has been used as a metaphor for their patriotism and Cubanness. However, the cultural production about the Chinese colony has failed to remember two important exceptions: the Chinese who, forced to fight in the wars of independence, fled or refused to comply, and those who chose to fight alongside Fidel Castro during the Cuban Revolution. In any event, these representations of the Chinese at war have offset the stereotypical, submissive image of the Chinese subject in Cuba.[44] Today, these strategies of representation and empowerment are evidenced in Havana's Chinatown in a mural painted by Chieng and Jorge Oviedo, where pedestrians can appreciate Chinese contributions to the nation. Among dragons, pictographs, exotic birds, Chinese masks, fans, Chinese instruments, the symbol of the yin and yang, martial arts practitioners, and a Chinese man wearing the traditional hat and carrying vegetables, one can also see the figures of four Chinese soldiers carrying rifles.

In all, the Chinese in today's Cuba have managed to go beyond the presence of the community itself (quite limited in numbers) to negotiate, instead, the symbolic act of representation anchored in the image of the Chinese *mambí*. Other metaphorical tactics exist, however: colony members, for example, are encouraged to appear in photographs of different Chinese societies (even if they are not members) to make membership appear larger than it actually is.

In the last chapter, we shift from Sino-Cuban self-representation to the way in which they have been seen by the rest of Cuba.

10

Exclusion and (Mis)representation

> I do not know how one can speak of honor among peoples [the Chinese] who can be made to do nothing without beatings.
>
> Montesquieu

Ien Ang argues that China is the "land/nation/culture that has loomed largest in the European imagination as *the* embodiment of the mysterious, inscrutable other" (*On Not Speaking Chinese* 11). As evidenced in previous chapters, the Chinese have also populated the imaginary of the Cuban nation for decades. However, a parallel destructive process of erasure exists whereby they have been excluded from the official discourse and from historical records. As García Canclini explains, cultural hybridization is a process "from which one can be excluded, or to which we can be subordinated" (xxx). This is evident, for example, in a contradictory passage in Fernando Ortiz's foundational work *Los negros brujos: apuntes para un estudio de etnología criminal* (The Black Shamans: Notes for a Study of Criminal Ethnology; 1906), which summarizes the exclusion suffered by the Chinese in the official discourse of hegemonic groups: "The yellow race knew how to isolate itself in such a way that it meant little for the psychology of Cuban society. However, it influenced other races more than they influenced it" (qtd. Francisco Morán 388).[1] This statement, while it devalues the past of a colonized ethnic group, may also be considered an example of internal colonialism. Incidentally, in the same book Ortiz accuses the Chinese of introducing opium addiction and homosexuality to Cuba (19).

Scherer has criticized similar flaws in other essays: "Although both José Martí's 'Our America' (1898) and Fernández Retamar's *Caliban and Other Essays* (1989) make place for the vanished American 'Indian' (that is, Taino or Carib) in their arguments concerned with *mestizaje*, they consistently ignore, and thus continue to erase in proper Orientalist fashion, the presence of Chinese immigrants on the island" ("Sanfancón" 168). Likewise, in another essay, "Nuestra América y Occidente" (Our America and the West), Fernández Retamar simultaneously defends the "Americanness" of blacks and Amerindians while ignoring the presence of Asians, the third largest ethnic group in Cuba: "Indians and blacks, therefore, far from constituting bodies foreign to our America for not being 'Occidental' belong to it on all counts: more so than the alien and uprooted 'civilizers.'"[2]

The exclusion of the Sino-Cuban community is also traceable across literary genres. Thus, while it is true that not much attention is paid to the Chinese in the works of Cuban author and patriot José Martí (1853–1895), he does mention a "yellow doctor" in the first stanza of the fifteenth section of his *Versos sencillos* (Simple Verses; 1881): "The yellow doctor came / To give me medicine / With a sallow hand / And the other hand in his pocket: / I have over there in a corner / A doctor who does not maim / With one very white hand / And the other on his heart" (*Selected Writings*).[3] Although the Chinese physician was the most admired figure of his ethnic group at the time, his prestige and symbolic capital had no effect on Martí: the poetic voice declares his distrust of the "yellow doctor"'s hands (the "sallow" one and the one in his pocket [i.e. with "something up his sleeve"]), and then professes his preference for the white hand of the Creole doctor he knows.

The same disparaging tone continues in Martí's essays, particularly when he briefly mentions the Chinese Cubans in "The Indians in the United States" ("Los indios en los Estados Unidos"; 1885):[4] "Another of those in attendance has seen the Indians squatting in circles to gamble away their year's pay, wagering nine out of every ten pesos they were given, just as the Chinamen in the cigar factories of a Spanish prison do the moment they receive, on Saturday evening, the part of their daily wage that is left after their debt to the establishment is deducted" (*Selected Writings*; 158–59).[5] Yet in his 1871 essay "Political Prison in Cuba" ("El presidio político en Cuba"), Martí wrote about the Chinese in Cuba in a compassionate tone:

> I remember it [the prison hospital] with horror. When cholera was gathering up its sheaf of victims, the body of a Chinaman was not sent to the hospital until one of his countrymen cut into the ill-fated man's vein and a drop welled up, a drop of black, coagulated blood. Then, only then, was it established that the sufferer was sick. Only then. And minutes later that sufferer died. (*Selected Writings*; 16)[6]

Whereas in his literary works he paid little attention to the trials of the Chinese in Cuba, on October 29, 1888, Martí wrote a chronicle, "A Chinese Funeral" ("Un funeral chino: los chinos en Nueva York"), which showed his sympathy for the marginalization suffered by the Chinese community in the United States:[7] "Liberty, too, has its scoundrels! And Li-In-Du did not want to be one of them, but instead busied himself with the trades of his land—that is, doing laundry and serving food—the two things the Chinese are allowed to do here. For if they work in mines or on railways, they are hunted down like wild beasts, chased from their shacks by gunshots and burned alive" (*Selected Writings* 237).[8]

Presumably, Martí's admiration for the deceased Chinese General Li-In-Du has much to do with his identification with him as a Freemason, a rebel, and a freedom fighter: "And with his Masonic hammer he went about softening up the Chinese emperor's head" (241).[9]

Paradoxically, Martí's condemnation of the Chinese Exclusion Act and defense of the rights of the Chinese are oddly intertwined with a not-too-gracious enumeration and description of Chinese types in New York's Chinatown. On the one hand, we read about the "Chinaman friar, a merry, mellifluous savant," the "shopkeeper Chinaman," and the aloof Chinaman who is "kept in poverty by the ignorant rich man who is pleased to avenge himself thus on one whose head is fully inhabited."[10] On the other hand, we also find the grotesque Chinaman of the laundries who "more often is an ungainly runt, meek and misshapen, without nobility in his mouth or gaze, or else a man who does not walk but drags himself along, slumped and gloomy, with two glass balls for eyes, drooling from opium" (238).[11] Despite the generally good intentions of the chronicle, the repeated mention of Chinese vices and the derogatory physical descriptions of the different Chinese types seen on Mott Street can hardly hide his deep rejection of the different and the unknown. And yet it is obvious that he feels compassion for them.

In the same vein, in his chronicle "Brooklyn Bridge" ("El puente de Brooklyn"), published in the New York journal *La América* in June 1883, Martí attacks the character of the Chinese again. He uses positive adjectives to describe the people of different races and nationalities who are admiring the new bridge, including blacks, Hebrews, Irishmen, Germans, Scots, Hungarians, Russians, Norwegians, and Japanese. Yet, when he turns his eyes to the Chinese, the adjectives become epithets and the remarks seem full of Orientalist contempt for them: "Lean and listless Chinamen. The Chinaman is the unfortunate son of the ancient world: thus does despotism wring men dry. Like worms in a trough its slaves writhe among vices. The sons of despotic societies are like statues carved out of mud. Their lives are not censers of incense, but are rank with the smoke of opium" (*Selected Writings* 141).[12]

Most noteworthy, however, is the suspicious silence about the Chinese in his extraordinary essay "My Race" ("Mi raza"), published on April 16, 1893, in *Patria*. Although Martí opens his essay with a diatribe against racism, by limiting the debate to the bipolar opposition between blacks and whites, he neglects the significant presence of the Chinese community in Cuba, which at the time consisted of approximately 150,000 members. In particular, it is difficult to understand how Martí could forget Chinese contributions to the independence wars when making statements like, "'Cuban' means more than white, more than mulatto, more than Negro. On the battlefields, the souls of whites and blacks who died for Cuba have risen together through the air."[13] Yet, in other texts, Martí did praise Sino-Cuban patriotism: "The Chinese were great patriots; there is no case where a Chinese has been a traitor: there is no concern with a Chinese, even if arrested: 'I not know,' no one can get more out of him than his 'I not know'" (qtd. Varela).[14] In accord with the ideas expressed in his famous essay "Our America" ("Nuestra América"), where Martí states that "there can be no racial animosity, because there are no races," in segments of "My Race" he eloquently denounces the logic of using alleged racial differences for political purposes:[15] "to insist upon racial divisions and racial differences of a people naturally divided is to obstruct both the individual and the public welfare, an approach that counters those elements to be stressed, those that bind the people."[16] One might add that, regardless of the reasons for his lapse, to ignore repeatedly the existence of a large ethnic group is another type of obstruction to the common happiness he expects. It would not be too far-fetched to assume that, as the Chinese Cuban Carlos Alay pointed out to me, Martí never considered the Chinese an integral part of the Cuban nation because of the language barrier. Ironically, today one can find a bust of the Cuban patriot (the same one found all over the city) in Havana's Chinatown, and a new book, *Martí en los chinos, los chinos en Martí* (Martí in the Chinese, the Chinese in Martí), has recently been published by Pedro Eng Herrera and Mauro García Triana.

Rather than being ignored, the Chinese are simply misrepresented in other works. Two texts published in 1887 by Cuban author Ramón Meza (1861–1911)—the novel *Carmela* and the essay "El mercader chino" (The Chinese Merchant), published in the journal *La Habana Elegante* on April 10—are indicative of how the Chinese were perceived by Creole and black Cubans.[17] A review of the vocabulary used in the essay to describe the shop of Chinese curios reveals concomitant feelings of rejection or curiosity and attraction. The narrative voice conceives of Chinese difference in terms of disharmony and stridence. Thus, the exotic objects "break the harmony" of other shops and the indecipherability and strangeness of the golden Chinese characters, or "scribbles," printed on a wooden sign "daubed" in black "end up engraved in one's retina"; and when the wind moves the sign, "the encompassed creaking hurts one's ears."[18] Everything Chinese seems strange and unpleasant, not only to the eyes and ears, but also to the nose: the penetrating mixture of licorice and other smells saturates the atmosphere. Even the widely admired refinement of Chinese drawings is seen here as flawed, in that the perspective is abominable and that there is no respect for gravity.

Not surprisingly, the Chinese are the ones accused of narrow-mindedness. According to Meza, their "selfishness" and the "narrow prism of their ideas" leads them to draw Roman Emperor Julius Caesar as a chubby man with a long mustache, fighting ten dragons.[19] Likewise, Meza sees the door not as an entrance to the store but as a barrier that prevents him from grasping that arcane world; it is, in his mind, like a piece of the "insurmountable wall behind which China took cover."[20] The description is equally derogatory once Meza shifts from the rare objects to their owner, a strange, silent, and expressionless Chinese man with a shaved head adorned with a long queue, whose glossy, yellow skin looks like marble.

At the same time, however, "El mercader chino" also shows the author's latent curiosity, bordering on fascination, for the mysterious world of the Chinese. The same sign that irritates his eyes and ears, and the same repulsive mixture of smells that makes him sneer, have drawn him into the shop and inspired him to write his text. Meza's ambivalent feelings toward Chinese culture are further exposed when his negative reaction to Chinese drawings is balanced by his admission that an "educated Caucasian patron" will be able to appreciate the exquisitely carved objects sold in the shop.[21]

Carmela displays a more sympathetic approach to the Chinese world. Unlike many of his peers, here Meza does not try to imitate or mock pidgin Spanish-Chinese. He focuses instead on the fact that Cipriano Assam, the main Chinese character, can communicate successfully despite his linguistic limitations. The novel also challenges the reader's potential stereotypes about Chinese docility. When Assam realizes that Carmela has dishonored him with her lies, he slaps her in public, thus subverting Creole power through the subjugation of a female from the dominating race. He also threatens to stab Tocineta, a black domestic servant who, jealous of him, constantly mocks him and sings songs deriding the Chinese. In spite of these occasions of temporary psychological relief, however, it is Tocineta who ends up killing Assam.

Mingled with other Sinophobic remarks, Meza comments on the monstrosity of the Chinese body in a passage that predates the literary subgenre of the *esperpento* (theater of the grotesque, popularized by Spanish writer Ramón María del Valle-Inclán (1866–1936).[22] In his play *Bohemian Nights* (*Luces de Bohemia*; 1923), Valle-Inclán compares the aesthetics of the *esperpento* to the deforming effects produced by the concave mirrors in Madrid's Callejón del Gato. That comparison is equally fitting of Meza's passage:

> How much laughter there was when Carmela asked Assam to look at himself in a mirror that was there! His face got flattened, his mous-

tache was lengthened, his little eyes looked like a line, his shoulders became square, his legs were reduced to a fourth their size; he looked like the bronze lion, under the arch of the Post Office, that gulps down all the correspondence without gagging.[23]

The protagonist's corporal disfigurement in the mirror becomes a comedic source as well as a trope for the monstrosity and foreignness of the Chinese body in general. By the same token, a character named Doña María de Jesús tries to commend Assam's behavior by telling her friends that "he was only Chinese in looks; in everything else he was a decent person."[24] In turn, Doña Justa and Carmela agree and observe that the only ways he was lacking "was having white skin and being Christian the way they were."[25]

Confronted with the impossibility of representing a culture in its totality, authors resort to concentrating on those fragments of it with which they are familiar. In this endeavor, they must walk a thin line between being selective and falling into obtuse stereotypes. With regard to the cultural production about the Chinese in Cuba, a handful of topics are quite recurrent. The perceptions of the Chinese may be summarized, for instance, by the presence of three predominant fictional characters: the libidinized *china mulata*, the *médico chino*, and the mythic elderly Chinese sage who, according to information recorded from my interviews with León Choy and other Chinese Cubans, has more to do with Hollywood than with authentic wise Chinese in Cuba. Indeed, one can easily identify the Hollywoodesque icon of the elderly Chinese sage in the following characters: Yuan Pei Fu in *El ciruelo de Yuan Pei Fu*, the uncle in the poem "El heredero," and Meng Ting in *La eternidad del instante*, among others.

The legendary herbalist, or *médico chino*, a figure that has become a fundamental part of Sino-Cuban mythology, is however one of the most recurrent and comprehensively developed Sino-Cuban characters. As Esteban Montejo points out in *Biography of a Runaway Slave*, people on the island trusted Chinese herbalists more than they did their Spanish physicians: "Witches and Chinese doctors were the most in demand. Around here there was a doctor from Canton called Chin. [...] Poor people only saw him from a long way off because he charged a lot. I've no doubt that he healed folks with those same herbs they put in bottles and sold in the pharmacy" (88).[26] Even when praising African medicine, Montejo shows his admiration for Chinese physicians: "A black Congo or Lucumí knew more about medicine than a doctor. More than a Chinese doctor! They even knew when a person was going to die" (151).[27]

Several novels also include *médicos chinos* among their characters. The term is often left in the original Spanish in English editions to underscore the cultural connotations ascribed to the most respected Chinese professionals on the island. Thus, besides the physician Lorenzo Chen, three other minor characters in García's *Monkey Hunting* are herbalists. This character resurfaces in Valdés's *La eternidad del instante*, where the author, probably taking information from Chuffat Latour's study, explains the origin of the popular saying "Not even the Chinese physician can save you":[28] "With such an anthological phrase she [Bárbara Buttler] made reference to the fame acquired by the coolie physician Cham Bombia, a sage of flora and fauna."[29] In fact, perhaps because of Bombia's known philanthropy, Mo Ying seems somewhat idealized in his daily activities and in his professional life.

In *The Messenger* and *La eternidad del instante*, the portrayal of the Chinese is also shaped by how blacks, the other racialized group on the island, view them. In *The Messenger*, Montero presents a picture of harmonious relations between the two communities. In fact, a mutual understanding begins when the first coolies arrive. Instead of laughing at them, as Creoles do, Lucumís identify with the image of Sanfancón the coolies bring, which reminds them of their Yoruba orisha Changó. At times, however, the Creoles' negative disposition toward the Chinese is shared by people of African descent. Consequently, although Aida is part black and considers herself Yemayá's daughter, Dominga and the Conga Mariate de-ethnify her and question her loyalty to Santería. They suspect that her Chinese blood makes her more partial to Sanfancón.

Similarly, Domitila contradicts Méndez Capote's assertions about Chinese husbands in *Memorias de una cubanita* when she tells her daughter Aida that a Chinese man "was the worst man a woman could marry but all a girl like her could hope for, since she was poor and had nappy hair" (13–14).[30] In fact, the only reason the mulatta Domitila and Noro Cheng Po, a Chinese émigré who became a tradesman in Cuba, marry is that they can aspire to nothing better. It seems then that the African and Chinese communities were "condemned" to understand each other and to intermarry whether they liked it or not. Whether or not the frequent marriage of Chinese men to black and mulatta women (and the transculturation that resulted from it) resulted from a lack of Chinese women, the fact that it took place leads us to question to what extent the Sino-Cuban colony was truly insular. Be that as it may, *The Messenger* implies that Chinese men married blacks reluctantly. Aida believes that her putative father, Noro Cheng, loves the calendars they send him from Canton so much because "in his heart he dreamed about those silent paisanas, dreamed about going to Canton to find a wife of his own race and make up for all the years he'd had to settle for a dark-skinned woman, which was all he could hope for in Cuba" (169).[31]

Contrasting perceptions of the Chinese in Cuba may be gleaned from *La eternidad del instante*. Gina, a mulatta maid, hums popular ditties about the Chinese that are subsequently glossed by her boss Maximiliano, in his role as cultural translator. Maximiliano clarifies, for instance, that the Chinese were indeed called "captains" and that there was a proverb stating that having a Chinaman standing behind one brought bad luck. Similarly, he confirms that the Chinese were liberal with their money and that they preferred mulattas over blacks, even though these were usually unfaithful. Unlike *Monkey Hunting*, however, this novel does not explain that, since very few Chinese women arrived with the coolies, and Creole women rarely were willing to marry Chinese men, women of African extraction were the coolies' only marriage choice. In a more positive light, numerous female characters find Mo Ying handsome and fall for him. In this sense, Valdés subverts the traditional image of the asexual Chinese man (a Chinese version of the black Mammy character) to introduce a rare fictional Chinese male character who enjoys an active sex life.

La eternidad del instante is also one of the few works that reflects the Cuban colonial authorities' initial attempt to "whiten" the country, or at least to create a buffer between blacks and whites, by using Chinese laborers: "In Cuba laborers are needed and landowners don't want any more black slaves, they want to whiten, in this case to yellow, the population."[32] However, in a Cuban version of "white but not quite," once Chinese laborers arrived in Cuba, the local population found it difficult to consider them white. The exception is the acceptance of Mo Ying and his father by the Cuban oligarchy, a case that suggests the socioeconomic and cultural implications of racial discrimination in Cuba.

Anthropologists and historians often point out that ties and lifelong obligations to family/kin and Chinese societies are the quintessence of Chinese personal relationships in Cuba. Frank Scherer has noted that "by 1954 there were fifty-six officially registered Chinese civic organizations, with thousands of affiliated members in Cuba. In 1997, only thirteen remain" ("Culture" 82).[33] Indeed, despite the fact that emigrating and leaving behind one's family could be perceived as a very individualistic act (in the cases where this emigration was voluntary), many coolies remained bound to a larger group, be it their family or a Chinese society. Emulating institutions they left behind, the Chinese in Cuba created their own schools, operas, temples, political parties, guilds, and brotherhoods. But perhaps the clubs that left the strongest imprint on the imagination of non-Chinese Cubans were their regional associations (*huiguan*), clan organizations (*fongs*), and secret societies (*tongs*).³⁴ While the clan and surname associations served as mutual-aid fraternities that shipped the remains of deceased Chinese back to China, provided hospitals, assisted in composing and sending letters, and maintained temples, secret societies provided illegal commodities and services, such as opium, gambling, and prostitution.³⁵

The importance of these brotherhoods within the Sino-Cuban community is underscored in Correa's *Cold Havana Ground* and in Padura Fuentes's *La cola de la serpiente*. In the opening scene of *Cold Havana Ground*, we learn that whereas some of these associations, like the Society of Seven Dragons, are clandestine, others operate in the open, like the Chung Wah Society (it owns the famous Chung Wah Casino) that provides a guesthouse for the protagonist's honeymoon.³⁶ The leaders of these clubs are very influential figures in the community. Thus, when the police are investigating the motives for the theft of Rafael Cuan's corpse, they question Antonio Choy who, for many years, has been the president of one of the most important Chinese societies.

Chinese societies and the Chung Wah Casino are usually described from the outside, a perspective that contributes to the aura of mystery around them. In contrast, Padura Fuentes's novella, *La cola de la serpiente*, tries to reveal the inner workings of a Chinese society in Havana; yet it does so through parody. Two old Chinese *compadres*, Juan Chion and Francisco Chiu, lead Lieutenant Mario Conde and Sergeant Manuel Palacios through the rooms of the decrepit headquarters of the Lung Con Cun Sol Chinese society, where time seems to have come to a standstill. This neglected building symbolizes the state of Havana's Chinatown, populated mostly by sad-looking, old Chinese men and described by Mario Conde as a "stinking hovel."³⁷ At the same time, it is also a synecdoche for the "tragic destiny" of the city of Havana. Although not written by a Chinese author, the work's bleak recreation of the Chinese world in the diaspora falls within Rey Chow's categorization: "In exile, Chinese writing [...] is condemned to nostalgia, often no sooner reflecting or recording the 'reality' of Chinese life overseas than rendering Chineseness itself as something the essence of which belongs to a bygone era" (16).

Similarly, the Chinese community in Cuba is often identified by three cultural hallmarks: cuisine, opera, and charades (*charada china* or *chi-ffá*) which, depending on the author, may or may not be pivotal elements of Cubanness.³⁸ Another (stereo)typical trait assigned to them is their exceptional patience.³⁹ For instance, in Valdés's *La eternidad del instante* Mr. Xuang writes a long essay on Taoist patience, and his son-in-law, Mo Ying, meditates by conversing with turtles on this topic. Aware of the potentially stereotypical dimension of this attribute, the author jokes about the cliché: "Moreover, the old man, endowed with great patience (Chinese, of course), listened to her daily tirade without protesting."[40]

The final Chinese character trait discussed in this chapter is their tendency toward silence, which is often mentioned as another form of resistance. Indeed, in Chinese culture, silence is appreciated and considered an essential element for meditation and concentration. This is repeatedly stated in the *Tao Te Ching*, in Buddhist thought, and in Huang Po's "The Dharma of the Heart."[41] This connection between silence and Chinese culture is pervasive as an identitarian trope in fictional works such as Padura Fuentes's *La cola de la serpiente*, García's *Monkey Hunting*, Valdés's *La eternidad del instante*, and "Chino olvidado" (Forgotten Chinaman; 1945), by the Spanish exile Antonio Ortega (1903–1970).[42] In some cases, silence is associated with Chinese characters' "millenary" smile, as we see in *La cola de la serpiente* and "Chino olvidado."

This last short story narrates the suffering of Antonio Chang, a Chinese laundry worker who, unable to pay a fine of thirty pesos for immoral conduct (because he was ironing before an open door while wearing a t-shirt), ends up being imprisoned. The character's most noticeable trait is his impenetrability. The narrator proceeds to examine the mysterious smile of the Chinese. The jailer and the other prisoners are equally intrigued with this man who is not interested in anyone or anything and whose facial features are indecipherable. In the end, terrified and aware of his inability to express himself in any language, Antonio decides to remain quiet in court and rehearses his decision in his mind: "Better to know nothing. To understand nothing. ('Chino not know nothing. Chino be ignolant!') That was the best thing to do. ('Nature does not speak,' said the venerable Lao Tse). He would not speak, he would not understand anything they said. (That would be like closing one's eyes, easy to do)."[43]

Along these lines, Padura Fuentes's *La cola de la serpiente* presents their impenetrable silence and mysterious smile as Chinese men's only shield against the terrible displacement and solitude they experience: "But the most painful thing was that invincible uprootedness that not even the economic success that some enjoyed had been able to mitigate. The only salvation from that malaise had been keeping a ghetto culture and answering disdain with silence, mockery with a smile."[44] As in other texts, here Chinese inscrutability and wiliness provoke the impatience of several characters: "None of them talked about that or about anything. This is screwed up. I don't understand the Chinese. These bastards pretend not to understand me," complains Sergeant Manuel Palacios.[45]

But undoubtedly, the work where the topic of silence predominates is Valdés's *La eternidad del instante*. Li Ying, the protagonist's father, admires his future wife, Xiao Ying, precisely because of her silence. Immediately after she predicts that her son, Mo Ying, will spend long periods of his life in silence, her husband praises that as a great virtue. Some years later, when Mo Ying nonchalantly tells his mother, Mei, that he likes the mountains she is painting because they do not speak, she answers that their quietness represents the very essence of the Chinese spirit. Also, at the age of twelve, Mo Ying travels with his master to a pagoda on a sacred mountain, where they spend three years silently meditating to become wiser. Years later, again returning to the leitmotif of the novel, Mo Ying asks his mother to break the silence into which she has fallen after her husband's departure for Cuba but, in line with the tenets of Taoism and Buddhism, she replies: "I'm a better person when I'm silent and I can be more humane dealing with other people's pain. He who doesn't speak is knowledgeable; he who speaks too much does not know the most important thing: to listen to others."[46] Eventually, Maximiliano Megía will follow in his mother's footsteps. After his wife abandons him and their five children, he falls into a profound depression and chooses to remain silent forever.[47] Yet rather than interpreting his decision as self-punishment, he feels that he is hiding a treasure in his throat: the pearl of silence.

11

Conclusion

> A national culture is the whole body of efforts made by a people in the sphere of thought to describe, justify, and praise the action through which that people has created itself and keeps itself in existence.
>
> Frantz Fanon

The body of works analyzed in this study constitutes a cultural mapping of the rugged history of the Chinese community in Cuba.[1] One by one, each Sino-Cuban character traces a collective identity in a process of uninterrupted articulation. Each unveils a human palimpsest that reflects the evolving image of this ethnic group, from a starting point of demonization and racism, to the Orientalist and strategically self-Orientalizing portrayals and, finally, to the more realistic approaches of recent novels. At the same time, we must not forget that beyond the simple, mimetic reflection of a historical reality, these representational strategies constitute a new reality in themselves, a new history that is able to produce independent sets of meanings and regimes of representation. Regardless of the authors' ethnic backgrounds, these aesthetic practices provide new histories to an oppositional discourse that challenges sanctioned versions of Cuban history, whether based on homogeneous cultural markers or on the equally mythical binary opposition between blacks and Creoles. They reshape the nation by calling into question nationalist projects that inexorably trap culture within the ideas of territory and state. Paradoxically, most of the cultural products considered here were created by authors and artists who lack the epistemologically privileged perspective of being either Chinese or Chinese Cuban. Notable exceptions are the testimonials *The Cuba Commission Report, La colonia china de Cuba 1930–1960*, and *Our History Is Still Being Written*, the works of Antonio Chuffat Latour and Regino Pedroso, the paintings of Flora Fong, Pedro Eng Herrera, and Wifredo Lam, and the photographs of María Lau.

Although a few of these authors and artists have more or less remote Chinese ancestors, most of them do not identify themselves as Chinese Cubans. This reality calls for caution or even skepticism on our part. Several questions come to mind. One is, Should Sino-Cuban literature be written in Spanish or in Chinese? That ethnic Chinese authors like Pedroso and Chuffat Latour chose to write in Spanish may have been a response either to their desire to reach a broader Cuban audience or to the fact that many members of the Sino-Cuban community could neither speak Cantonese nor write Chinese. Some may also wonder whether, by being considered a Latina author and thus an ethnic minority in the United States, Cristina García is given "cultural authority" to comment on the cultures of other minority groups such as Chinese Cubans. In this regard, Severo Sarduy, in an interview with Emir Rodríguez Monegal, acknowledged the inevitable shortcomings that plague Westerners when dealing with Eastern cultures:

> But I am not dealing with a transcendental, metaphysical, or profound India but, on the contrary, am emphasizing the superficial and, I would say, even Indian tackiness. I believe, and I would have liked Octavio Paz to have agreed with me (I believe he does) that the only decodification we can make as Westerners, our only possible non-neurotic reading, considering our logocentrism, is the one that exalts that country's superficiality. To do otherwise yields a Christianizing translation, syncretism, true superficiality.[2]

Yet, while ethnic writing has traditionally been associated with nationalistic claims and refutations, one can hardly imagine how a Sino-Cuban literature could be nationalistic if it is being written, for the most part, by authors from other ethnic backgrounds.

In fact, it could be argued that literature and other cultural manifestations about the Chinese diaspora in Cuba have followed *indianista* and *indigenista* literature in Latin America. Whereas in some works Chinese subjects are idealized and used almost to embellish or exoticize the plot, in others (which could be termed "Chineseist") Creole authors condemn their exploitation and defend their right to be considered an integral part of Cuban identity and culture, in spite of the shortcomings associated with the term "national identity." As with *indigenismo*, besides the fact that most authors are Creoles, one must take into account that the modes of production determining these literary and cultural texts reveal an unequivocal Western influence, as reflected in the different literary genres and artistic styles. Moreover, that some novels were originally written in English reveals an implied reader, one who is probably neither Chinese Cuban nor Cuban (at least not resident in Cuba), but who is part of the North American market in general. Likewise, the recurrent and detailed explanations of Chinese and Sino-Cuban cultural idiosyncrasies in these texts prove that the works are intended for a reading public that is unfamiliar with the history and culture of this ethnic group.

A considerable crisis of representation therefore exists. On the one hand, we find ambivalence with respect to the figuration of the Chinese world. Within the same work this world may be represented as a foreign subjectivity imported from a mysterious, faraway land, only to be vindicated a few pages later as something that, far from being exotic, is an intrinsic part of Cuban national identity and should not be considered peripheral to the concept of Latin American culture. On the other hand, despite timid claims of Chinese ancestry by a few of these authors, we find an obvious cultural and ideological displacement between the objects of representation and the axiological system of the (at times sympathetic) women and men who fictionalize them. Severo Sarduy and Leonardo Padura Fuentes attempt to solve this dilemma through the use of parody. Other authors, consciously writing on behalf of Chinese Cubans, attempt to distance themselves (with varying degrees of success) from their own Western epistemological perspective in order to apprehend the Chinese worldview in their works. That is the case, for example, with Mayra Montero and Cristina García, two novelists lacking the cultural capital normally assigned to people of Chinese extraction. Since neither is of Asian origin, each is susceptible to the suspicion of creating paternalistic or hegemonic representations of the postcolonial subject. In any case, they successfully transcend the merely mimetic transcription of reality to delve into the Chinese worldview and psychology beyond the mere incorporation of Chinese words. To accomplish this, Montero and García rely on renowned Chinese thinkers as well as popular culture in the forms of religious beliefs, superstitions, witchcraft, legends, proverbs, and other cultural practices.[3] Despite the inevitable limitations attached to the fact that both authors still write from a Western prism, their novels bring a new perspective to the field. They incorporate strong female characters, avoid the reinforcement of tedious generalizations and stereotypes, and acknowledge the extensive process of hybridization that has taken place in the blood and in the life of the Sino-Cuban community. More importantly, they place the Chinese diaspora in Cuba beyond parochialisms and within the sphere of geopolitical forces, deterritorialization, and globalization.

In fact, Cristina García is a unique case. Considered a member of an ethnic minority in the United States, she has used her own family's memories of exile and of living on the margins of two cultures to extrapolate the Chinese experience in Cuba. In addition, she stands out as one of the writers who have been most successful in conceiving their story from a global perspective that universalizes and, in a way, deterritorializes the Chinese diaspora. Like García, other women writers such as Mayra Montero and Zoé Valdés, have contested (or complemented) the contributions of their male counterparts by inscribing the categories of gender and sexuality into the collective discourse about cultural difference and hybridity. In their works, they ethnicize gender by adding the dimension of modes of reproduction to the literary representation of economic production and international division of labor. Likewise, they often intersect the notions of cultural difference and sexual difference.

In one of the definitions of Orientalism in the introduction to his book, Said highlights Western intellectuals' manipulative (and flawed) attempts to understand and even to incorporate something that is manifestly a different world. From his perspective, even the most progressive and embracing cultural production analyzed here would be categorized under that label, since it often tries to incorporate Chineseness as an integral part of Cubanness. However, it seems safe to say that finding a hegemonic and Orientalist perspective in Montero's and García's novels would not be easy. Rather, they tend to mine colonial ideology by revealing the problematic of postcolonial subjectivity, with a particular emphasis on personal and cultural identity, double consciousness, cultural difference, and hybridity. In contrast with other works that force the Chinese subject to be a "mysterious Oriental" or a demonized "Chinkie," the success of *Monkey Hunting* and *The Messenger* in representing (nonessential) Chinese Cubans lies in their resistance to the temptation to racialize or "Chinesize" them. Fortunately, García and Montero do not feel the need to tell readers why their characters are "typical Chinese." Indeed, I believe that these authors have successfully met Said's appeal to find nonrepressive and nonmanipulative alternatives to Orientalism.

Likewise, albeit less successfully, Regino Pedroso and Zoé Valdés (authors who rightfully claim Chinese ancestry) also establish a dialogue between their works and Chinese culture, both popular and high culture. In contrast with *Monkey Hunting* and *The Messenger*, however, in their works Chineseness becomes more of an exotic object of study; hence, they are more in tune with traditional anthropology, cultural diversity, and multiculturalism. Predictably, they lack the emphasis on that "third space" of liminality and hybridity that is prominent in the novels of García and Montero. Instead, Chineseness tends to be conceived as a homogeneous, cohesive, "pure," and separate entity, with few references to the negotiations and translations of cultural identity dominating the life and subjectivity of Chinese Cubans.

As García does in *Monkey Hunting*, Valdés, in *La eternidad del instante*, ventures to place the action in mainland China. In this respect, both novels participate in the broadening of the interpretation of Chineseness by non-Chinese intellectuals, a phenomenon termed "cultural China" by Tu Weiming in "Cultural China: The Periphery as the Center." Sheng-mei Ma has summarized Tu's "three symbolic universes":

The first consists of mainland China, Taiwan, Hong Kong, Singapore—
"populated predominantly by cultural and ethnic Chinese" ([Tu] 12).
The second refers to the "twenty to thirty million... huaqiao (overseas
Chinese)" (12–13) throughout the world. The third domain includes
individuals "who try to understand China intellectually and bring
their conceptions of China to their own linguistic communities," a site
which has shaped the "international discourse on cultural China" for
"the past four decades" (13). (Ma 97)

In the cases of García and Valdés, however, the issue of periphery, as it is used in the title of Ma's article, is relative. Although their position is peripheral with respect to mainland China, they produce their works in Western metropolitan centers: Cristina García was born in Havana, grew up in New York, and now lives in Los Angeles; likewise, Zoé Valdés was also born in Havana but has lived in Paris since 1995.

Although most of these authors are unable to dispense completely with their Western and contemporary episteme, at least their approaches bring them closer to the specificity of the dynamic Sino-Cuban worldview. It is important to note, however, that whereas *indigenista* novels appeared in Latin America at the end of the nineteenth century, this "Chineseist" bonanza (a mini-boom of sorts) in the Cuban novel has taken place at the end of the twentieth century and through the beginning of the twenty-first. Why this sudden Sinophilia and literary interest in the coolies and their descendents? Could it be because of the rise of the PRC as an economic and geopolitical superpower, or because of the current "trend" toward multiculturalism, or because of the international success of novels such as *Monkey Hunting* and Isabel Allende's *Daughter of Fortune* (*Hija de la fortuna*; 1999) and *Portrait in Sepia* (*Retrato en sepia*; 2000)? While the answer is unclear, the fact remains that the vindication of the Chinese in Cuba's history and the publication of these works by anti-Castro authors have paralleled efforts by the Cuban government to revitalize Havana's Chinatown as a tourist attraction.[4]

Recent examples of this new Sinicization of Cuban official discourse are the biannual conferences on the Chinese diaspora sponsored by the University of Havana and the yearly Festival of Overseas Chinese (Festival de Chinos de Ultramar) that has been sponsored by the Chinatown Promotional Group since 1998. Also revealing is the creation at the University of Havana of an endowed chair (*cátedra*) in studies on Chinese immigration to Cuba. In addition, the 2006 edition of International Fair Cubadisco (devoted to the promotion of music) was dedicated to China.[5] Along the same lines, as part of the 1997 celebrations of the sesquicentennial anniversary of the Chinese presence in Cuba, the government issued a new stamp commemorating the event, a gesture that acknowledges the coolies' saga as part of the island's national iconography.[6] We can therefore conclude that the most recent manifestation of this literary and cultural cycle, termed here "Chineseism," indeed has something to do with the increasingly powerful economic and political influence of the PRC, and also with the marketability of the Chinese (and Afro-Cuban, for that matter) ethnic label as a valuable commodity in Cuba and abroad.

On the other hand, Cristina Apón Peña, the first president of the Chinatown Promotional Group (1995–2000), argues that the government's involvement in the internal affairs of the Chinese colony has been a very positive development, one that is unique in the Americas. She also points out that improved diplomatic relations with China have come about only in the last few years, while the constitution of the Chinatown Promotional Group was drafted and endorsed in 1995. In fact, now that the revitalization of Chinatown is the responsibility of the office of the official historian for Havana, economic support from the Chinese embassy has decreased.

This newfound interest in Chinese culture has also coincided with the government-backed commodification of African-rooted religions for the benefit of the tourist industry that, since the decline in sugar production, has become the main source of revenue in the country.[7] Along with other attractions, tourists find a Santería museum in Havana's Guanabacoa district and a museum devoted to the orishas in downtown Havana that is maintained by the Yoruba Association of Havana. Likewise, the Callejón de Hamel in Havana, which is decorated with Afro-Cuban cultural and religious murals by the painter, muralist, and sculptor Salvador González Escalona (1948–), has become a tourist attraction.[8] Several authors have even commented on government-sponsored tours of these sites, a surprising about-face from a government that, until recently, had frowned on all forms of religion. It is worth recalling, for example, Zoé Valdés's bitter criticism, in *I Gave You All I Had*, of the "discourse of *mestizaje*," that is, the official appropriation and manipulation of miscegenation as a rhetorical and demagogical symbol of Cuban nationalism. Another passage that comes to mind is Daína Chaviano's condemnation, in *El hombre, la hembra y el hambre*, of how Cuban religions and folklore are being "wholesaled" for the tourist industry.

A reason for this sudden literary and cultural interest in everything Chinese may be found in Jesús Díaz's (1941–) short story "Confesión" (1991).[9] In it the unnamed protagonist attempts to create "a new literature," different from the Western canon, by drawing from the Chinese sources around him. Yet he is depicted as a dishonest character who, as a child, had repeatedly insulted and thrown rocks at Manuel Wong (the Chinese man who is now his benefactor). All at once, his mixture of disdain for and fascination with Chinese culture turns into an opportunistic attempt to appropriate something that is not his in order to achieve literary success. In his defense, however, although he lies to Manuel Wong by telling him that his deceased son's manuscript has no literary value, he does acknowledge the sophistication of Chinese literature and culture and feels remorse for having been disrespectful in the past. Consequently, the protagonist has found, like many Cuban and Cuban American authors included in this study, a fertile path to originality by reflecting the Chinese component in Cuban culture.

It is noteworthy that the protagonist fails in his first attempt to create a new literature inspired by a text that he plans to plagiarize. After concluding that he is not a Western author, he also realizes his potential to devise a new type of writing. Yet, once he begins to write, he is unable to overcome Western literary influences and ends up unconsciously plagiarizing the first sentence of Jorge Luis Borges's short story "Tlön, Uqbar, Orbis Tertius." We thus understand the impossibility of ridding ourselves of our Western literary heritage and worldview, even when surrounded by non-Western cultures. In any case, each reader must decide which Cuban and Cuban American authors, if any, have achieved the originality and freshness for which Díaz's protagonist is striving.

The extreme changes in attitude toward the Chinese in Cuba are a poignant example of how race relations are historically contingent. Now that the Chinese colony has almost disappeared and presents no threat to the official black-Creole *mestizo* national identity, the Chinese and their culture have gained a new acceptance on the island. After decades of being denied their own culture, the Chinese in Cuba have gone from being virtually silenced (even the lion dance was forbidden in 1961) to being officially celebrated and marketed.[10]

This rearticulation of meanings once again proves that, rather than being a notion based solely on genetic or biological traits, race is also a social construct. Symbolic signifiers such as "Chinese" and "Chineseness" have evolved and fluctuated in Cuba depending on the politics of the time. Although when planters first decided to hire coolies, the latter were officially considered white and docile, they were soon thereafter treated as slave labor. Some time after the coolie trade ended, the Chinese came to be known, along with the Spaniards, as the island's principal business owners, a reputation that, after the Cuban Revolution, was associated with a capitalist petite bourgeoisie. The Chinese community, consequently, was perceived as primarily separatist and counterrevolutionary.[11] In contrast, today, perhaps because the few remaining members of that community no longer pose a threat to national unity, the politics of cultural discrimination seem to have vanished. However, this new freedom has not prevented the Chinese colony from being seen as an exotic draw for the profitable tourist industry and as a symbol of a multicultural past and a passing era that need to be recaptured for proper anthropological study.

This cultural production reveals the instability of personal and collective identities. It also exposes the unrealistic claims of homogenizing nationalistic projects and the simplism of the binary logic (such as black-white or Creole-indigenous) through which many nationalistic discourses in Latin America and the Caribbean have been constructed. Rather than defining the West by negation—that is, the West is not what its cultural rival (the East) is—we rediscover, as Julia Kristeva explains, the "Orientals" among us, that foreigner or "Other" who lives within us: "we shall never be able to live at peace with the strangers around us if we are unable to tolerate the otherness in ourselves. [. . .] By recognizing our uncanny strangeness we shall neither suffer from it nor enjoy it from the outside. The foreign is within me, hence we are all foreigners" (191–92). Several of the "strangers" in these works incarnate a palimpsest of multiple diasporas, histories, and oppressions that goes beyond any reductionistic duality. Ultimately, those "strangers" redirect the domain of (Cuban, Chinese, Chinese Cuban) ethnicity toward the notion of cultural difference and place it above nationalistic claims.

The undeniable significance of this large cultural production for future re-elaborations of cultural canons in Latin American and Chinese diaspora studies should not be overlooked. These works rescue from oblivion essential aspects of the oral and written history of the international division of labor and labor migration. More importantly, they unearth a terrible history of internal colonialism and genocide. While the genocide of Chinese nationals described in *The Cuba Commission Report* (which despite plausible exaggerations is still the third largest genocide in the history of the Americas) cannot be compared to the genocides of Amerindians and Africans in overall numbers, it is significant when we compare it as a proportion of the overall population.

As noted, Chinese and Chinese Cubans have had their struggles for self-representation—*The Cuba Commission Report* is a great example of their difficulties. In recent years, other Chinese Cubans (Chuffat Latour; Pedroso; Seuc; Fong, Generals Choy, Chui, and Sío Wong) have contributed different perspectives. With various degrees of double consciousness and self-Orientalization, they have been representing themselves from the position of legitimacy that their Chinese ethnicity provides them, rather than allowing the Creole Other to represent them. Other contributions have come from writers of more or less distant Chinese ancestry (José Lezama Lima, Severo Sarduy, Zoé Valdés) who have at times used the "ethnic capital" of having a Chinese ancestor to claim an "authorial right" to access the cultural representation of the Chinese on the island.

My interpretation of the cultural production by and about the Sino-Cuban colony comes from the outside, from the perspective of a European working in U.S. academia. Although I claim no ethnic immunity, I have tried to avoid the pitfalls detailed in Said's *Orientalism* and in Spivak's "Can the Subaltern Speak." These works assert that any attempt by a European or North American to "know the Orient" as a single entity is ultimately a hegemonic act of oppression.[12] I have consciously tried to avoid romanticizing, fetishizing, commodifying, or exoticizing Chinese and Chinese Cubans.

As indicated in the quotation from the *Tao Te Ching* that opened this study, "Understanding others is knowledge." Perhaps through these fictional explorations of the historical relations between the West and the "Orient," we may reach a deeper mutual understanding of cultural similarities and differences between the two. Even better, this increasing knowledge about the cultures of the historical Other may eventually eliminate the distinction of "Orient" versus "Occident," as Said proposed at the end of his introduction to *Orientalism*.

I write these last lines while sitting in one of several Chinese restaurants in the "Cuchillo" of Havana's Calle Zanja, a restaurant managed by Roberto Vargas Lee, the grandson of a "natural" or "legitimate" Chinese, as they call the Chinese who were born in China. I see Creoles dressed in traditional Chinese attire, inviting tourists to taste "authentic" Chinese food and serving Chinese tourists who are playing Chinese chess with Roberto's father-in-law, one of the very few recent immigrants from China. I am surprised to see that Chinese Cubans no longer use chopsticks; this tradition has been completely lost. Waiters hang lettuce leaves in the restaurant's entranceway to appease the ferocious lion of the traditional lion dance, known for its determination to ruin the harvest. Suddenly, two Chinese lions come along, dancing, threatening people with their sharp teeth, and eating the lettuce that is hanging in every restaurant. These dances, they say, take place more frequently in Havana's Chinatown than in other Chinatowns in the Americas. To my surprise, however, when the lions lift their necks to eat the lettuce, I see not Chinese Cuban but Creole young men under the costumes. Likewise, none of the youngsters who follow the dragons and show off their martial arts skills seems to be of Chinese origin. Yet, rather than recalling the uprootedness and "a world threatened by extinction"[13] that Padura Fuentes emphasizes so much in *El viaje más largo* (The Longest Journey), what Havana's Chinatown arouses in me is mostly admiration for the resiliency and pride of the "legitimate" Chinese and their descendents. Instead of lamenting that miscegenation and the lack of recent immigration from China have undeniably limited the Chinese presence in Cuba, they struggle to teach their culture and traditional values to non-Chinese Cubans.

The new generation of Chinese Cubans has realized that, beyond the emphasis on a monolithic originary identity based on a "received" set of traditions, there must be an ongoing negotiation of the act of representation. They have developed a "double vision" that enables them to mediate between cultures successfully. "Social differences," claims Homi Bhabha, "are not simply given to experience through an already authenticated cultural tradition; they are the signs of the emergence of community envisaged as a project—at once a vision and a construction—that takes you 'beyond' yourself in order to return, in a spirit of revision and reconstruction, to the political *conditions* of the present" (*Location* 3). In this light, in spite of their limited resources, Chinese Cubans continue to celebrate their traditional festivities, allowing and encouraging the participation of non-Chinese Cubans.[14] They also teach *wushu* (martial arts, including tai chi shuan), the lion dance, Chinese traditional medicine, massage and relaxation techniques, and Chinese languages to anyone who is interested in learning.[15] Thanks to the enthusiasm and efforts of Yrmina Eng Menéndez, Alejandro Chiu Wong, Cristina Apón Peña, and others, the Chinese colony has managed to keep its Chinese pharmacy, Chung Wah, open, and to continue publishing its bilingual newspaper, *Kwong Wah Po*.[16] In addition, they have established two *casas de abuelos* (houses for the grandparents) for Chinese elderly, and streets and buildings continue to be restored for use as Chinese restaurants and businesses. There is even a cultural radio program in Mandarin and Cantonese every Wednesday at 8:00 p.m. on Radio Habana 106.9 FM. Current efforts are focusing on the creation of a better residence for the elderly and on building a teaching hospital for Chinese traditional medicine.[17] All these activities may also be interpreted as strategies for active cultural resistance against Creole dominance.

Through this book I pay homage to my dear friend Yuli Chung and to all Chinese Cubans at home or abroad, past and present. I am also hopeful that this study will be complemented in the near future by analogous studies on the cultural production of and about other Chinese communities in Latin America (particularly in countries like Peru, Mexico, Brazil, and Panama) or supranationally.

Epilogue

The unsung and relatively prosaic lives of "legitimate" Chinese and people of Chinese descent are just as fascinating as those of Wifredo Lam, Regino Pedroso, Flora Fong, and other well-known Chinese Cubans.[1] The recording of their testimonies is, therefore, a valuable resource in apprehending the ever-changing world of the Chinese Cubans and their diaspora from the point of view of the protagonists themselves. I will now summarize some of the information gathered from different interviews with members of the Sino-Cuban communities in Cuba and the United States.

Most of the Chinese and their descendants in Havana considered Alejandro Chiu Wong, the eighty-year-old president of the Lung Kong Society in Cuba and vice-president of the Pan-American Lung Kong Association who died in 2007, one of the main leaders of the colony. He generously invited me to eat lunch in the restaurant of the society (several Chinese societies have restaurants, some of them quite successful, as is the Chan Li Po), together with four other members of the society. His clan society, located in Calle Dragones Number 364, provides free meals for elderly Chinese. This service was created by the Chinatown Promotional Group during the Special Period to assist elderly Chinese men and women who were in desperate need of help.

As María del Carmen Wong pointed out during this interview, before 1991 Chinese societies were not very active and sponsored almost no social activities. In 1991, however, Chiu contributed his own money to create a free kitchen for the elderly and to revitalize Chinatown and its societies. He also won a first-place prize at an event dedicated to tourism with a presentation in which he maintained that the revitalization of Chinatown would create an excellent source of income. The opening of the societies to everyone of Chinese descent in 1985 also contributed to the revitalization of the *barrio chino*.

Chiu was born in Canton and, before he migrated to Cuba to become a merchant in 1953, he had a wife and four children in Hong Kong, where he grew up and worked in the film industry. His wife and children moved to San Francisco, California, and the children still visit him once or twice a year. Once in Cuba, Chiu married another woman and had three more children. As he explains in Spanish with a heavy Chinese accent, "after the Revolution, most of the Chinese left the country, especially the richest. Those who stayed were poorer and most were married."[2] However, he decided to stay and to hand his little business over to a revolution that he fully endorsed: "I was in the Cuban army for twenty years, and during the Missile Crisis of October 1960, I was in the trenches," he states proudly.[3]

A perennial figure in the Chung Wah Casino is Luis Chao, a native Chinese from Canton who arrived in Cuba in 1953 at the age of fourteen. He is a man of few words who agreed to answer my questions on the condition that I asked only personal questions: he refuses to answer questions dealing with the casino, Chinatown, or politics. While reading one of the outdated newspapers donated by the Chinese embassy, Luis explained that when he arrived in Cuba he was hired by his uncle, who had a Chinese restaurant.[4] It took him an entire day of traveling to arrive in Hong Kong, whence he embarked for Cuba. Luis had a son with a Cuban woman, but they live abroad now. Although it took him a long time to learn Spanish, he earned a degree in chemistry at the University of Havana with the generous help of his Cuban classmates. Luis is the only board member of the casino who holds a university degree. He also works as the administrator of the Chung Wah Pharmacy and as president of the Ching Tak Tong Clan Society. For most of his life he lived in Havana's Marianao District, but he moved to Chinatown in 1985. For years, he would go to the casino to send remittances to China, but all his family members there have now passed away. Of all the people I interviewed in Cuba, Luis is undoubtedly the most nostalgic: although his life improved after he emigrated to Cuba, he considers himself Chinese (not Cuban) and states that the two most important things in his life are, first, his health and, second, China. In 1996, he returned to China for the first time, with the support of the Chinese embassy. When I asked Luis if he suffered discrimination in Cuba, he answered that even today people use the racial slur *narra* and address them with the words "Oye, chino" (Hey, Chinaman) and "Oye, narra."[5] However, Luis states, "they say it without thinking. Deep inside, Cubans are not bad people."[6]

Guillermo Chiu, another native Chinese who arrived in Cuba in 1953 at the age of twenty to work in his father's store, has heard the same insults. He also explained that they used to call him "manisero" (because the Chinese used to sell peanuts) and would mock him by wiggling their index fingers up and down while whistling "Chinese music." Chiu is the treasurer of the casino and also the editor of the Chinese newspaper. He married a Cuban woman and had two children who live in New York. On the fiftieth anniversary of the creation of the PRC, the Chinese embassy invited him to return to China, where his family members and friends still remembered him.

One of the few native Chinese women still alive in Havana's Chinatown is eighty-year-old Ofede Lau Si. She was also reluctant to answer my questions, but she finally agreed to do so over lunch at the Casa de Abuelos of the Lung Kong Society. Lau Si was twenty-three years old when she arrived from Canton to marry a Chinese man who is now deceased. Besides having three children with him, she studied at the university, taught Chinese culture, and worked as a linotype technician for fourteen years at the Chinese newspaper. In her broken Spanish, Ofede stated that she considers herself both Chinese and Cuban and that Cuba resembles Canton. She finds Cuban people lovely and claims never to have suffered discrimination in Cuba. In 1985 she was lucky enough to be able to spend three months in China with her family. She now feels nostalgic because she thinks that "Chinatown is changing."[7]

One of the few native Chinese who speaks Spanish without a Chinese accent is León Choy, a very friendly journalist who used to work on the official newspaper *Granma* and now writes the Spanish page of the Chinese newspaper. Fleeing from the ravages of World War II, his family left the Cantonese town of Nam Hoi T'sa Han and arrived in Cuba in 1940. At the time, he was only four years old and, for that reason, he feels more Cuban than Chinese. According to Choy, the discrimination suffered by the Chinese was subtle, not as harsh as that suffered by blacks. His knowledge of Spanish, he argues, was the key to his never having suffered discrimination. He believes that Cuban society is aware of the positive influence of the Chinese and has learned to appreciate their culinary art and their businesses, among other things. As he explains, immediately after the Cuban Revolution some Chinese were happy because rents became much cheaper, but when private property was abolished, most of them ceased to support it and many left the country. Chinese cultural manifestations also declined considerably. Since the practice of religion was forbidden, people had to hide their saints and Sanfancón figures. As to the process of transculturation among the different ethnic groups, in his view the syncretism between blacks and Creoles was much more evident than that between blacks and Chinese.

Overall, Chinese Cubans seem to be much more communicative and open to interviews than the "legitimate" Chinese are. A good example of this is sixty-two-year-old María del Carmen Li, the daughter of a Cuban mother and a Cantonese father. She remembers that, along with other Chinese, her father would smoke tobacco that was placed in a can of boiling water. He would put a sheet of wet newspaper on the wall and then would roll it up to inhale the smoke. Li was born in Cuba and was never able to finish grade school. After her father became seriously ill with tuberculosis, she was forced to get married at the age of fifteen and the following year she had a son. She remembers that male chauvinism characterized Chinese men in those times. According to her, they would bring young women from China as wives, and in many cases the latter had only seen photos of their future husbands taken when they were much younger. Once in Cuba, some of these women were kept in the back rooms of the houses and rarely went out. Although her father was "un chino aplatanado" (a Chinese man assimilated to Cuban culture), she explains, he was as uncommunicative and mysterious as most "legitimate" Chinese men. He spoke very little and never let her get close to the table where they played mahjong because "she ruined his good luck."[8] He never wanted to teach her this game, a sort of betting on dominos. Although Li never experienced much discrimination, her schoolmates would tease her by saying that the Chinese eat slugs. They also made fun of her Chinese last name and would insult her by saying "Chino Manila Kalimbambó." She also remembers that children often threw oranges at the Chinese, and her father was once hurt when a potato was thrown and hit him in the back while he was working in a laundry.

A summary of the experiences of members of the Chinese colony in Cuba should, of course, be complemented with the ordeals of their compatriots who chose to (or had to) leave Cuba. My reading of literary, cultural, and historical texts about the Chinese community in Cuba was preceded by numerous conversations with one of the many Chinese Cuban women who managed to survive successive migrations and oppressions: Yuh Lah (Dominga) Chung, known to her friends as "Yuli." With a constant smile on her face—occasionally interrupted by tears—she would tell me about her trials and tribulations in China, Cuba, and the United States. Although Yuli Chung turned seventy-eight on December 20, 2007, she still has vivid memories of her life in those countries. She was born in the Cuban town of Sagua la Grande to a Cuban mother of Spanish ancestry and a Chinese father, a Freemason who had arrived in Cuba during the time of the Spanish colony with a contract to cut sugarcane. Chung's mother died during her delivery and, in the early 1930s when she was four years old (or five, since the Chinese date the age of a child to her conception), her father decided to take her to his hometown in Kwangtung (Shung Shan or Shenzhen?), to live with his new Chinese wife, Yu Mui. Shortly after a ninety-day voyage during which Chung almost died from an illness, her father returned to Cuba, where he made a good living by smuggling Chinese immigrants into the country with false identities taken from deceased Chinese men.

Once in China, Chung had to learn Cantonese and was exploited by her stepmother, who underfed her and made her work very hard, cooking and cleaning at home. In fact, she still has back and shoulder problems from all the heavy loads her stepmother made her carry from an early age.[9] From the day she turned ten until she was eighteen, Chung also worked barefoot in the rice fields, even when it rained. As she recalls, when she was thirsty, she had to drink the rice-field water. At home, since she was fed only leftovers, Chung often had to steal food to survive. Her life, she remembers, was very sad. She often thought about committing suicide, and the only reason she did not do so was that she thought God would punish her. She would spend the entire year waiting for Chinese New Year, the only day when she did not have to work: "It seemed that time didn't pass," she recalls.[10]

Chung still has a scar on her head from the time her stepmother struck her on the only occasion she dared to make an impertinent reply: when Chung's stepmother tried to marry her to an old man for money, the young girl told her that if the man was as good as she said, she should marry him herself. At the time, several men visited the house to see Chung; only later did she realize that they were coming in search of a spouse. According to an ancient custom, women were not allowed to look men in the face, so she never had a chance to see her suitors. In fact, Chung knew of an aunt of hers who only met her husband a month after their wedding.[11] Once she was finally allowed to see him, she cried for a long time because the man had only one eye and was extremely unattractive. Frightened by her aunt's experience, after she learned about their intentions, Chung would instinctively hide every time suitors came to her house.

On several occasions, Chung's stepmother threatened to kill her so that her father would never find out about the way she was being mistreated. Yu Mui also tried to sell her to an old woman who had previously taken four girls from the town's most underprivileged families. Initially, feeling that she had nothing to lose, Chung agreed simply to avoid her stepmother's mistreatment. Later, however, she began to mistrust the old woman, despite her promises of a better life. Chung had heard rumors about rich families buying a boy and a girl to bury them alive inside a mausoleum with food and water, so that they would burn incense for the dead person until they ran out of food and died themselves. Moreover, no one knew whether the old woman was selling the girls for marriage, prostitution, or as domestic servants. One night, the old woman arrived at Chung's home, but when the neighbors found out, they sent the local guards to drive her away. Led by Chung's cousin, people in Shung Shan who loved "Fan Kuei" ("the Little Foreigner [Devil])," as they called Chung because of her Western phenotype, decided to protect her.[12]

Chung recalls many other aspects of daily life in southern China. In those days, she states, a man would return his wife to her parents if she did not bear him children. Likewise, old men married young girls or used them as sex slaves because this was popularly believed to restore their youthful vigor. In her town, for example, there was a rich man who had twelve wives and would take the youngest (who was fourteen years old) with him everywhere. Chung adds a further insight into the ordeals of Chinese women by mentioning that, although she did not see this personally, she heard from her aunt that, in old times, women who were unfaithful or who were not virgins when they married were punished by being put in cages normally used for pigs and submerged in water up to their necks. The more fortunate brides were sent back to their dishonored families, who, in turn, had to return all the money, pigs, and sweets the groom had given them in exchange. As for the tradition of footbinding, even though it was an outdated custom by the time Chung arrived in China, she once saw a five-month-old baby girl whose feet were being bound. She also remembers that most old women limped and could barely walk.

In 1949, at the age of twenty, Chung returned to Cuba, where she experienced culture shock again, since she did not know the language and was unfamiliar with local customs: "I had to learn again to wear shoes, drink milk, eat bread, and speak Spanish."[13] For the first time, she heard the radio and interacted with black people, of whom she was at first afraid (the only time she had seen a black person before was in Macao, now Aomen, many years earlier). Some time later, Chung's father arranged a marriage with a Chinese Cuban man she had never met. Since this husband would not allow Chung to leave the house by herself, she cannot say she knows Cuba, even though she lived in that country for fourteen years. She had two children with him, but ended up getting a divorce and marrying Juan Alberto Chung, a much gentler Chinese Cuban man. Three years after Castro's takeover, Yuli and Alberto Chung had to leave all their possessions behind (a requirement of being allowed to leave the island) and migrate as political refugees to Florida. After living in Denver, Colorado, for a few years, Chung convinced her husband to move to Alhambra, California, where she had Chinese Cuban friends and knew other *paisanos* (people of the same ethnicity). Yuli and Alberto Chung still live in that town.

Chung shares similar life experiences with other Chinese Cuban women of her generation. In Los Angeles, she reunited with Josefina Chang, one of her childhood friends, who had followed exactly the same migration patterns. When Chang was living in China, she bought land with the remittance her husband would send from Cuba. Later, however, the communists took her land and she was publicly humiliated. Her family had to start anew in Cuba, but she lost all her possessions again after the Cuban Revolution.

Chang, who is ninety-two years old, now lives by herself in Los Angeles's Chinatown and has completely forgotten her Spanish.

Dr. Amado Lay, another Chinese Cuban, had quite a different experience. He is a professor emeritus of the Department of Modern Languages, Literatures, and Cultures at Gustavus Adolphus College in Minnesota, where he was a professor from 1965 to 1996. Dr. Lay was born in 1928 in San Juan de los Remedios, in the former province of Las Villas, and lived there and in Havana. His paternal grandfather was the first member of his family to arrive in Cuba, at the end of the nineteenth century. He was from Canton and, like so many other people in his community, moved to Cuba in hopes of a better life. There, he married a Chinese Cuban woman. Although he has never denied his ethnic heritage, Dr. Lay considers himself first and foremost Cuban and is proud of his nationality. During his years in Cuba, he never felt discriminated against, although people sometimes made jokes that today would be considered "politically incorrect." In 1962, disagreeing with the politics of the new government, he moved to the United States as a political refugee. He came to the United States with a doctorate from the University of Havana, and then received an MA from the University of Texas, Austin, and a PhD from the University of Arizona. Dr. Lay feels very sad over the political turn Cuba took after Castro's advent to power and over the decrepit state of Havana, which he has seen on television and in newspapers. Although he does miss the Cuban sea breezes and weather, he has no desire to visit the country because the situation that precipitated his exile continues to exist: "I cannot feel nostalgia for Cuba, since the Cuba I knew no longer exists."[14]

Dr. Lay believes that the second generation of Chinese became completely assimilated to Cuban culture and, as a result, a new syncretistic culture was born out of the mixture of ethnicities. This is apparent in, for example, the religious practices in his family (although he remembers seeing his grandfather burn candles to Sanfancón, the rest of the family was Catholic) and in the attitudes of Chinese Cuban women:

> In my experience, I have always seen Chinese Cuban women as very determined women and liberated from their husbands' tutelage. I can cite as an example my mother-in-law, who was a very enterprising woman, with great business skills. And I remember two other women like her. In the second generation, there were Chinese Cuban women who became professionals: pharmacists, medical doctors, dentists, etc.[15]

Although Dr. Lay never learned Cantonese, he still remembers some colloquial expressions he heard at home and some customs, such as receiving a gift wrapped in red paper at Christmas and New Year. He also remembers the *teatro bufo* (bouffe, or comic, theater) at the Shangai Theater, where the Chinese protagonist was almost always betrayed by his mulatta concubine.

Dr. Lay is married to Miriam Wenchang Lay, another Chinese Cuban. Now retired, she worked for the Bank of America from 1987 to 2004. Her maternal grandfather was the first in her family to emigrate to Cuba, in the first decade of the twentieth century. He was a six-foot-tall man (unusual for the time) from northern China (also unusual among Chinese Cubans), who decided to move to Cuba for economic reasons. Miriam Wenchang Lay was born in the municipality of Jagüey Grande, Matanzas, in 1938. Her family moved to Havana when she was seven, and she lived in Havana's La Víbora neighborhood until she left Cuba in June 1962. Her father, Amado Lau, was Chinese and her mother, Lila, was Chinese Cuban (born in Cuba). Although she is aware that the stereotype of Chinese women of the time is that they were totally submissive, her mother was educated and progressive. She always tried to provide her daughters with a good education and encouraged them to attend college. Wenchang Lay never noticed any inequality between her mother and her father in terms of authority or making decisions.

Wenchang Lay's reason for leaving Cuba was her desire for freedom. Consequently, the only Cuba she would like to visit today would be a free and democratic one. Although she does feel nostalgic, she is aware that the Cuba she remembers has disappeared: "Rather, there is sadness because one misses everything that used to exist and which could have existed."[16] She remembers how hard it was to leave all her possessions behind and adjust to her new situation. In order to overcome her nostalgia, she would remind herself of the need to pay attention to certain priorities. Since Wenchang Lay was twenty-four when she left Cuba, she has strong memories of her life there: she had a happy childhood, her adolescence was full of dreams, and she had just begun her university career, studying pharmaceutical sciences, when the revolution began in November 1956. Although her family "always lived in neighborhoods inhabited by Cubans," she still remembers going to the movies in Chinatown with her uncle and to gatherings of the Chinese society to which her father belonged.[17] It is interesting to note here that many Chinese Cubans refer to Creoles simply as "Cubans," thus unconsciously leaving Chinese Cuban subjects in the margins of the national imaginary. The Chinese Cuban exile Joaquín Li offers the same perspective in his testimony: "We associated with Cubans, too, in and outside of business" (43).

Wenchang Lay grew up with the example of her parents' pride in their ethnic heritage and feels equally proud of being Chinese and Cuban. However, she never learned Chinese nor did she attend a Chinese school. She, her sister Judith, and her mother attended Catholic schools and never had any influence from Chinese religions. From time to time they would go to Chinese parties, however, since her father was an active member of the *colonia china*. In addition, since her father enjoyed cooking Chinese food, Miriam would help in the kitchen and learn from him. Miriam also underscores the process of hybridization that took place in Cuba: Chinese restaurants served both Chinese and Creole food and "Cubans would use certain words taken from Chinese."[18]

As for the topic of racial discrimination, the only case she experienced happened when she was a young girl: "Only a small incident as a child in school, but I solved the problem by myself just through a little conversation with the girl who offended me. I believe I taught her a lesson."[19] When asked about the way she is seen by others, Miriam answered that in Cuba she was considered Chinese Cuban, which is also the way she identifies herself (in contrast with her husband, who defines himself as Cuban). When she meets a Cuban person in the United States, it is enough to say she is Cuban; however, other people in the United States seem to have difficulty understanding that concept, just as they have a hard time understanding that a Chinese American or a Mexican American is indeed an American.

Of course, many other examples of people of Chinese descent living in Cuba and abroad could be cited, but these brief summaries of selected experiences illustrate to a certain degree the much more complex and variegated collective experience. Their answers remain in the realm of popular (self-)perception of Chineseness.

Notes

Chapter 1. Introduction

1. The terms "the Orient" and "the West" are in quotation marks because, in many cases, they do not necessarily coincide with geographical locations, but are geopolitical notions. Thus, few people would doubt that Spain is a Western country; yet Morocco, the neighboring country to the south, is not generally conceived of as a Western nation by people in Europe and the United States. That Morocco is indeed geographically located in "the West" in the Arab worldview is proven by the fact that it is considered, together with Algeria and Tunisia, part of the Maghreb, an Arabic word that means "sunset" (and, therefore, West). For the same reason, sometimes Latin America is not considered part of "the West" and Amerindian cultures are not considered "Western."

2. Frances Wood, in her book *Did Marco Polo Go to China?* (1996), argues that the Venetian traveler never went to that country. She bases her speculation on the fact that Marco Polo never mentioned aspects of Chinese culture that most other European travelers found fascinating, such as footbinding, Chinese writing, tea, chopsticks, woodblock printing, and the Great Wall. He did mention, however, porcelain and the use of coal and paper money, which, according to Wood, he probably found in Persian or Arabic guidebooks to China.

3. The Havana Chinatown began to be built in the 1850s. However, according to Homer H. Dubs and Robert S. Smith, there was a Chinatown in Mexico as early as 1635: "By 1635 there was already at least the beginnings of a Chinese colony in Mexico City" (189). Later, in 1806, the British government took 182 Chinese men and one woman as coolies to the island of Trinidad.

4. In his study *La colonia china de Cuba 1930–1960* (1998), Napoleón Seuc claims that, in spite of its flaws, pre-Castro Cuban society was "relatively speaking, the least discriminatory of all known societies." ("Relativamente hablando, la menos discriminatoria de todas las conocidas" [164]).

5. During a stay in Havana, I had many opportunities to witness firsthand some of the racial dynamics in the country. I remember, for example, how a tour guide was quick to announce that there was no racism in Cuba only minutes before she completed, with a smile on her face, a joke started by the driver: "whenever you see a ball, stop because a boy is coming after it; whenever you see a hen . . . accelerate because a black man is coming after it." A few days later, when a cab driver got lost, he told me sarcastically that he was going to have to ask "those dark complected [verde oscuro] gentlemen on the corner, because, as you know, there is no longer racism in Cuba." In the same vein, I had several conversations with Cubans who laughed at the official claim that the revolution had eradicated racism from the island. "If you are

having a conversation with a tourist on the street," an Afro-Cuban bartender told me, "this color of ours doesn't help much; you will be stopped by the police much more often than if you are white"; "if you are black and you are dreaming about becoming a member of the national ballet," a black dancer explained, "forget about it because that domain is only for white people ... even if the person making decisions is a black woman." These are only a few of the comments that I heard during my conversations with Cubans. Several of the Chinese I interviewed also mentioned the mockery they had had to endure all their lives: being called "narra," being addressed "Hey, Chino," children throwing things at them, and so on.

6. "Las desigualdades raciales persisten en Cuba, y se han hecho más visibles principalmente a partir de la crisis económica de los años 90. Se trata de la consecuencia de la funcionalización de formas de racismo que han permanecido agazapadas en la subjetividad de muchas personas. [. . .] En las representaciones raciales predomina una evaluación negativa de los negros y una positiva de los blancos, lo que configura una de las barreras fundamentales que limita la movilidad de los negros hacia los sectores más ventajosos" (10).

7. According to Henley C. Adams, however, the people rioting in Central Havana in August 1994 and demanding political and economic changes were mostly "young nonwhites" (169).

8. In the case of Peru, the first coolies were taken in the mid-nineteenth century from Macao and Guangdong to work mainly on the construction of railroads, the coastal sugar and cotton plantations, and the guano fields. According to Watt Stewart, the first seventy-five Chinese laborers arrived at the port of Callao on October 15, 1849. Later, more "colonists" were taken to Peru: "According to the official report of Peru's Minister of Government in mid-1853, between the dates of February 25, 1850, and July 5, 1853, 3,932 colonists were brought, of whom 2,516 were Chinese. From another Peruvian source (César Borja's *La inmigración china* [Lima, 1877]) is derived the statement that in the years 1850–1859 the Chinese introduced numbered 13,000" (Stewart 17). The coolies soon realized that they were de facto slaves and that they would not be able to return to their homeland or regain their freedom after their eight-year term of labor. According to the census of 1876, there were 2.5 million people in Peru, of which 49,956 were Chinese (2 percent of the population) (Derpich 28). While Stewart marks the year 1856 as "the termination, more or less, of this early period in the history of Chinese immigration to Peru" (23), Humberto Rodríguez Pastor extends the period of semi-slavery until 1874 (33). Between 1849 and 1874, 100,000 contract laborers, mostly male, arrived in Peru. According to Derpich, between 1890 and 1930 a second wave of entrepreneurs from Hong Kong migrated to Peru to invest in different areas (17). Lima's Chinatown was one of the two earliest Chinatowns in the Americas, and today Peru has one of the largest Chinese communities in Latin America. One of the key elements of Chinese Peruvian culture is the *chifa* (Chinese Peruvian restaurant; this term is also used in Ecuador). While the first generation of Chinese is known as Wa Kiu, the Chinese born in Peru are known as Tusáns.

The Chinese community in Panama was inaugurated in 1854, when approximately 1,600 Chinese laborers came from Canada and Jamaica to work on the construction of the Panama Railroad. "With an estimated 175,000 Chinese living in the Republic," explains the Chinese American anthropologist Lok C. D. Siu, "they make up about 6.5 percent of the total population of 2.7 million" (33). Siu also points out that the majority of Chinese Panamanians live in Panama City and the surrounding suburb of Chorrera. As a result, the capital city has two Chinatowns (33–34). Today, there are thirty-eight fraternal societies in Panama (Jackson n.p.). With regard to the treatment of Chinese immigrants and their descendents in this country, Juan Tam, a member of the Chinese Association of Panama, reports that anti-Chinese legislation was passed during the presidencies of Arnulfo Arias and Belisario Porras (Jackson n.p.).

The first Chinese to move to Mexico were Philippine-born and were taken aboard the Manila Galleon. In fact, the first picaresque novel written and published in Latin America, *El Periquillo Sarniento* (written in 1816 by Mexican author José Joaquín Fernández de Lizardi [1776–1827] and published in 1831), contains depictions of Chinese. While Mexicali, Baja California, is the city with the largest concentration of Chinese Mexicans in Mexico, the state "home to the largest Chinese community in Mexico" is Sonora (Rénique 211). As to the Chinese Brazilian community, it is mostly located around the Liberdade district in São Paulo. There are approximately 100,000 Chinese in Brazil. According to José Roberto Teixeira, the biggest wave of Chinese migration to Brazil took place in 1825 and 1826 (269).

9. Although I use the phrase "Atlantic slave trade" in this study, I am aware of its implicit contradictions. As Lisa Yun points out, "Historically, the 'transatlantic' and the 'transpacific,' often perceived of as discrete epistemological geographies, meet in the history of the slave and coolie. In fact, 'transpacific' is actually a misnomer for essentializing Asian migration, since many Asians (including coolies) also came via transatlantic routes and were situated within transatlantic colonial and maritime systems" (41).

10. "Devil ships" was the term the Chinese commonly used to refer to the clippers and steamboats transporting coolies.

11. The pejorative term "coolie" initially referred to unskilled hired workers in India, China, and eastern Asia, but it was later applied to Chinese and other Asian contract emigrant laborers employed by colonial powers in their colonies, particularly after the abolition of the black slave trade under British pressure (*Encarta Encyclopedia*). The Spanish derogative term *culí*, or *culi*, is a derivative from English "coolie" or "cooly," which in turn comes from the Hindi word *kuli*, meaning "day laborer" (*Diccionario de la Real Academia de la Lengua*). As Joaquín Li explains, in Cuba the coolies were also known as *zhuzai* (little pigs). I enclose the term in quotation marks on first use in this study to acknowledge that I am aware of its derogatory origin.

12. According to section 16 of *The Cuba Commission Report*, 200,000 Chinese immigrants participated in the coolie trade. Ch'en Lan Pin (or Chin Lanpin) led the

commission, which resulted from the Cantonese viceroy's refusal to sign a treaty allowing the recruitment of coolies in 1872. The arbitration carried out by ministers of Russia, Britain, France, Germany, and the United States recommended an investigation into the treatment of Chinese contract workers in Cuba. Another imperial commission was sent to Peru in 1878.

13. I translate *colonia china* as "Chinese colony," even though today the English word "colony" is seldom used in the sense of "community."

14. "Donde residía, desde muchas generaciones atrás, una importante población cantonesa. Hablaban castellano, eran avezados en costumbres españolas y se dedicaron al servicio doméstico o como horticultores o floristas" (n.p.). In fact, most of the Chinese in the Philippines were not Cantonese but from the Fujian region. There are other theories about the earlier arrival of Chinese people to the Americas. Gavin Menzies, an amateur historian and a former submarine commander in Britain's Royal Navy, claims, in his widely debated alternative history book *1421: The Year China Discovered America* (2002), that a Chinese fleet under the command of Emperor Zhu Di's eunuch admirals arrived in America and established colonies in the Caribbean and other places seventy years before Christopher Columbus. After circumnavigating the globe and mapping the coasts of Australia, New Zealand, Africa, America (Patagonia, and the Andes Mountains), the Antarctic mainland, the Shetland Islands, and many other places with remarkable accuracy, the enormous fleet led by Admiral Zheng supposedly returned to China, but Zhu Di was no longer in power. Subsequently, the records of the journey were destroyed.

15. After the Treaty of Nanking in 1842, the ports of Amoy, Canton, Fuchow, and Shanghai were opened to foreign trade.

16. José Baltar Rodríguez, in *Los chinos de Cuba: apuntes etnográficos*, lists a total of 338 ships from seventeen countries: 97 from France, 81 from Spain, 37 from Great Britain, 33 from the United States, 21 from Portugal, 19 from the Netherlands, 12 from Russia, 7 from Germany, 6 from Peru, 5 from Italy, 4 from Chile, 4 from Norway, 4 from El Salvador, 3 from Austria, 3 from Belgium, 1 from Denmark, and 1 from Sweden (18).

17. "El grueso del poblamiento chino se asentó en las provincias occidentales (más de un 80%), sobre todo en La Habana y Matanzas" (63).

18. Hence the Cuban proverb "Lo engañaron como a un chino Manila" (They fooled him like a Manila Chinese).

19. More specifically, as the map "Presencia china en Cuba" (Baltar Rodríguez et al. 1999) explains, they came from Amoy (today Xiamen), Shantou (Swataw), Hong Kong (Xianggang), Huangpu (today Wampoa), Fuzhou, Annan, Macao (today Aomen), and Manila.

20. At the time, the *enganchadores* were known in China as Chu Chay Tau ("pig brokers," or "overseers of pigs").

21. Corbitt explains that it was Simón Peón, a native from Yucatán, who proposed the importation of *indios yucatecos*. Despite the fact that the Indians refused to leave their homes, in 1849 a private company "made a contract with Miguel Barbacharo,

the Governor of Yucatán, for a number of Indians taken prisoner in the Civil War then being waged" (13). The kidnapping of Indians continued until 1871. A total of 1,047 Yucatecan Indians would be sold to Cuban planters. As to the Apaches, Ramón Gutiérrez explains, "Indian captives regularly were marched south to work in the Parral [Chihuahua] silver mines. Some went on to plantations in Veracruz, and after 1800 many were shipped off to Havana and to Yucatan. Don Mariano Varela's 1788 accounts book noted that he had delivered 108 Apache slaves to Chihuahua" (188).

22. Depots were originally created for the detention of black runaway slaves, but were later used for Chinese who refused to sign new contracts. There, they were forced into hard labor such as repairing roads.

23. In order to maintain control over the African slaves, the plantation owners purposely divided their families and mixed members of different African ethnicities. Later, the Catholic Church in Cuba gave permission for the creation of societies called *cabildos*, through which blacks were able to maintain and reconstruct their cultural heritage. It was in these *cabildos* that the African slaves practiced their Santería ceremonies.

24. I am indebted to Evelyn Hu-DeHart for this explanation about the presumed participation of the Chinese in the Ladder Conspiracy.

25. According to the map "Presencia china en Cuba," 59,077 coolies arrived between 1848 and 1860, 63,227 between 1861 and 1870, and 19,211 between 1871 and 1874.

26. Both Arnaldo Correa, in his novel *Cold Havana Ground*, and Mayra Montero, in *The Messenger*, mention these Chinese societies.

27. Incidentally, the same problem affected the Jewish Cuban community, which saw most of its members leave the island for the United States and Israel in the 1960s, after their shops were confiscated and peddling was forbidden by Castro's government. As Ruth Behar explains in her documentary *Adio Kerida* (2002), today there are only about one thousand Jews left in Cuba.

28. As army chief of staff, Batista ran Cuba from behind the scenes from 1934 to 1940, using puppet presidents (Carlos Mendieta [1934–1935], José A. Barnet [1935–1936], Miguel Mariano Gómez [1936], and Federico Laredo Brú [1936–1940]).

29. "At the height of the Cuban Chinese restaurant 'craze,' an estimated five thousand Cuban Chinese lived in New York" (Meyer 148).

30. The Chung Wah Casino was opened in 1893. The original meanings of the word *casino* in Spanish are "association," "club," "society," or the place where such meets: "meeting hall," "clubhouse," or "country house." Chung Wah Casino means "Chinese association."

31. "Muy lejos de convertirse en un vegetal, como había ocurrido con tantos de sus viejos compatriotas, los que todavía vivían" (147).

32. This project has also secured support for the Chung Wah Casino and various Chinese societies, and has been instrumental in the creation of the Chinese House of Arts and Traditions, which holds exhibits, contests, and literary competitions. Thanks to the efforts of the Chinatown Promotional Group, some Chinese societies

have been allowed to operate restaurants collectively. The embassy of the PRC has supported the Chinatown Promotional Group in different ways, including the donation of the archway at the entrance of Havana's Chinatown.

33. Allen Chun has pointed out the limitations of terms such as "Chineseness": "If we, on the other hand, view China as an unambiguous political entity and Chineseness as a feature shared by ethnic Chinese on the basis of discrete traits and traditions, it is really because we are influenced by a homogeneous notion of culture that is essentially modern, if not national, in origin" (113); "when ethnic consciousness is used to construct cultural discourses that in turn function as the basis for inculcating national identity in both thought and practice, it is difficult to distinguish the various dimensions of political orthodoxy, social value, and life routine, all of which serve to engender 'Chineseness'" (117).

34. Incidentally, Napoleón Seuc proposes the Taiwanese example as a future model for Cuba.

35. "Eso que llamamos 'cultura cubana' no es más que la construcción simbólica, en el lapso de dos siglos, del metarrelato de la identidad nacional. Un metarrelato que postula un sujeto, el Sujeto Blanco, Masculino Heterosexual Católico o Marxista, cuyos valores históricos legitiman los discursos y las prácticas hegemónicas de las elites nacionales" (105).

36. José Barriero has proven that there are still Taino people and customs in eastern Cuba: "the historic and ethnographic record supports the Indian presence in eastern Cuba—the existence of its actual population of descendents and its cultural extensions throughout a great deal of Cuban culture" (31).

37. "En Cuba durante muchos siglos se ejerció abiertamente un prejuicio racial muy grave contra los negros. Pero no nos dábamos cuenta que había al mismo tiempo otro, tan grave como el primero, contra los chinos. Los chinos han sido muy importantes en Cuba porque, aparte de su influencia en el orden cultural, están dentro de la concepción del mundo cubano" (Rodríguez Monegal, "Diálogo" 18).

38. The term *huaqiao* has also been translated as "sojourners" or "temporary workers."

39. *Criollos* are sons and daughters of Spanish (or other European) settlers born in the Americas, or their direct descendents. Although some nuances of the English word "Creole" may differ from those of the term *criollo*, I will use "Creole" to refer to *criollos* in this book.

40. Eighty percent of the Chinese laborers consulted by the Ch'en Lan Pin commission claimed they were either deceived or abducted.

41. Exceptions are Mayra Montero, who considers herself Cuban Puerto Rican, and José María Eça de Queiroz, who was the Portuguese consul in Cuba.

42. The trilingual foldable map "Presencia china en Cuba," mentions two other Chinese instruments that have become part of Cuban culture: The Cu drums used during the lion dance and the wooden *cajita china* (Chinese little box), a percussion instrument used by danzón, rumba, and son bands.

43. The first war of independence, the Ten Years War (Guerra de los Diez Años, also known as the Great War; 1868–1878), began on October 10, 1868 and ended on May 28, 1878. It was led by the attorney Carlos Manuel de Céspedes (1819–1874). After a brief rebellion known as the Small War (La Guerra Chiquita), which began in August 1879 and ended a year later, the second Cuban war of independence (1895–1898) started on February 24, 1895, under the intellectual leadership of José Martí. By January 1, 1899, the government of Cuba was officially in the hands of the United States.

44. Among the main Chinese institutions were schools, churches, occupational guilds, political parties, chambers of commerce, cemeteries, theaters, clan associations, hospitals, residences for the elderly, and newspapers. During the 1940s and 1950s, there were four Chinese-language newspapers in Cuba. Today, *Kwong Wah Po* is the only Chinese newspaper left in Havana. It is published every fifteen days by the eighty-one year-old Ángel Chiong.

45. "Se puede conjeturar que han de existir textos artísticos en chino y japonés, es decir, una producción cultural en lenguas originales que en alguna instancia esté dando cuenta de las tribulaciones de sus con-nacionales en tierras latinoamericanas, sea o no que hayan regresado a sus países de origen." (114).

Chapter 2. Chinese Bondage

1. Miguel Barnet is an anthropologist, novelist, and poet. He founded the National Union of Writers and Artists of Cuba (Unión Nacional de Escritores y Artistas de Cuba). Besides *Biografía de un cimarrón*, he has published the following testimonials and testimonial novels: *Canción de Raquel* (1969), *Gallego* (1981), *La vida real* (1986), and *Oficio de ángel* (1989). He has also published the collections of poems *La piedra fina y el pavorreal* (1963), *Isla de Güijes* (1964), *Orikis y otros poemas* (1980), *Carta de noche* (1982), *Mapa del tiempo* (1989), *Con pies de gato* (1993), and *Poemas chinos* (1993); the essays *La fuente viva* (1998) and *Cultos afrocubanos* (1995); and the collection of Cuban fables *Akeké y la jutía* (1978).

2. "Como poeta de la memoria quiché, Menchú es consciente de su presente y de su público y ajusta su discurso para que un tiempo concuerde con el otro. Si el pasado es importante para el poeta, el presente determina cómo se conmemora el tiempo anterior" (Luis, "De la oralidad" 234).

3. Along with these official members of the commission, the delegation that interviewed the captain general of Havana was made up of the consular representatives of Great Britain, France, Russia, the United States, Germany, Sweden, Norway, Denmark, Holland, Austria, Belgium, and Italy.

4. Alejandro Lee Chan mentions in his study the sad reality of those Chinese children who were sold to wealthy Cuban planters as curiosities or as toys for their children. One of those children was the mother of the Sino-Cuban artist Candelario Chiu (also known as Candelario Ajuria and Candelario Chiu Chi Koc). During World War II, Chiu's mother was fleeing from the war zone on foot, holding onto her mother's skirt, when she got lost. The man who found her sold her to a Cuban wealthy man

who, in turn, took her to Cuba as a present for his daughter. Chiu's mother, who was four years old at the time, is believed to be one of the first Chinese women to go to Cuba.

5. Those who arrived after February 1861 did not receive a *cédula*.

6. Confucius's Chinese name was K'ung-fu-tse (551–479 BCE). He is popularly known as Kongzi in China. *Lun Yü* literally means "selected sayings."

7. Napoleón Seuc associates this proclivity to suicide with the belief in reincarnation: "Many believe in reincarnation. Consequently, if this life is bad, full of illness and suffering, many commit suicide, normally hanging themselves, with hopes of being reborn (reincarnated), with better *karma* in their next life." ("Muchos creen en la reencarnación, por lo que si esta vida es mala, de enfermedades, sufrimientos, muchos se suicidan, ahorcándose generalmente, con la esperanza de renacer [reencarnar], con mejor *karma* en su próxima vida futura" [45]).

8. Jiangnan is a region to the south of the Yangtze River that includes the southern part of the Yangtze Delta. The most important cities in the area are Shanghai, Nanjing, Ningbo, Hangzhou, Suzhou, Wuxi, and Shaoxing.

9. The suicide rate was also very high among the approximately 100,000 Chinese coolies who arrived in Peru between 1849 and 1874 to work mainly on the excavation of guano, on the construction of railroads, and on sugar plantations.

10. "Si bien las condiciones de trabajo significaron un impacto cultural profundamente regresivo que condujo a la pérdida de la condición humana y por lo tanto a un tipo de suicidio masivo (el mayor del mundo por millón de habitantes en la década de 1850–1860), éste adquirió voz propia como elocuente denuncia social de lo que significa el tráfico humano" (Guanche Pérez "Juan Pérez de la Riva y los culíes" n.p.). Yet he claims that the suicide rate among indigenous people in Cuba was even higher: "To what extent was suicide responsible for the disappearance of the indigenous population? Perhaps some 30 percent, perhaps more. [. . .] The chronicles indignantly recount individual and collective suicides by the desperate Indians; strangling themselves, ingesting the poisonous juices of the bitter yucca, or also eating earth, a last remnant of their native religion. [. . .] The archives contain innumerable tales of horrendous punishments committed by the *encomenderos* in their haste to contain through terror the uncontainable desire for self-destruction that took hold of the Indians" (Guanche Pérez "Cuestión" 23).

11. "A los propios mayorales los mataban a palos y puñaladas. No creían en nadie los chinos. Eran rebeldes de nacimiento. Muchas veces, el amo les ponía un mayoral de su raza para que entrara en confianza con ellos. A ése no lo mataban" (40). Indeed, in *The Cuba Commission Report* many Chinese workers admit to having killed their overseers: "on one occasion four Chinese killed an overseer—a Negro—they were confined in the plantation prison six months, after which two men were hanged, and the two others shot on the plantation, in the presence of all the other labourers" (59).

12. "Ellos sí se mataban. Lo hacían callados. Después que pasaban los días apa-

recían guindados a un árbol o tirados en el suelo. Todo lo que ellos hacían era en silencio" (40).

13. "Los chinos no volaban ni querían ir para su tierra" (40). Later, however, Montejo contradicts himself by recalling the Chinese claim that after they died, they came back to life in Canton (117). Probably inspired by this passage, Zoé Valdés, in *La eternidad del instante*, describes Mei's death in the following way: "It happened in silence, without pain, but with the sadness of knowing that the spirits of the Chinese cannot cross the oceans" ("Sucedió en silencio, sin dolor, pero con la pena de que los espíritus de los chinos no pueden atravesar los océanos" [295–96]).

14. "En esas sociedades se reunían y conversaban en sus idiomas y leían los periódicos de China en alta voz. A lo mejor lo hacían para joder, pero como nadie los entendía, ellos seguían en sus lecturas como si nada" (86).

15. "El fundamento de la religión de China" (87).

16. The film *Nadie escuchaba* was the winner of an award from the International Documentary Association.

17. Pabellón de castigo.

18. "Era de origen chino y esa era su forma. No iba a cambiar y no cambió nunca."

Chapter 3. Cuban Sinophobia

1. These restrictions must have already been in place in 1949, given the testimony of the Chinese Cuban Joaquín Li, who relates how he had to overcome them in order to join his father in Cuba: "I had to buy someone else's papers because of restrictions on Chinese immigration. I bought the papers of a young man also named Li" (43).

2. In *Lo chino en el habla cubana* Beatriz Varela quotes two popular songs, "Esa lengua china" (That Chinese Language) and "El idioma chino" (The Chinese Language) that attest to this curiosity about the foreignness of the Chinese language.

3. "No aprendían el español de los amos sino de los compañeros de trabajo, muchos de los cuales no eran hablantes nativos" (103).

4. "¡Chino no lava lechuga donde mimo lava calzoncillo! 'Mentila, chino son pelsona lecente!'" (*Cuentos populares de humor* 152).

5. "—¡Qué calajo, viva quien quiela!" (*Cuentos populares de humor* 146).

6. "Como muchos chinos que se alzaron" (*Cuentos populares* 94).

7. "—¿Tú quiele cambia?" (*Cuentos populares* 94).

8. "A un chinito que iba por primera vez a la escuela, la maestra le preguntó:
Chinito, ¿cómo tú te llamas?
Y el chinito contestó:
—Me llamo Tin Malín.
Y la maestra agregó:
—De dos pingüé.
A lo que el chinito replicó:
—No, de un solo pingüé!" (*Cuentos populares de humor* 150)

9. "—Anoche le sentaba bien el tlaje de valón—dijo Won Sin Fon con su acento cantonés, *tlaje* por traje y *valón* por varón" (Valdés 186–87).

10. Although Hernández Catá (1885–1940) was born in the town of Aldeávila de la Ribera, in the province of Salamanca, and wrote most of his dramatic production in Spain, he considered himself Cuban. Among others, he published the collections of short stories *Cuentos pasionales* (1907), *Los siete pecados* (1920), *Piedras preciosas* (1924), and *Cuatro libras de felicidad* (1933). He also published several novels, including *Novela erótica* (1909), *Pelayo González* (1909), *La juventud de Aurelio Zaldívar* (1911), *La piel* (1913), *Los frutos ácidos* (1915), *Zoología pintoresca* (1919), *El placer de sufrir* (1920), *El drama de la Señorita Occidente* (1921), *Estrellas errantes* (1921), *El nieto de Hamlet* (1921), *La voluntad de Dios* (1921), *Una mala mujer* (1922), *La muerte nueva* (1922), *El corazón* (1923), *Libro de amor* (1924), *El bebedor de lágrimas* (1926), *El ángel de Sodoma* (1928), and *Fuegos fatuos*. In addition, along with Alberto Insua, he co-authored the plays *Amor tardío* (1913), *En familia* (1914), *Cabecita loca* (1914), and *El bandido* (1919). Later, he published another play titled *Don Luis Mejía* (1925).

11. "When the Chinese entered the urban manufacturing centers of California, they were successfully used as strikebreakers on the East Coast. For example, in September 1870, seventy-five Chinese laborers were transported from San Francisco to North Adams, Massachusetts, to break a strike by white workers in a local shoe factory. During the same period, Chinese laborers were also used as strikebreakers in Beaver Falls, Pennsylvania, and Belleville, New Jersey. Their use as strikebreakers in California first occurred in 1869, when a large number of Chinese laborers were brought in to break a strike in the San Francisco boot-and-shoe industry" (Almaguer 173).

12. "¡Pobres macacos amarillos! ¡Qué iban a resistir el trabajo tremendo! [. . .] excelentes para guisar en sus fonduchos, o para lavar y planchar con primor. . . ¡Oficios de mujeres bien! Pero para aguantar el sol sobre las espaldas ocho horas, y agujerear el hierro, ¡hacían falta hombres muy hombres!" (48).

13. "Si un chino nos infunde siempre una invencible sensación de repugnancia y de lejanía donde hay algo de miedo, un chino muerto es algo pavoroso. . . ." (50).

14. Indeed, throughout his career, Hernández Catá explored racist hostility toward mulattos in several works: his novella *La piel* (The Skin; 1913); "El drama de la Señorita Occidente" (The Drama of Miss West), included in *Libro de amor* (Book of Love; 1924); and *Cuatro libras de felicidad* (Four Pounds of Happiness; 1933). Although the *Oxford English Dictionary* states that the term "mulatto" is "now chiefly considered offensive," many people disagree, as one can read at the website www.mulatto.org.

15. "Desde el borde de la escotilla veíase, abajo, el grupo lamentable de esqueletos estrechamente forrados de amarillo, con ojos y bocas angostas llenas de un silencio antiguo o de un gritar corto y gutural que nada tenían en común con nuestras voces" (135–36). Incidentally, this stereotypical shout assigned to Asians in Western popular culture reappears in "Bagazo" (Bagasse; 1950), a short story by the Cuban author

Ramón Ferreira (1921–), and it has also been mocked in the titles of two anthologies of Asian American literature edited by Frank Chin, Jeffrey Paul Chan, and others, *Aiiieeeee!* (1974) and *The Big Aiiieeeee!* (1991).

16. "Por aquel pedazo de carne amarilla que después de reptar por la cubierta se habría deslizado hasta el muelle a lo largo de un cable, no iba a malograr mi carrera. [. . .] ¡Ah, eso no, por un chino, por un maldito chino, menos aún!" (134).

17. "Para mí, como para todos los occidentales, un chino era un muñeco color de hiel, viscoso, más extraño a nuestra sensibilidad que el último de los animales domésticos. No era un prójimo: era . . . *Un chino*, es decir, una especie de carne mecanizada, sin facciones precisas, imbricado en serie por un país inmenso en donde los hombres no estaban hechos a semejanza e imagen de Dios" (136).

18. This novel later became the screenplay for a Cuban-Spanish coproduction, a 1988 film by the Cuban director Manuel Octavio Gómez.

19. "El que nace aquí vive con sangre caliente en las venas. Eso lo da la mezcla del africano con el peninsular. Porque al chino lo que le corre por las venas es cocimiento de tilo. Los chinos siempre han sido muy tranquilos" (194).

20. "Era inútil. Tenían una guerra muy grande con la divulgación. Eran tumbas de verdad" (137–38).

21. There is even an album titled *De Zanja a Flagler. El Chino Wong*, recorded in Miami in May 1974 by the artist, along with actors Eugenio Pérez and Hortensia Lamar and guitarist Evaristo Quintanilla. The cultural importance of the Shangai Theater (usually spelt without the second h in Cuba) is reflected in its recurrent appearance in several works about the Chinese and Chinese Cubans, including Arnaldo Correa's *Cold Havana Ground*, Zoé Valdés's *I Gave You All I Had* and *La eternidad del instante*, and several of Severo Sarduy's novels.

22. "El teatro chino fue un gran acontecimiento para los cubanos, por su música tan rara, para los criollos. Los chiquillos, cantaban en chino por las calles y daban una 'lata' tremenda en el hogar" (57).

23. Antonio Orlando Rodríguez has published several books for children, including *Abuelita Milagro* (1977) *Siffig y el vramontono 45–A* (1978), *Cuentos de cuando La Habana era chiquita* (1984), *Un elefante en la cristalería* (1991), *Pues señor, este era un circo* (1993), *El sueño* (1994), *Concierto para escalera y orquesta* (1994), *Yo, Mónica y el monstruo (1994)*, *Tiquiriquití, Tiquiriquitó* (1996), *Struff* (1997), *Mi bicicleta es un hada y otros secretos por el estilo (1997)*, *Farfán Rita vs. el profesor Hueso* (1998), and *Disfruta tu libertad y otras corazonadas* (1999). He currently lives in Bogota.

24. The play *El chino* won the first dramatic contest of the Adad Theater. Along with Virgilio Piñera and Rolando Ferrer, Carlos Felipe was among the most important Cuban playwrights of his generation. *El chino* is one of his most famous plays, together with *El travieso Jimmy* (1951) and *Réquiem por Yarini* (1965).

25. "Sufre alternativas curiosas, así es vivo y locuaz en algunos momentos y en otros, depresivo y silencioso, acusando siempre una lesión mental, que se manifiesta en algunas situaciones por la idiotez" (64; in italics in the original Spanish).

26. With regard to this use of the word "captain," Chuffat Latour points out that "the Chinese were good friends and faithful to their masters, whom they called captain, as if they said father." ("Eran los chinos buenos amigos y fieles a sus dueños, les llamaban a éstos Capitán, como si dijeran padre" (18). By the same token, in Zoé Valdés's *La eternidad del instante* Maximiliano explains that Cubans used to call all Chinese "Captain," and in Antonio Orlando Rodríguez's *The Last Masquerade*, the ninety-year-old former coolie Fan Ya Ling also repeats the word *capitán*. The Spanish soldier Miguel de Luarca adds insight in *Verdadera relación de la grandeza del Reino de China* (1575) when he states: "They bring these captains, for they call captains all who are ministers of the king" ("Traen estos capitanes, que así se da a entender capitanes a todos aquellos que son ministros del rey" [38]).

27. "¡Canalla! ¿Será necesario que le refresque la memoria, como al chino? En él se comprende; en usted, un hombre saludable...." (69).

28. "¡Te odio, chino infernal! ¡Aborto de los infiernos! ¡Ay, si fueras de barro para despedazarte, para hacerte polvo...." (92).

29. Padura Fuentes has published "Las cuatro estaciones" (the four seasons), a quartet of detective novels featuring Lieutenant Mario Conde: *Pasado perfecto* (*Havana Blue*; 1991); *Vientos de cuaresma* (*Havana Yellow*; 1994); *Máscaras* (*Havana Red*; 1997); *Paisaje de otoño* (*Havana Black*, which won the 1998 Hammett Award of the International Association of Crime Writers). He has also published two other works featuring the same protagonist, the novella *Adiós Hemingway* (2001) and the novel *La neblina del ayer* (2005); and the nonfiction books *The Story of My Life* (2002), *Faces of Salsa: A Spoken History of the Music* (2003), and *Culture and the Cuban Revolution* (with John M. Kirk; 2001).

30. "Se murió uno y vienen los otros, ¿no dicen que los chinos son como las hormigas?" (145–46).

31. "Chino son jodeloles y también son misteliosos" (182).

32. "Sí, eso mismo es un chino, se dijo después de meditarlo un rato, pero concluyó que, pensándolo bien, aquel personaje fabricado apenas era un chino *standard*, construido por una esquemática comprensión occidental" (140).

33. "—Tú ve mucha película, Conde. Ya no hay mafia china en el balio" (163).

Chapter 4. Orientalism

1. Although Eça de Queiroz was Portuguese, he is included in this chapter on Cuban Orientalism because *O Mandarim* deals indirectly with Chinese Cubans. Similarly, because it deals with a Sino-Cuban character, in another chapter I analyze the short story "Chino olvidado" (Forgotten Chinaman; 1945), by the Spanish exile Antonio Ortega.

2. This historical fact is remembered in Zoé Valdés's *La eternidad del instante* (2004), where the protagonist, Mo Ying/Maximiliano Megía, scolds one of his friends for having forgotten Eça de Queiroz's generosity toward the Chinese (312).

3. The cruelty and mercilessness of Chinese emperors are again stressed in another short story in the same collection: "El pirotécnico Li-Shiao" (The Pyrotechnist

Li-Shiao), by Cuban author Manuel Herrera (1943–). Early in the story, readers find a typically Orientalist introduction to a China of despotic emperors, wanton morality, and submissive subjects. The narrator describes how Li-Shiao, the protagonist, throws himself at the feet of the emperor of Cathay and bows submissively "as if his spine were activated by a spring" ("Como si su columna vertebral estuviera accionada por un resorte," 268). The emperor lives in extreme luxury and his orders are followed by the sound of a gong.

4. Severo Sarduy published the novels *Gestos* (1963), *De donde son los cantantes* (1967), *Cobra* (1972), *Maitreya* (1978), *Daiquiri* (1980), *Colibrí* (1984), *Cocuyo* (1990), and *Pájaros de la playa* (published posthumously, 1993). In addition, he published the collections of essays *Escrito sobre un cuerpo* (1969), *Barroco* (1974), and *Para la voz* (1977); the collections of poems *Flamenco* (1971), *Mood Indigo* (1971), and *Big Bang* (1974); and the radio scripts *La playa* (1971), *La caída* (1971), *Relato* (1971), and *Los matadores de hormigas* (1971).

In 1557, the Portuguese established a trading post in Macao, which became a free port in 1849 and returned to Chinese control fifty years later. In 1859, Macao was the only seaport available to the Cuban coolie trade. In 1873 Portugal put an end to this trade.

5. "Leng T'che, la tortura china de los cien pedazos" (89).

6. "Se trata de esa foto tomada durante la ejecución de una tortura china cuyo nombre se escribe con los ideogramas Leng y Tch'e, que quieren decir cien pedazos. [. . .] La foto me traumatizó a tal punto que decidí seguir su 'eco' o su recepción en Occidente" (Conversación 338–39).

7. "Se dieron finalmente, las dos, a la resistencia pasiva. Practicaban la no intervención, el *wouwei*. Para ello, como los antiguos soberanos chinos, adoptaron grandes sombreros de los cuales caía una cortina de perlas destinada a cubrirles los ojos. Llevaban orejeras. Obturando esas aberturas se cerraban al deseo" (35).

8. "El mundo chino me parece un mundo de percepción, un mundo estático más bien, un mundo que se sitúa en la dialéctica de la contemplación y de la acción extrema" (Rodríguez Monegal, "Diálogo" 19).

9. As Victor H. Mair explains, "Tao is the all-pervading, self-existent, eternal cosmic unity, the source from which all created things emanate and to which they all return" (132–33).

10. Zoé Valdés (1959–) has written the following novels: *Sangre azul* (1993), *La hija del embajador* (1995), *Cólera de ángeles* (1996), *Te di la vida entera* (1996), *Café Nostalgia* (1997), *La nada cotidiana* (1998), *Querido primer novio* (1999), *El pie de mi padre* (2000), *Milagro en Miami* (2001), and *La eternidad del instante*, which won the 2004 Ciudad de Torrevieja Novel Award. She has also published several collections of poems: *Vagón para fumadores* (1999), *Todo para una sombra* (1986), *Respuestas para vivir* (1986), *Los poemas de La Habana* (1997), and *Cuerdas para el lince* (1999); essays: "Del poema al guión" (1992), *En fin, el mar . . . (Cartas de balseros)*; a collection of short stories: *Traficantes de belleza* (1998); and a children's book: *Los aretes de la luna* (1999). Valdés has received numerous literary awards, including

the Roque Dalton and Jaime Suárez Quemain Poetry Award (1982), Frankfurt's Literatur Preis (1997), and the Novela Breve Juan March Cencillo Award (1995). She was also a finalist for the Narrativa de Mujeres and La Sonrisa Vertical Awards (1987), the Casa de las Américas Award (1988), and the Planeta Award (1996).

11. We learn, for instance, about Chinese opera, Chinese painters and poets, the Chinese calendar, the symbolism of jade and incense, and popular pastimes such as collective showers, cricket fights, and the game of mahjong. The novel also dwells on the topos of Chinese patience, proverbs and legends about the creation of rice and silk, the tea ritual, and Chinese calligraphy. As in Cristina García's *Monkey Hunting*, in *La eternidad del instante* poetry (along with silk, opera, and other customs and cultural practices) also serves as proof of the refinement of Chinese high culture.

12. "The name Sanfancón, also San Fancon, San-Fan-Con, or San Fang Kong, represents a Western corruption of Cuan Yu, who, after his death, became the 'Venerated Ancestor Kuan Kong' and eventually the 'patron' of all Chinese immigrants to Cuba. This mythical figure is traced to the Han period (ca. 220–280 CE), when a brotherhood was formed between three legendary ancestors/warriors/philosophers named Lau Pei, Cuan Yu, and Chiong Fei (here given in hierarchical order by age). These were later joined by a fourth member, Chui Chi Long, but it is the second of these, Cuan Yu/Kuan Kong, who became crucial to the Cuban invention of Sanfancón, the owner of the sword and thunder. The appearance of Sanfancón coincides with the establishment, in the year 1900, of the first clan society on the island, the Lung Con Cun Sol" (Scherer, "Sanfancón" 164–65). In Cuba there is a popular saying related to him: "¡Yo no creo ni en San Fang Kong!" (I don't even believe in San Fang Kong!). Within the religious syncretism that took place in Cuba, Sanfancón is identified with the Catholic Saint Barbara and the African Shango.

13. Perhaps having in mind the French market as the implicit audience for her novel (she wrote the book in Paris), Valdés, awkwardly, chooses to mention French authors and painters, such as Molière (1622–1673), who is compared to the Chinese author Li Yu; François Rabelais (1494?–1553); Pierre Loti (Louis Marie Julien Viaud; 1850–1923); and Georges Seurat (1859–1891), whose pointillist painting is compared to the blooming of different flowers. She also mentions other European authors, among them British poet and artist William Blake, who provides the inspiration for the title and is quoted by Maximiliano Megía in the novel.

14. "En el patio, Xue Ying ejecutaba movimientos de danza, valiéndose de un sable antiguo, mientras entonaba una preciosa melodía" (76).

15. "Y de un triple salto ascendió hasta caer sin hacer el menor ruido en el techo correspondiente al Salón de la Armonía" (95).

16. "En lugar de cerrar filas junto a mamá y sus hijos, prefirió argumentar que partiría lejos a buscar fortuna. Tal vez tú lo hayas creído, yo sólo considero su decisión un vulgar pretexto, eligió la vía más fácil. Zafarse del compromiso familiar y dejar a mamá con el peso de todo encima de sus espaldas" (92).

17. "Yo estoy enferma de los oídos. Los ruidos me hacen mucho daño. Supongo

que desde que papá se marchó no deseo escuchar nada que no sea su voz" (99–100).

18. The emphasis given in *La eternidad del instante* and in García's *Monkey Hunting* to the importance of poetry in the Chinese tradition is one more way of presenting the sophistication of this culture. Likewise, Regino Pedroso points out in the introduction to *El ciruelo de Yuan Pei Fu* that, for the Chinese, poetry is "an emotional way of feeling and seeing life." ("Un modo emocional de sentir y ver la vida" [18]).

19. "Ritual sensual de primavera" (45).

20. Indeed, Jonathan D. Spence has described Polo's writings as "a combination of verifiable fact, random information posing as statistics, exaggeration, make-believe, gullible acceptance of unsubstantiated stories, and a certain amount of outright fabrication" (1). See also the arguments of Frances Wood.

21. "[Era] algo que me interesaba mucho para conocer la historia del ideograma chino y del dibujo erótico" ("Zoé Valdés gana" 1).

22. Both Wood and Spence point out that even though Marco Polo claimed to have lived in China for seventeen years, he never mentioned Chinese calligraphy in his writings. This is highly suspicious precisely because most other Westerners did find it fascinating. For instance, three decades before Marco Polo, the Franciscan friar William of Rubruck noticed that the "Cataians" he met in the Mongol capital of Karakorum wrote "with a brush of the sort painters use, and in a single character make several letters that comprise one word" (Spence 2). The Dominican friar Gaspar da Cruz and the soldier Miguel de Luarca also described Chinese characters being written from top to bottom, with each word being represented by a character. Likewise, British Commodore George Anson, who traveled to China in 1743, disparaged their writing methods (Spence 55) and Montesquieu suspected that the origins of this writing system might lie in some secret fraternity (Spence 89).

23. Luis Rogelio Nogueras was born in Havana in 1945. Among his works are *Cabeza de zanahoria* (1967), *Las quince mil vidas del caminante* (1977), *Imitación de la vida* (Casa de las Américas Award; 1981), *Nosotros, los sobrevivientes* (1981), *El último caso del inspector* (1983), *Y si muero mañana* (1983), *Nada del otro mundo* (1988), *La forma de las cosas que vendrán* (1989), and *De nube en nube* (2003).

24. "Mirando un grabado erótico chino / tú me preguntaste / que cómo era posible hacerlo de ese modo / Lo intentamos / ¿recuerdas? / Lo intentamos / Pero fue un fracaso / China tiene sus arcanos / China tiene sus secretos / China tiene sus murallas infranqueables."

25. "El humo amarillo / de una estirpe deshecha"; "ideogramas negros / que ya no dicen nada"; "En compañía de un coro de eunucos."

Chapter 5. Chinese Women as Exotica

1. "The highest number of Chinese women on the island," explains Alejandro Lee Chan, "reached only 4.09% of the total of the Chinese population in 1953." ("La cifra más alta de mujeres chinas en la isla alcanzó solamente el 4,09% del total de la población china en 1953" [100]).

2. "If a woman commits adultery and she is caught in the act by her husband, he can kill the two of them, and if the husband officially complains once he knows of her committing an adulterous act, the wife receives fifty very cruel lashes; the husband may thereafter sell her into slavery, to recoup the dowry he gave for her. Nevertheless, Chinese men are such scoundrels that, for profit, many 'pimp out' their wives; this is very common among them." ("Si las mujeres cometen adulterio y los coge el marido juntos, puédelos matar, y si da queja de ellos averiguando el adulterio, le dan cincuenta azotes muy crueles y puede luego el marido vender a la mujer por esclava y servirse de ella por haberla dado el dote. Con todo, son tan bellacos que por interés hay muchos que son alcahuetes de sus mesmas mujeres y esto es entre ellos muy ordinario" [125–26]).

3. The libidination of Chinese mulattas continues in Antonio José Ponte's short story "A petición de Ochún" ("At the Request of Ochún;" 1964), included in his collection *Tales from the Cuban Empire* (*Cuentos de todas partes del imperio*; 2000). In it, Luminaria Wong, another beautiful *china mulata*, is characterized by her exotic sex appeal: "Luminaria Wong, unlike Ignacio, was not completely Chinese. In other words, she was a *china mulata*. The color of her skin could not be determined and it would change as the color of other women's pupils change. That skin was at its best after dark, for sure" (48). ("Luminaria Wong, a diferencia de Ignacio, no era completamente china. Para usar una manera rápida de describir tanta belleza, Lumi era una mulata china. Tenía un color de piel que no acababa de resolverse y que cambiaba como cambia en las demás mujeres el color de las pupilas. Lo mejor de aquella piel se ganaba, seguramente, en la oscuridad" [45]).

4. Mayra Montero was born in Cuba. In 1973, she moved to San Juan, Puerto Rico, where she still lives. She is of Galician descent and prefers to be considered a Cuban–Puerto Rican *mestiza* or mulatta writer. She has published a collection of short stories entitled *Veintitrés y una tortuga* (1981), a book of articles entitled *Aguaceros dispersos* (1996), and the following novels: *La trenza de la hermosa luna* (finalist for the Herralde Award in 1987); *La última noche que pasé contigo* (finalist for the Sonrisa Vertical Award in 1991); *Del rojo de su sombra* (1992); *Tú, la oscuridad* (1995); *Como un mensajero tuyo* (1998); *Púrpura profundo* (2000); and *El capitán de los dormidos* (2002).

5. "Una costurera mulata a la que para colmo le decían 'la china'" (32).

6. "Yo era una mulata clara, con los ojos achinados por la parte de mi padre, y la nariz sospechosa de la parte de los lucumíes. Estaba tan mezclada como la fiebre napolitana" (80).

7. "No hice más que recibirlo en mí, pero él se empecinó, se hundió por su gusto en esta carne china, una carne que en la intimidad se mulateaba" (213).

8. *Te di la vida entera* was a finalist for the prestigious 1996 Planeta Award, one year after Valdés left Cuba and moved to Paris, France, where she still lives. According to the author, she wrote 175 pages of this novel in Cuba.

9. "Es que ella caminaba con un meneo, muy propio de su paciencia china y de su

pasión dublinense contenida, que era un p'aquí, p'allá, de allá p'acá, que ponía duro al más blando" (62).

10. Leonardo Padura Fuentes (1955) is a Cuban journalist and writer known for his essays, screenplays, and detective novels. See chap. 3, n. 29 for his corpus.

11. "Tras la maraña del vello el Conde recorría el surco que ascendía hacia un pozo profundo y musgoso, devorador, por el que entraba su mano, su brazo, y todo su cuerpo después, succionado por un remolino implacable" (189).

12. "La materialización del exotismo chino" (Balán n.p.).

13. In his novel *Cobra* (1974), Sarduy also introduces footbinding uncritically. Cobra, a transvestite and the main attraction in a Moroccan theater-brothel, practices the ancient Chinese custom of wrapping the feet and washing them in hot and cold water to impede their development. This obsession leads her to use drugs and Chinese herbs that will eventually shrink her entire body as well as that of Madam, her lover.

14. Another historian, Jonathan D. Spence, observes that as early as 1556, the Dominican friar Gaspar da Cruz described footbinding in his writings. In fact, the practice was praised by the Jesuit Matteo Ricci and the Dominican Domingo Navarrete during the sixteenth and seventeenth centuries, because it kept women submissively at home (Spence 26).

15. "—No es sólo tradición, para nosotros es el resultado de siglos de respeto estético al pasado de la naturaleza. Aquí, las mujeres somos consideradas flores o nubes, y además chamanas. Invocamos la lluvia con nuestra danza infinita, para que no se malogre la cosecha de arroz" (173).

16. As with footbinding, Valdés never questions arranged marriages. However, she does indirectly criticize male chauvinism; Xuang, Mei's father, is aware of her talent, yet he is sorry that, because she is a woman, she will never be considered wise.

17. "Cerrando con prudencia el paraván, entró al cuarto Luis Leng. Descorrió la cortina. Cauto, se arrodilló entre los muslos de las mujeres que se acariciaban. Ya cuando iban a venirse, les separó los bollos con las manos, interponiendo el miembro entre ambos" (118). Through Luis Leng, a character borrowed from José Lezama Lima's novel *Paradiso*, Sarduy pays homage to its author, who had passed away in 1976. In *Paradiso*, the cook Juan Izquierdo explains that he learned his culinary art from "that proud Chinaman Louis Leng, who added the mastery of confection to his ancient and refined cooking while he loafed around the Cuban Embassy in Paris. Later he worked in North Carolina, with lots of pastry and young turkey breasts" (13). ("El altivo Luis Leng, que al conocimiento de la cocina milenaria y refinada, unía el señorío de la *confiture*, donde se refugiaba su pereza en la embajada de Cuba en París, y después había servido en North Caroline [sic], mucho pastel y pechuga de pavipollo" [19]).

18. "Escogieron a dos indonesias recién llegadas que rociaban la cama con agua de jazmín, masturbaban con la punta de los dedos empapados en alheña y alcanzaban las dilataciones cuadales gracias a un método respiratorio que escandían samsáricos suspiros" (215).

19. As Suzanne Jill Levine indicates in the translator's note, in this phantasmagoric parody of Cuban history Sarduy chooses to ignore the Taino presence on the island.

20. The novel *Cobra* received the Prix Médicis Étranger.

21. "Es una ausencia pura, es lo que no es" (38).

22. "A la vez fijo y vertiginoso de deseo. Es un mundo de deseo" (Rodríguez Monegal, "Diálogo" 19).

Chapter 6. Self-Orientalization

1. The concept of Occidentalism has been analyzed extensively in three recent books: Xiaomei Chen's *Occidentalism: A Theory of Counter-Discourse in Post-Mao China* (2002), Ian Buruma's and Avishai Margalit's *Occidentalism: The West in the Eyes of Its Enemies* (2004), and Alastair Bonnett's *The Idea of the West: Culture, Politics and History* (2004).

2. Other works by Regino Pedroso are the following collections of poems: *Antología poética (1918–1938)* (1939), *Más allá canta el mar* (1939; National Award), *Bolívar, sinfonía de libertad* (1945), *Poemas* (1966), *Sólo acero* (1979), *La ruta de Bagdad (1918–1923)* (1983), *Concepto del nuevo estudiante*, and *El Heredero*. Nicolás Guillén, in his "Crónica de Yucatán," describes Pedroso as follows: "The author of *Nosotros* is the same as always. Skinny (although he eats in a solid and appropriate manner), nervous, and . . . Chinese. He never talks; he walks with lead feet, or silk feet, to find a more appropriate material to the Asiatic side of his blood mixture." ("El autor de *Nosotros* es el mismo de siempre. Flaco (a pesar de que se alimenta de una manera sólida y adecuada), nervioso y . . . chino. No suelta prenda jamás; avanza con pies de plomo, o de seda, dicho sea para encontrar el material más adecuado al lado asiático de su mezcla sanguínea"; n.p.).

3. In his oeuvre, Nicolás Guillén also treats the Chinese colony as an integral part of Cuban society. Thus, in his didactic "Poema con niños" (Poem with Children) he advocates respect for ethnic difference. In a scene with four Cuban boys of different ethnicities (white, black, Chinese, and Jewish), each one tells the rest about the experiences of discrimination he has suffered. Soon, however, they begin to quarrel over which skin color is better, until the mother of one of them teaches them tolerance through the following poem: "Blood bathes the body / Of the black of black skin: / The same blood, running, / Boils under white flesh. / Who saw the yellow flesh, / When the veins exploded, / Bleeding with nothing but the red / Blood with which all bleed?" ("Al negro de negra piel / la sangre el cuerpo le baña: / la misma sangre, corriendo, / hierve bajo carne blanca. / ¿Quién vio la carne amarilla, / cuando las venas estallan, / sangrar sino con la roja / sangre con que todos sangran?" [267]). Guillén also makes reference to the Chinese in his poem "Médico chino" (Chinese physician; written on January 28, 1949, and included in *Sátira política [1949–1953]*), where he uses this reference to criticize contemporary U.S. policy in Asia (*Obra poética*).

4. "Negro-amarilla. (Sin otra mezcla)" (9). Debbie Lee's doctoral dissertation ex-

amines in depth not only Pedroso's works but also those by other Asian authors in Latin America.

5. "La vieja tierra de Li Tai Pe" (21). Li Tai-pe (c. 701–c. 62), one of the greatest Chinese poets, is also known as Li Po, Li Bo, Le Pih, and Ly Pe.

6. "Nos ligan doblemente los vínculos / de la estirpe y la nueva inquietud ideológica" (35–36).

7. "La amenaza odiosa del bárbaro nipón" (50).

8. "Mandarines / venales y enfermizos" (8–9); "Negra noche del pasado" (11).

9. "Soy de tu misma raza hombre amarillo" (7). In his poem "Hermano negro" (Black Brother), included in the collection *Los días tumultuosos (1934–1936)* (The Tumultuous Days [1934–1936]), there is a very similar line: "I am also your race!" ("También yo soy tu raza!" [8]) (*Antología poética)*.

10. "Y del quietismo inútil de tu filosofía, / brote el clamor de guerra" (56–57).

11. Incidentally, the last two sections are completely ignored by the critic Osvaldo Navarro in his foreword to the book.

12. "Una inquietud curiosa ha insomnizado mis / ojos oblicuos / y para otear más hondo el horizonte, / salto sobre la vieja muralla del pasado. . . / Yo fui hasta ayer ceremonioso y pacífico. . ." (35–38).

13. "Se ha desnudado en mis ojos el alba de / Occidente. / Entre mis manos pálidas, la larga pipa de los siglos, / ya no me brinda el opio de la barbarie; / y hoy marcho hacia la cultura de los pueblos / ejercitando mis dedos en el gatillo del / máuser" (25–30).

14. "Sol nuevo" (32); "Arcaica ideología" (44).

15. "—Transmutación de sangre y de sudores de culíes—" (20).

16. "—Aunque yo soy hijo de la Revolución, / son mis antepasados ilustres—" (3–4).

17. "Apenas sí han encontrado mayor eco en la poética de los hijos de Confucio" (19).

18. "Mandarín de botón encarnado" (13).

19. "Amarillo antepasado" (13); "Ojos oblicuos, alargados como sables" (13).

20. "¡En lo alto, oro, sedas, impúdicas orgías, y abajo un pobre pueblo cargado de triste infamia!" (9–10).

21. "No juzgues lo absoluto, / pues nada eterno es y todo fluye eterno; / mas nada es siempre lo mismo" (32–34).

22. "A veces llegamos a dudar que hayan sido del todo auténticamente chinos" (17).

23. "Para el hombre de esta raza milenaria, la poesía no es un simple juego del intelecto [. . .] sino un modo emocional de sentir y ver la vida [. . .] nace de un profundo estado contemplativo ante la naturaleza, o más bien, de su cósmica inmersión en ella, y está en lo estelar de su alma y no en el simple juego de hacer literatura" (18).

24. "Sólo que al occidental siempre le será difícil penetrar hasta donde sonríe su sonrisa" (20).

25. "Y es que para el amarillo, aunque materialista y perseverante defensor de su diaria ración de arroz [. . .]" (19).

26. "Aunque un día sabrás que nunca nada sabes" (75).

27. One of the translations of the *Tao Te Ching* is "The Law (or Canon) of Virtue and Its Way." As he does in *Nosotros*, in *El ciruelo de Yuan Pei Fu* Pedroso educates the reader about the culture of his ancestors by proudly displaying his knowledge of Chinese religions, philosophy, and poetry. Besides quoting the *Tao Te Ching*, he mentions and quotes the Chinese poets Li Tai-pe and Du Fu (712–770) as well as Chuang-tzu (or Zhuangzi). Moreover, in the endnotes the poet provides information about different Chinese deities, customs, and expressions; Mongol conquerors; and other historical characters. He also claims to have consulted contemporary scholars like Dr. Chung and numerous historical texts, such as those of the ancient Chinese historian and court astrologer Sze Ma-chien (c. 145–c. 90 BCE; also known as Ssu-ma Ch'ien or Sima Qian), who wrote the classic *Shih Chi* (Records of the Historian), the first comprehensive history of China.

28. Flora Fong was born in Camagüey in 1949. She works in sculpture, ceramics, stained glass, textile design, and Asian-style artistic kites. She has received numerous awards, including the 1988 Distinción por la Cultura Nacional (Distinction for National Culture), and the Distinción 23 de Agosto (August 23 Distinction) of the Federation of Cuban Women in 1989. *Nube de otoño* is also the title of an art video directed by Alejandro Gil in 1993 and based on Fong's biography and works.

29. "[La escritura china] constituye un punto de partida de mi quehacer plástico a partir de la década del 80. Un ejemplo de ello lo tenemos en el carácter BOSQUE, cuyo significado y apariencia sirvieron de base en la representación y síntesis de mi bosque tropical. [. . .] Otros recursos compositivos tienen su base en los signos cuadrados de la escritura china, en un juego intencional" (5). Other Cuban painters such as Baruj Salinas (1935– ; whose origin is not Chinese but Sephardic) have also found a source of inspiration in the Chinese pictograph. Salinas left Cuba in 1959.

30. As Adelaida de Juan explains, Fong was surprised by the aerial perspective of some classical Chinese paintings ("Autumn Cloud" 11).

31. "Asume, por voluntad expresa de la artista" (10).

32. "Así, en un proceso consciente reivindica su antecedente chino, una de las presencias indiscutibles en el bien común de nuestra cultura" (56).

33. "La sangre que corre por las venas de Flora Fong marcó su pintura antes de que ella hiciera el viaje que la llevó a la tierra de sus abuelos" (77).

34. Flora Fong's children, Li and Liang Domínguez Fong, are also artists and have exhibited their works in Cuba and the United States. Liang Domínguez Fong has followed in her mother's footsteps, becoming interested in the Asian world. Li Domínguez Fong (1978–) has received two awards in the exhibitions *Salón Varadero Internacional* (2001 and 2002), has had two personal exhibitions in Havana in 2000 and 2002, and has participated in several collective exhibitions, including two dedicated to Chinese culture: *Manos de la cultura china* (2003) and *Festival de la cultura china* (2003), both in Havana.

35. "En la Casa de Arte y Tradiciones del Grupo Promotor del Barrio Chino está una obra mía en la que quise expresar la esencia entre las dos culturas: El Castillo del Morro y la Muralla China, intercalados" (Sariol n.p.).

36. "Los girasoles son las flores de la vida porque siguen al sol y un rayo de sol fecundó a An Dong, la diosa de la fertilidad, madre de Yan Di" (Sariol n.p.).

37. These bamboo divination sticks can be found in an altar to Sanfancón at the Lung Kong Society in Havana. Each of the one hundred sticks of the oracle has a number (written in both Arabic and Chinese numbers) and represents a historical Chinese character. One shakes the box until a stick falls out.

Chapter 7. Religious Syncretism

1. Santería is also known as Lukumí (friends) or Regla de Ocha (these terms can also be spelled Lucumí or Regla de Osha). One of the key traits of this religion is the personal relationship that its followers develop with a particular orisha (also spelled *orisa* or *orixa*), who may possess the believer's body during worship and speak through her or him.

2. "The *orishas*," according to Suzan Moss, "are personifications of spiritual power. Each one manifests according to his or her particular rhythmic energy. Each can help people to develop specific skills" (n.p.).

3. When I interviewed Leandro Chiu (Chiu Pan), the guide of the Kung Long Society, he mentioned that many Afro-Cuban people go to the altar on the second floor of the society's building to ask Sanfancón to grant their wishes. Likewise, I noticed that the practice of Santería is not uncommon among Chinese Cubans.

4. In addition, the novel includes segments about breathing and meditation techniques, and lessons on Taoist burial traditions, Buddhist monastery life, and Buddhism. For instance, by explaining the properties of different kinds of incense, Maximiliano introduces the Buddhist precept of the divine nature of humanity.

5. Eleggua, the trickster child-god, is the Santería orisha of doorways and crossroads, and the mediator between humans and all of the other orishas.

Even before Mo Ying migrates to Cuba, he dreams about a woman named Trebisonda San Fan Cong, whose surnames coincide with the name of the Chinese Cuban "saint."

6. "No veo gran cosa en que un sabio deje de comer. Debes vivir en tu época, aceptar la naturaleza y sobre todo respetarla. Conserva tu independencia, despréndete de las cosas materiales sólo cuando estés listo para hacerlo; pero deshacerte de lo material no significa que el sabio se vuelva indiferente a los sentimientos, a la libertad, a la felicidad" (119).

7. "Yo aprendí—afirmó Confucio—que cuando el país está perdido y uno no se da cuenta es que uno no es inteligente; si uno lo percibe sin luchar para defenderlo, entonces lo que no se tiene es fidelidad; si uno se cree fiel sin sacrificarse por su país, entonces lo que no tiene es integridad" (318).

8. "Lo incierto, cierto es, y lo cierto es incierto" (9).

9. "Pienso en la cruz sangrante de un cruel martirologio" (31).

10. "Aunque espíritu taoísta-confuciano, tales razonamientos de Yuan Pei Fu son signos evidentes de que su mente no era extraña a las seráficas esencias del más puro cristianismo" (177).

11. "El Hijo del Cielo" (17).

12. "Sufriréis hambre, sed, la vara del castigo; pero tendréis un cielo al que entraréis, como todos los seres de la tierra" (104).

13. Thus, in the poem "La profecía del Santo de Hu-Pe" (The Prophecy of the Saint from Hu-Pe), we read, "My eyes already contemplate the eternal light of Tao" ("Ya mis ojos contemplan la eterna luz de Tao" [21]); and in the poem "En la muerte de Tien Lo" (In the Death of Tien Lo): "Tao astonishes you with the light of a miracle" ("Tao te maravilla con la luz de un milagro" [25]).

14. Arnaldo Correa was born in the Escambray Mountains of Cuba. In 1966 he published his first book of short stories, *Asesinato por anticipado*. In addition to *Cold Havana Ground* (I was unable to find the original version in Spanish), he has published four collections of short stories and a novel, *Spy's Fate* (2002). He is considered, along with Ignacio Cárdenas Acuña, the cofounder of the Cuban crime-fiction genre.

15. "El igualamiento de la religión africana y la historia" (105).

16. Although this time the plot takes place not in Haiti or the Dominican Republic—as her previous works do—but in Cuba, *The Messenger* still is part of the quest for a pan-Caribbean identity that Latin American writers like Alejo Carpentier and Gabriel García Márquez began in their works years before. This starting point is in itself problematic, if we consider that most of the cultural production by and about Chinese Cubans delineates imaginary borders around the notion of ethnicity. Along this line of thought, Abraham H. Khan has stressed that "the notion of Caribbean identity does not conceptually cohere with notions of personhood for culturally diverse groups of people forming the socio-historical reality of the geographical region, and therefore is suspect" (138). Among Mayra Montero's previous works set in Haiti or the Dominican Republic are the short story "Corinne, muchacha amable" and the novels *La trenza de la hermosa luna* (1987), *La última noche que pasé contigo* (1991), and *Tú, la oscuridad* (1995).

17. This argument is made in Leonardo Padura Fuentes's *La cola de la serpiente*: "Those religions, first stigmatized by slave owners who deemed them heretical and barbarous, and later by the bourgeoisie who considered them to be matters of ignorant and dirty blacks, and currently marginalized by dialectic materialists who described them scientifically and politically as holdovers from a past that atheism had to overcome, had nevertheless for Mario Conde the charm of resistance." ("Aquellas religiones, eternamente estigmatizadas por esclavistas que las consideraban heréticas y bárbaras, luego por burgueses que las estimaban cosas de negros brutos y sucios, y en los últimos tiempos marginadas por materialistas dialécticos capaces de calificarlas científica y políticamente como rezagos de un pasado que el ateísmo debía superar, sin embargo tenían para Mario Conde el encanto de la resistencia" [175]).

18. "Se mantiene en el estrecho límite que comparten superstición y razón, si bien asomándose a aquélla desde ésta" (120).

19. In Santería, Yemayá, patroness of fishermen and sailors, is the queen of the sea; Changó (or Shangó), the master of thunder, fire, and war, is an orisha de insatiable virility.

20. "El Mensajero de la Muerte, que se llama Chui Chi Lon, es siempre el mensajero de nuestros propios corazones" (200; the story told by Enriqueta Cheng appears in italics in the novel). "En el momento en que alguien muere sin arreglar sus cuentas, un mensajero del alma sale del lugar de la muerte y vuela hacia el lugar de su destino" (245).

21. The name of the first character, Yuan Pei Fu, comes from the title of Regino Pedroso's collection of poems *El ciruelo de Yuan Pei Fu*. Likewise, the name of the second character also seems to coincide with that of a man named Calazán Herrera, mentioned in Lydia Cabrera's *El monte*.

22. "Lo que no puede la *nganga* negra, siempre lo ha podido la *nganga* china" (38).

23. *Babalawos* are also called *gran olúos* (grand olúos) and *brujos mayores* (high priests). These geomantic divination specialists are sons of the orisha Orula. Rómulo Lachatañeré provides this definition for the label: "Rank conferred on the sons of St. Francis, or, those who are deemed suitable for the dispensations of this saint considered a superior being in the hierarchy of the santería pseudoreligion. Only the babalao has the right to perform divination using the Ifá divining chain. The officiant should have absolute sexual integrity. A man who is weak-spirited may not receive the necklaces of St Francis" (145–46). The Chinese community in Cuba still remembers the names of Chinese babalawos, such as Julio Liao Sin and Felipe Cong.

24. "Ay, Cheché, viejito, ¿no ves que me comí un resguardo chino y que contra la brujería china no hay quien pueda?" (225). The same aura of infallibility of Chinese witchcraft reappears in Antonio Orlando Rodríguez's (1956–) *The Last Masquerade* (*Aprendices de brujo*; 2002). There, José Chiang, a Chinese mulatto, tells the two protagonists about the powers of Fan Ya Ling, a *babalawo* who owns a store of Chinese curios and pharmaceutical products called El Crisantemo Dorado in Havana's Chinatown: "'That guy is hell,' Chiang said. 'You have to watch him, because he's really into witchcraft. And Chinese witchcraft is the worst! Even blacks fear it! Because, since it is done with practically nothing, no one can undo it'" (260)." ("—Ese primo es la candela—comentó Chiang.—Con él hay que andar al hilo, porque le mete a la brujería en la misma costura. ¡Y la brujería china es la peor! Hasta los negros le tienen miedo, porque, como se hace con humo, no hay quien pueda deshacerla" [261]).

25. "The witches would gather together and celebrate their festivals on the slope of La Vigía. They would go up there at night and come down at dawn, and along the trail they scattered a powder that smelled of fish" (190). ("Solían reunirse y celebrar sus fiestas en la loma de La Vigía. Subían de noche y bajaban al amanecer, y por el camino esparcían un polvito que olía a pescado" [231]). These witches from the Canary Islands are said to be white, so they are not Guanches, the native Ber-

ber people from the islands who no longer survive. Esteban Montejo also mentions these witches in *Biography of a Runaway Slave*: "the Musundi Congo were the ones who flew the most. They disappeared through witchcraft. They did the same as Canary Island witches but without a sound" (Barnet and Montejo 43). ("Los congos *musundi* eran los que más volaban; desaparecían por medio de la brujería. Hacían igual que las brujas isleñas, pero sin ruido" [40]). They are also mentioned in Lydia Cabrera's *El monte*: "Also very frightening is the witchcraft of the *isleños*—natives of the Canary Islands—who have transmitted a great number of superstitions to us and 'who fly'—the Canary Islands women at least—'just like the shamans from Angola'—although they do not suck blood." ("Muy temible es también la brujería de los isleños— naturales de Canarias—quienes nos han transmitido gran número de supersticiones y 'que vuelan'—las isleñas—'como los brujos de Angola,'—aunque no chupan sangre" [23]).

26. "Los santos son iguales en todas partes, son los mismos en China que en Guinea" (39).

27. "Matan con papeles y trabajan con grillos y caballitos del diablo" (187).

28. "Con la brujería china lo amarraron, que dicen que no hay Dios que la desamarre. Al poco tiempo, murió en Nueva York, dicen que se pudrió por dentro" (107).

29. "Camino de Pueblo Grifo me encomendé una vez más a Dios, le pedí al Padre Olofi que alejara a su mensajero—se lo pedí, y luego me mordí la lengua—y al final tuve un recuerdo para Sanfancón, el Changó de los chinos" (184).

30. A *palero* is a Palo Monte, or Regla Mayombe, priest. In Cristina García's *Monkey Hunting*, Domingo Chen also remembers that the *paleros* coveted the skulls of suicide victims.

31. Kathleen López explains that, in October 1893, "the Chinese cemetery (Zhonghua Zongyishan) was established under the Consul General, who purchased land with donations from members of the Chinese 'colony.' Burial plots and mausoleums were arranged according to home district and clan or surname associations" (104). In January 2003 the Cuban media reported the theft of human bones from different cemeteries:

> There is a certain "black market" in human bones—whose sources are the burial places—destined for Santería (also called witchcraft). Skulls and tibias are of particular importance and value. If the skull belonged to an Asian, the demand is greater. In terms of Santería, it is said that a Chinese man's bones cost more because of the proverbial intelligence, patience, and perseverance of this race, a fact that makes them "stronger." It is said that a Chinese skull goes for between twenty and thirty U.S. dollars. (Existe cierto "mercado negro" de huesos humanos—cuya fuente son las necrópolis—con destino a la santería [también llamada brujería]. Particular importancia y valor tienen cráneos y tibias. Si el cráneo perteneció a algún asiático, la demanda es mayor. En términos de santería se dice que un chino cuesta más por la proverbial inteligencia,

paciencia y constancia de esta raza, que los hace más 'fuertes'. La calavera de un chino se "cotiza"—dicen—entre veinte y treinta USD. [Cosano Alén n.p.])

32. Even today, the term *legítimo* is used by Chinese Cubans to refer to those among them who were born in China.

33. These explanations about the power that a Chinese skull can provide a *nganga* are corroborated by a character named Alcides Varona in Leonardo Padura Fuentes's novella *La cola de la serpiente*: "Look, if you want to make a Jewish nganga, to do evil, you must look for a deceased person who was really bad during his life . . . because the spirit continues to be as bad as the person when alive on earth. And sometimes it is even worse. . . . That's why the best bones are those of crazy people, and even better than those of crazy people are those of Chinese, who are the most ill-tempered and vengeful folks on the face of the earth. . . . I inherited my *nganga* from my father and it has the kiyumba [skull] of a Chinaman who committed suicide out of rage because he didn't want to be a slave, and you don't even imagine the things I've done with that nganga. . . . God forgive me." ("—Mira, si quieres hacer una nganga judía, para hacer mal, debes buscarte un difunto que en vida haya sido bien malo . . . porque el espíritu sigue siendo tan malo como el vivo que fue en la tierra. Y a veces es peor. . . . Por eso los mejores huesos son los de los locos, y mejor que los de los locos, los de los chinos, que son los tipos más rabiosos y vengativos que hay en el plano de la tierra. . . . La mía yo la heredé de mi padre y tiene la kiyumba [cráneo] de un chino que se suicidó de rabia porque no quería ser esclavo, y tú no te imaginas las cosas que yo he hecho con esa nganga. . . . y que Dios me perdone" [176]).

34. A *nganga* is an iron pot in which the Palo Monte priest stores, along with other magical elements, the bones of a dead person whose spirit will obey him. The qualities that the person had in his lifetime will be transferred to the *nganga*. This understanding is the essence of Palo Monte.

35. Besides *El Monte*, Lydia Cabrera is the author of *Por qué (cuentos negros)* (1948); *Refranes de negros viejos* (1955); *Anagó, vocabulario lucumí (el Yoruba que se habla en Cuba)* (1957); *La sociedad secreta Abakuá: narrada por viejos adeptos* (1958); *Otán Iyebiyé (Las piedras preciosas)* (1970); *Ayapá (cuentos de Jicotea)* (1971); *La laguna sagrada de San Joaquín* (1973); *Notas sobre África, la negritud y la actual poesía Yoruba* (1975); *Anaforuana (Ritual y símbolos de la iniciación en la sociedad secreta Abakuá)* (1975); *Francisco y Francisca (chascarrillos de negros viejos)* (1976); *Regla Kimbisa del Santo Cristo del Buen Viaje* (1977); *Itinerarios del insomnio: Trinidad de Cuba* (1977); *Reglas de congos: Palo Monte–Mayombe* (1979); *Yemayá y Ochún (Kariocha, Iyalorichas y Olorichas)* (1980); *Koeko Iyawo (Aprende novicia): pequeño tratado de Regla Lucumí* (1980); *Cuentos para adultos, niños y retrasados mentales* (1983); *La medicina popular en Cuba (Médicos, curanderos, santeros y paleros: Hierbas y recetas)* (1984); *Supersticiones y buenos consejos* (1987); *La lengua sagrada de los ñáñigos (Vocabulario abakuá)* (1988); *Los animales en el folklore y la magia de Cuba* (1988); *Cuentos negros de Cuba* (1989); *Consejos, pensamientos y notas de*

Lydia H. Pinbán (1993); *Páginas sueltas* (1994); *Arere Marekén: cuento negro* (1999); and *Vocabulario Congo (El bantú que se habla en Cuba)* (2001).

36. "Lo que hace un brujo otro lo deshace: 'bastón que mata perro blanco mata perro negro.' A menos que el 'daño' lo haya lanzado un brujo chino, pues la magia de los chinos se reputa la peor y la más fuerte de todas, y al decir de nuestros negros, solo otro chino sería capaz de destruirla. Y aquí nos encontramos con algo terrible: ¡ningún chino deshace el maleficio, la 'morubba,' que ha lanzado un compatriota! Como en el caso de la desventurada E., hija de mulata y de chino, muerta no hace muchos años en la flor de la edad. Del tremendo maleficio de que fué [sic] víctima inocente, no pudo, no quiso librarla, de seguro, el médico, también nativo de Cantón, que llevó su padre a su cabecera de moribunda como última esperanza" (22).

37. "La brujería china es tan hermética que Calazán Herrera [. . .], quien 'para saber ha caminado toda la isla,' jamás pudo penetrar ninguno de sus secretos ni aprender nada de ellos. Solamente sabe que comen a menudo una pasta de carne de murciélago en la que van molidos los ojos y los sesos, excelente para conservar la vista; que confeccionan con la lechuga un veneno muy activo; que la lámpara que le enciden a Sanfancón alumbra pero no arde; que siempre tienen detrás de la puerta un recipiente lleno de agua encantada que lanzan a las espaldas de la persona que quieren dañar y que alimentan muy bien a sus muertos" (23). A few pages later, Cabrera narrates the supernatural experience of a daughter of Oyá nicknamed La Chinita (41).

38. "Con los ojos fuera de las órbitas" (178).

39. "Hicimos lo que teníamos que hacer, y en cuanto el pozo se tragó la prenda, el monte se quedó callado, y nuestro buen Chino S., libre de aquella fuerza demasiado violenta para él" (179).

40. "San Fan Con no mata así, él usa cuchillo" (155). By way of contrast, Leandro Chiu, the guide of the Kung Long Society, states that in the Chinese pantheon there is no room for curses and bad actions. One could never ask Sanfancón to hurt someone.

41. "[Mi] abuelo decía que alguien que era más malo que San Fan Con, es porque era malísimo" (155).

42. "—¿Pero no era santo, verdad?—preguntó el Conde. [. . .] Quiero decir, no lo santificaron como a los santos católicos. . . ¿Por qué San Fan Con? [. . .]

—Eso fue aquí. Vino Cuang Con pelo se cubanizó en San Fan Con, y como es santo cololao, los neglos dicen que es Changó, mila tú, capitán" (160).

43. "—Yo no cleo en eso, capitán, pelo hay gente que sí, ¿tú sabes? Eso es cosa de paisanos que hacen blujelías de neglos y neglos que hacen blugelías con cosas de chinos" (160).

44. Daína Chaviano was born in Havana and, since 1991, has lived in the United States. She has also published the novel *Fábulas de una abuela extraterrestre* (1989), for which she received Berlin's Anna Seghers Award; *El hombre, la hembra y el hambre* (Azorín Award; 1998); and *Gata encerrada* (2001). In addition, she has published the collections of short stories *Los mundos que amo* (1980), *Amoroso planeta* (1983),

El abrevadero de los dinosaurios (1990), and *País de dragones* (2001); the collection of novellas *Historias de hadas para adultos* (1986); the collection of poems *Confesiones eróticas y otros hechizos* (1994); and *La anunciación* (1990), a script based on an eponymous account cowritten with Tomás Piard.

45. "Es peor el hambre espiritual, sobre todo cuando uno empieza a preguntarse cómo es posible soñar o tener experiencias paranormales si sólo existe lo palpable, lo visible, lo mediable, lo fotografiable. Así empezó el hambre devota de mi generación. Necesitábamos de orishas y milagros. Y ahora nos hemos convertido en polífagos. Engullimos como anarquistas. Estamos ansiosos por devorar a Dios. He aquí el resultado de mezclar la sangre europea con la africana, y cocerlas a ateísmo lento durante cuarenta años: somos los mayores depredadores de dioses del hemisferio occidental" (54).

46. The *I Ching* (Book of Changes) is "A Chinese book of ancient origin consisting of 64 interrelated hexagrams along with commentaries. The hexagrams embody Taoist philosophy by describing all nature and human endeavor in terms of the interaction of yin and yang, and the book may be consulted as an oracle" (*Encarta Encyclopedia* 1998).

47. "Esta isla se vende. Ni siquiera se subasta: se vende al por mayor. No sólo su mano de obra, sino también su alma; cada creencia, cada versículo, cada canto de sus religiones, cada pincelada de quienes la dibujaron durante siglos" (23). Claudia, the protagonist, was fired from the museum where she worked for complaining about the sale of its paintings on the black market.

48. "Ni a los orishas respetan ya, y eso sí que es preocupante. Nada bueno puede esperarle a un pueblo que se deja robar sus santos" (25). In another work by Chaviano, the erotic novel *Casa de juegos* (House of Games; 1999), she uses a character's complaint about tourists' ignorance as a vehicle to explain the differences between the various European and Afro-Caribbean creeds to the (presumably non-Cuban) reader (103–04). Perhaps unintentionally, here Chaviano connects with Mayra Montero's *The Messenger* by insinuating that the existence of European-rooted spiritism should make the other beliefs less "exotic" to the reader. Later, the protagonist also claims that the transculturation of faiths on the island is something genuinely Cuban (159).

Chapter 8. Painful Transculturations

1. The father of Yuli Chung, to whom I dedicate this study, was also a Chinese Freemason in Cuba.

2. "Yo veía que los más aislados eran los chinos. Esos cabrones no tenían oído para el tambor. Eran arrinconados. Es que pensaban mucho. Para mí que pensaban más que los negros. Nadie les hacía caso. Y la gente seguía en sus bailes" (27).

3. "El Chi-ffá verdadero lo jugaban los chinos en grandes apuestas. Aún no conocemos este juego, debido a los signos clásicos chinos. La charada semi criolla de majá, ratón, gato, piedra fina, etc. es una charada figurada, llena de pillaje" (Chuffat 50). Beatriz Varela provides additional examples of transculturation, such as the popular-

ity of some Chinese medicines among Creoles, the participation of women during the festivities of the Lunar New Year, and the influence of Chinese music in Cuban cultural production and music. She also points out the use of kites and the playing of a Cuban game called "la valla de gallos" (the gamecock's arena) during the Chinese festivity of the lamps (12–16).

4. Zoé Valdés's grandmother was an Irish actress, Zoé Buttler, who migrated to Cuba. She also has a Chinese grandfather (to whom she attributes her young-looking face), African great-uncles, and ancestors from the Canary Islands. Cuca Martínez claims to have the face of a young girl from the Canary Islands.

5. Arnaldo Correa's *Cold Havana Ground* also depicts a contemporary Chinese community that, far from being ghettoized in the *barrio chino*, is fully integrated into mainstream society. While some of its members, like Antonio Choy and Donald W. Chang (Rafael Cuan), are industrialists and importers, others, like Francisco Lin and Pablo Chang (Rafael Cuan's son), are officers in the Cuban army. Here, as in previous novels, *chinos californianos* such as Donald W. Chang (Rafael Cuan) are the wealthiest in the community.

6. Here, the English translation provided by Nadia Benabid for the sentence "Más por exótica que por asiática" (14), "more for exotica than for Eastern Asia," is not very successful. The narrative voice is underscoring the fact that the mother was attracted to him more because he seemed exotic than because he was Asian.

7. This first contact with Santería is preceded in the novel by a section entitled "Prayer for my head" ("Rogamiento de cabeza"), which is a Santería salutation to Obatalá (the creator of human bodies and the owner of their heads) and the orishas, performed to strengthen one's guardian angel.

8. "Si bien no era una africanóloga, por lo menos tenía bien claro que de por aquellos lares descendía buena parte de mi cultura y de mi religión. Porque aquí, el que no tiene de congo tiene de karabalí" (109).

9. Chinese Cubans are also a thing of the past in Daína Chaviano's *El hombre, la hembra y el hambre*. Although two different Chinese characters are briefly mentioned, their presence is mostly felt through ancestors and spirits. Thus, we read about the spirit of a Chinese mulatto and that of someone called El Indio, who uses words with tonal variations reminiscent of Chinese languages. Likewise, coolie grandfathers are remembered through objects they left behind and that are being classified by a character named Aquiles (64).

10. "Con ese karma asiático que funciona tan bien, cuando conviene, en esta islita reina del mestizaje. El mestizaje: nuestra salvación. En fin, cuando no es manipulado, en tanto que insignia nacional, en cualquier discursito de ministro folklorista" (129).

11. "En cada uno juró que se moría de amor por ella. Y por su ciudad. Como si mujer fuera sinónimo de ciudad. Y la ciudad tuviera útero" (90).

12. Likewise, in *El hombre, la hembra y el hambre* the main character, Claudia, regrets the fact that a city that was declared a World Heritage Site by UNESCO has become the "Beirut of the Caribbean." For her, preserving the city becomes a way to

preserve the essence of Cubanness. In the end, the protagonist's own degeneration, from working as an art historian to becoming a prostitute, is also a metaphor for the physical and moral decline of Old Havana and, by extension, of Cuba.

13. Also spelled Oshún, Ochún is the orisha of the rivers, sensuality, and love in Santería.

14. Pastor Pelayo was born in Canton and died in Cuba in 1913. His descendant Blas Pelayo Díaz, who still lives in Cuba, is currently writing a historical-biographical testimonial novel about his life. Blas Pelayo Díaz is also writing his own memoirs, which deal with the Chinese presence in Cuba, his participation in international events, and the time he spent in other countries.

15. Méndez Capote recalls the memorable day when all the Chinese in Havana cut their long braids, as these had begun to be considered unhygienic and a symbol of backwardness and submission to the emperor.

16. "Papelito jala lengua" (256). Napoleón Seuc quotes it as "Papelito jabla lengua": "In English, 'no ticket, no laundry.' If you don't give him the laundry receipt, the Chinese man will not give you your clothes" ("Equivale al inglés 'no ticket, no laundry.' Si no le das el comprobante del tren de lavado, el chino no le entrega la ropa" [Seuc 201]).

17. "Después de todo había aprendido a soportarlos, hasta se contaminó de sus defectos y asimiló sus virtudes. Desde hacía infinidad de años Mo Ying se sentía chino-cubano, dicho así en una sola palabra. Cuba era su segunda patria. A China no regresaría, estaba demasiado viejo, era demasiado pobre y demasiado cubano para morir tan lejos" (240).

18. There is no English translation for the fabled *piedra de rayo*. It is an axe made from a polished stone, which some people mistakenly believe to have been made from a lightning bolt. Maximiliano also remembers one of his best friends, the blue-eyed Chinese Eduardo Wong, who, besides a white suit and a thick gold chain on his chest, would always wear Chinese sandals sewn with henequen straw, claiming that it kept him in touch with his past: "I don't want to forget my ancestors." ("'No quiero olvidar a mis ancestros'" [211]).

19. A *guayabera* is a man's shirt with vertical tucks and sometimes embroidery; it has pockets on the chest and on the tails.

20. "Un poco de desorden en el orden, ¿no? No van a pedirme que aquí en la calle Zanja, junto al Pacífico (sí, donde come Hemingway), en esta ciudad donde hay una destilería, un billar, una puta y un marinero en cada esquina les disponga un 'ensemble' chino con pelos y señales" (28).

21. "El Bosque de La Habana es el Palacio de Verano, y las aguas del Almendares son las del Yang-Tzé. . . ." (28).

22. "Guachinangas y regordetas, se desnudaban en verano para beber guarapo con hielo molido" (90).

23. "Luego, como había aliñado el pudor dinástico de los cantoneses con las manías toscas de los cubanos, se rascó irritado los huevos y dedicó a la Tremenda una muequitaoísta de repugnancia ofendida" (115).

24. For a better understanding of the connotations of the term *jabao*, Umi Vaughan explains: "Jabao is another category. A kind of median, like the mulatto, however stripped of the idyllic qualities of sensuality and beauty. Jabaos usually have fair skin with kinky hair and clear African facial features (wide noses, thick lips, etc.). Some have reddish or even blond hair and are said to be *la candela*, extremely mischievous and picaresque. It is said that los jabao no tienen raza (jabaos have no race) and that they do not mix well (genetically) with other races. Los jabaos son malos (jabaos are bad) is another often heard phrase" (n.p.).

25. "Para devolverlo al gaupachá santiaguero, cuando en compañía de jabaos y guachinangos desciframiento sus insomnios en los balluses libaneses del puerto, desasosegado por los fuacatazos de la corona leibniziana del Bacardí" (119).

26. "Al conocimiento de la cocina milenaria y refinada, unía Luis Leng el señorío de la confitura, donde se había refugiado su pereza en la Embajada de Cuba en París. Había servido, más tarde, mucho pastel y pechuga de pavipollo en North Caroline [*sic*]. De regreso a Cuba, formó al mulato Juan Izquierdo, que añadió a la tradición la arrogancia de la cocina española y la voluptuosidad y las sorpresas de la cubana, que parece española pero se rebela en 1868" (114).

Chapter 9. Self-Definition and the *Chinos Mambises*

1. "¡Nadie ha relatado en prosa, ni cantado en verso, los hechos de los hijos del Celeste Imperio en la épica guerra de Cuba!" (*Páginas escogidas* 81).

2. For more information on the promotion of assimilation by Jewish Argentine authors such as Alberto Gerchunoff (1884–1950), Carlos Grünberg (1903–1968), and Enrique Espinosa (Samuel Glusberg; 1897–1987), see Edna Aizenberg's "*La gesta del marrano* y el sefaradismo literario argentino."

3. "Necesitaba que se le inyectara e iluminara con la ilustración del progreso humano. [. . .] Los adelantos de los pueblos civilizados" (9).

4. "Mal llamados hombres civilizados" (10).

5. "Rancia aristocracia china" (8).

6. "La sujeción, el esclavaje, la abyección en que vivía el chino, le hacía tímido, obediente, cobarde; siendo digno de consideración por su inteligencia y amor al trabajo" (9).

7. "Una raza sumisa y obediente" (10).

8. "El refinamiento de la raza blanca" (15–16); "civilizarse" (16).

9. "Mientras que la otra raza perdía lastimosamente el tiempo en sandeces y boberías, sin aspiraciones ni pretensiones a nada" (16).

10. "La intelectualidad adquirida por los chinos es el factor principal que ha superado a otras razas en todo el orden social. El chino se considera blanco y basta. La superioridad de inteligencia" (16). Incidentally, we have a similar perspective, this time based on inherited cultural and traditional values, in a recent study by the Chinese Cuban author Napoleón Seuc entitled *La colonia china de Cuba 1930–1960* (1998). After pointing out the economic success of the East Asian Tigers (Hong Kong, Taiwan, Singapore, and South Korea) and particularly of overseas Chinese

in Thailand, Malaysia, the Philippines, Indonesia, Singapore, and Taiwan, he states, "The dissimilitude in economic growth among different peoples and ethnicities in this century makes us think that there are factors of a traditional and hereditary nature—but of a cultural not a genetic origin—that provide a margin of advantage for certain races—in the free and competitive world market of the modern economy, in the free-trade doctrine of open (not protectionist) societies—over other races and peoples of the earth." ("La disimilitud en el crecimiento económico de este siglo de pueblos y etnias diferentes nos inclina a pensar que hay factores tradicionales, hereditarios, pero de origen cultural, no genético, que dan cierto margen de ventaja a ciertas razas—en el libre y competitivo mercado mundial de la economía moderna, en el librecambismo de las sociedades abiertas [no proteccionistas]—sobre otras razas y pueblos de la tierra" [172]). Later, Seuc reveals some of the survival tactics used by the Chinese in Cuba: "They managed to gain an influential friend—a judge, chief of police, or rural guard in the countryside—to whom they resorted in times of need." ("Ellos se las agenciaban para conseguirse un amigo influyente—un juez correccional, jefe de la policía o de la guardia rural en los campos—a quienes acudían en momentos de necesidad" [162–63]).

11. "Hat Min Gan Ga / Toy pok ton un hay yan / Sen mai mon / Go sion ni chi yau / Tun lin / Go sion ni fac tak / Chiok Fi / Shi Chung Chay / Chan sen pen tan / Chi yau-Chi yau / Go shion." (Cara negra, diente de plata / Lo maltratan como si no fuese persona / Despierta del letargo / Yo deseo tu libertad / Rompe la cadena / Yo deseo tu felicidad / Vuela como el pájaro / Muera el tirano / Viva la democracia/ Libertad, libertad / Yo lo anhelo [89]). (Black face, silver tooth / They mistreat him as if he were not a person / Awake from lethargy / I long for your liberty / Break your chains / I long for your happiness / Fly like a bird / Death to the tyrant / Long live democracy / Freedom, freedom / I desire it).

12. "He recorrido las Provincias de Santa Clara, Camagüey y Oriente, en busca de datos, entre aquellos chinos que pertenecieron al Ejército Libertador, y de los otros chinos pacíficos que trabajaron por la causa de la Independencia de Cuba" (5).

13. "Fruto de mis largos años de constancia cumpliendo un sagrado deber en bien de mi país [. . .] en bien de Cuba, nuestra Patria" (5).

14. "Yo no he visto soldados más valientes que los chinos; peleaban con abnegación, y fieles a sus compromisos, jamás traicionaron a la causa por la independencia de Cuba. Eran hombres sinceros, amigos buenos y obedientes. Siempre ocupaban la extrema vanguardia, sonrientes y alegres. Muriendo sin lamentarse como héroes que eran. Cuando terminaban el fuego, después del combate, usaban chacoterías y espeluznantes bromas del peligro" (26).

15. "Cumplíamos con el sagrado deber con la patria cubana" (26).

16. "Los chinos también se dieron exacta cuenta de su lamentable situación. Habían de pensar en algo patriótico que los pusiera en condición de hombres dignos; de hombres libres para que cesara aquel estado vejaminoso" (25).

17. General Choy is a founding member of the Communist Party of Cuba and belongs to the Association of Soldiers of the Cuban Revolution. During 1980–1981,

he participated in the internationalist mission in Angola and, from 1986 to 1992, he was ambassador to the Republic of Cape Verde. General Choy retired from active duty in the Revolutionary Armed Forces in 1992 and is currently the president of the State Working Group for the Cleanup, Preservation, and Development of Havana Bay. General Chui was born in Santiago de Cuba and is a founding member of the Communist Party of Cuba. He also helped establish military missions in Nicaragua, Ethiopia, and Mozambique. In the internationalist mission in Angola, General Chui commanded the 90th Tank Brigade in Malanje, where he was seriously wounded and lost a leg. He also headed the Office of Finance and Supplies for the Association of Soldiers of the Cuban Revolution, which is responsible for a national political education program. He retired from active military duty in 1998. The third general, Sío Wong, was born in the province of Matanzas and is a founding member of the Western Army, the Rebel Army's military police, and the Communist Party of Cuba. He is president of the Cuba-China Friendship Association and has been president of the Parliamentary Group for Friendship with China. He is also a member of the National Assembly of Popular Power and its International Relations Commission and, since 1986, has been president of the National Institute of State Reserves (INRE).

18. During his second term as president, Batista was responsible for a ruthless repression that led to Fidel Castro's uprising. He was deposed by Castro's revolutionaries on January 1, 1959.

19. Sío Wong considers himself "a Cuban of Fidel" (159).

20. The three Sino-Cuban generals were interviewed by the editor, Mary-Alice Waters, and by Arrin Hawkins, Martín Koppel, Luis Madrid, and Michael Taber.

21. In Arnaldo Correa's *Cold Havana Ground*, Francisco Lin, a lieutenant-colonel of Chinese descent, explains the impact of the revolution on Havana's Chinatown: "That whole world began to disappear when the Revolution wiped out the economic system. The big Chinese merchants returned to San Francisco, where they'd come from originally" (66).

22. José Woong was a "revolutionary from Canton, China, who arrived in Cuba around 1927 and became leader of the Workers and Peasants Protection Alliance, based in the Chinese community. He joined the Cuban Communist Party, founded the Chinese-language newspaper *Gunnun Hushen* (Worker-Peasant Call), and served as its editor. In May 1930 he was arrested and imprisoned in Havana's Castillo del Príncipe, a renowned detention center, together with other Communist Party leaders. Three months later, in a politically motivated assassination, he was strangled to death in his jail cell by agents of Machado" (Choy, Chui, and Sío Wong 208; I made changes to the translation to make it sound more idiomatic). As Mercedes Crespo Villate explains, other outstanding members of the Asociación Protectora de Obreros y Campesinos (Worker and Peasant Protection Alliance) were Antonio Lejang, Luis Li, Julio Su Leng, Jorge Lem, Julio Chang, Octavio Ling, and Ángel Wong (59–60). Other Chinese men who were members of the clandestine struggle against the dictatorship were Felipe (Tang Lay) Alay, Vicente Hung, Manuel Luis (member

of the Cuban Chinese Socialist Alliance), Juan Moc Eng (first president of the Chung Wah Casino after the Cuban Revolution), and Óscar Chiong (second president). Napoleón Seuc also includes his father, Armando Seuc, and his father's cousin, Pepe Cuan Cuan, who was deported to China by Machado, accused of being a communist (10).

23. "Los chinos residentes apoyamos la Revolución Cubana y a su jefe Fidel Castro!" (The proclamation is also written in Chinese).

24. Patria o Muerte.

25. "Esteban Lazo Hernández, ideological secretary of the party Central Committee; his grandfather was Chinese. Bárbara Castillo Cuestas, minister of domestic trade; her grandmother was Chinese. Lázaro Barredo, vice president of the International Relations Commission of the National Assembly; he too had Chinese grandparents" (60).

26. As Ángel T. González points out, a few days earlier the president of the casino escaped with the association's money and sought asylum at the Guantánamo Naval Base.

27. "La lucha anticomunista y por el Estado de Derecho, en lo que a mí concierne, no ha terminado, pero desde aquella década renuncié por encontrarla inútil a toda actividad revolucionaria militante que valiera la pena. Ahora sólo soy un combatiente en el campo de las ideas, con la pluma y la palabra" (158–59).

28. Agustín Blázquez is a Washington-based documentary film producer and director. Among his films are *Covering Cuba* (1995), *Cuba: The Pearl of the Antilles* (1999), *Covering Cuba 2: The Next Generation* (2001), *Covering Cuba 3: Elián* (2003), *Covering Cuba 4: The Rats Below* (2006), and *Covering Cuba 5: Act of Repudiation* (2007). He is also coauthor of *Covering and Discovering* (2001).

29. For this reason, Napoleón Seuc chooses an image of the monument to the *chinos mambises* for the cover of his *La colonia china en Cuba* and devotes several pages of its introduction to the Chinese participation in the Cuban wars. In his book he also includes a 1957 photograph of the Chinese community's float during Carnival (*los carnavales*) in Havana, where one can see a group of Chinese children standing around a placard printed with General Gonzalo de Quesada's adage "There was not a single Chinese Cuban deserter. There was not a single Chinese Cuban traitor."

30. "Los tratantes de culíes habían cometido, entre otros, un error capital: junto a los desesperados agricultores del sur, habían aceptado, a bajo precio, una gran cantidad de prisioneros políticos procedentes del gran movimiento revolucionario chino Taipings" (*Viaje* 28).

31. It is very difficult to know the exact number because, as General Sío Wong points out, many Chinese took their masters' surnames or simply changed their own names and surnames to Spanish ones (60). Jiménez Pastrana also claims that four hundred Chinese took part in the battle of Las Minas de Juan Rodríguez (Guáimaro) (130).

32. The definition of *mambí* in the glossary of *Our History* is the following: "Fighters in Cuba's three wars of independence from Spain between 1868 and 1898. Many were freed slaves and other bonded laborers. The term 'mambí' originated in the 1840s during the fight for independence from Spain in nearby Santo Domingo. After a black officer in the Spanish army named Juan Ethninius Mamby joined freedom fighters there, colonial forces began calling guerrillas by the derogatory name 'mambíes.' Later 'mambises' was applied to Cuban fighters, who adopted it as a badge of honor" (198).

33. "Ellos combatían contra la bandera que los había esclavizado, ellos serían compañeros y hermanos de sufrimientos de los que sufrían, como ellos, el yugo colonial" (70).

34. As Alejandro Lee Chan explains, this episode has been studied by Diego Barros Arana in "Esclavitud y tráfico: culíes en Chile," Diego L. Chou in "Los chinos en la Guerra del Pacífico," and Patricio Quiroga Z. in "De la Guerra de 1879 y la participación de los coolíes chinos" (72).

35. The glorification of the *chino mambí* continues in Arnaldo Correa's *Cold Havana Ground*, where a Sino-Cuban character named Francisco Lin apprises the protagonist of his heroism. Likewise, in *Monkey Hunting*, Cristina García points out the outstanding roles of Commander Sebastián Siam and Captain Liborio Wong in military campaigns against Spanish troops. In addition, the protagonist, Chen Pan, donates money and weapons to the cause and becomes an auxiliary for the liberating army during the wars of independence. His descendent, Domingo Chen, fights for the United States in the Vietnam War. In his case, however, the idea of fighting someone else's war is explicitly dramatized. During the battle, for example, he is constantly afraid of being taken for a Vietcong by his fellow soldiers.

36. "Yo no sé si la atracción inmensa que ejerce todo lo chino sobre mí se debe a oírle llamar chino a mi padre [. . .] si se debe al contacto que en mi infancia se tenía con los chinos, o a los cuentos de la heroica conducta y el limpio proceder de los chinos en las guerras de Cuba" (52).

37. "Libertad a los esclavos o colonos chinos que se hallan hoy en las filas insurrectas."

38. "En Cuba no hubo nunca un chino traidor ni chino guerrillero" (Méndez Capote 54). "No hubo chino cubano desertor, no hubo chino cubano traidor" (Quesada 90). This adage was immortalized in the inscription on a monument to the Chinese men who fought for Cuban independence, located in Havana's Calle Línea.

39. As Méndez Capote explains, at times paraphrasing Gonzalo de Quesada's *Páginas escogidas* (1892), in spite of being more than eighty years of age, the wealthy commander Siam insisted on fighting again in order to unite the veterans of the 1868 war for independence, initiated by Carlos Manuel de Céspedes, with those of the 1895 war. He showed his courage in the 1870 victory at Mines of Guáimaro, under the command of U.S. Captain Thomas Jordan. Another patriotic officer praised for his prowess is Juan Anelay (Juan Han Lai), who fought under the command of Henry "El Inglesito" Reeve. He did not even groan once while being lynched during the 1868 war, but only let out "a whisper that was rather a moan of love . . . 'Long live free

Cuba!'" ("Un suspiro que más parece un quejido de amor...—¡Viva Cuba libre!" [58]). She also mentions Lieutenant Tancredo (or Rancredo, as his name appears in other historical texts), who showed his lifelong ethnic pride and rancor toward Spaniards at the time of his death in Las Villas (the place where the Cuban Liberating Army had the largest number of Chinese troops): "Spaniard, you despise the Chinese because you have made them slaves in Cuba. I am Chinese, but now I am to you Lieutenant Tancredo, an officer in the Cuban army. I am your enemy. Finish me off." ("—Español, tú desprecias a los chinos porque tú en Cuba has hecho de los chinos esclavos. Yo soy chino, pero ahora yo soy para ti el teniente Tancredo, oficial del ejército cubano. Yo soy tu enemigo. Remátame" [55]). The map "Presencia china en Cuba" mentions other outstanding Chinese combatants (Baltar Rodríguez et al.). From Pinar del Río: Sergeant Luis Achón; from Havana: Captains José Achón, Víctor, Genaro, and Francisco Arocha; from Matanzas: Sergeant José; from Las Villas: Commanders Antonio Moreno and Sebastián Siam, Captains Pablo Jiménez, José Tolón (Lai Wa), José Cuang (Kau Kon Cuang), Juan Díaz, Andrés Lima, Liborio Wong (Wong Sen), and Facundo; Lieutenants Manuel Pau, Pío Cabrera, Achón, and Tancredo; Sergeants José and Crispín Rico; and Privates Juan Cuan, Pedro Lau, and Juan "El Loco" Anclay; from Camagüey: Captains José Bu (who fought under the command of Generalissimo Máximo Gómez), Juan Sánchez (Lam Fu Kim), who had already been a soldier in China, and Bartolo Fernández; Lieutenants José Pedroso and Pío Cabrera; Sergeants Andrés (Cao Lion Kao) and José Fong; from Oriente: Liborio Wong (Wong Ceng).

40. "No creo que emigrar sea la solución a nuestros males, por mucho dinero que puedas enviar a la familia. De hecho, nosotros no sólo no nos hemos hecho ricos con las heroicidades de Weng Bu Tah en Cuba: no aspiramos ni a comer de ello" (63).

41. "Sin hablar de la guerra. No olviden al gran mambí José Butah, pariente mío, por cierto, y a otro mambí de reconocida trayectoria, José Tolón; no por gusto se habrá construido el monumento al combatiente chino" (313).

42. Here the novel probably alludes to the fact that in Article 65 of the new constitution signed in 1901, after the final war for independence, there was a provision that "any foreigner who had fought for ten years for Cuba's freedom, arms in hand, would be considered Cuban by birth. He could even be president of the republic" (Choy, Chui, and Sío Wong 62). After the Dominican General Máximo Gómez refused to accept the implicit offer of that provision, written specifically for him, only three other foreigners qualified to be president: General Carlos Roloff, who was Polish, and two Chinese officers: Lieutenant Colonel José Bo (or Bu) and captain José Tolón (Lai Wa), who had fought in the three wars of independence (Choy, Chui, Sío Wong 62).

43. This information about captain José Bú was probably taken from Chuffat's study: "[Bú] provided numerous and important services during the Cuban War of Independence. Now he lives in the capital of the Republic, forgotten by his friends, those who in other times, in his prime, he protected." ("[Bú] ha prestado múltiples e importantes servicios en la Guerra de la Independencia de Cuba. Actualmente vive en la Capital de la República, olvidado de sus amigos, aquéllos que en otra época, en sus buenos tiempos, había protegido" [Chuffat 29]).

44. Not all the belligerent Chinese characters in these works leave a positive im-

age, however. For instance, in "Aquella noche salieron los muertos" (1932), by Lino Novás Calvo (1905), we have the ruthless second-in-command, a former pirate who is suspected of being a sorcerer and who does not seem interested in anything but war.

Chapter 10. Exclusion and (Mis)representation

1. "La raza amarilla supo concentrarse, aislarse en tal forma que significó psicológicamente poco en la sociedad cubana, aunque influyó más en las otras razas que éstas sobre ella" (12).

2. "Indios y negros, pues, lejos de constituir cuerpos extraños a nuestra América por no ser 'occidentales,' pertenecen a ella con pleno derecho: más que los extranjerizos y descastados 'civilizadores'" (qtd. Walter Mignolo, "Posoccidentalismo," 681). This antagonism toward the Chinese community is shared by several other Latin American intellectuals during the first decades of the twentieth century. The Peruvian José Carlos Mariátegui, for example, posits, in his most famous work, *Seven Interpretative Essays on Peruvian Reality* (1928), that they did not contribute "either cultural values or progressive energies to the formation of nationality" (279). In Peru, he states, they never introduced their culture; only their race: "Probably the only direct importation from the Orient of an intellectual order is Chinese medicine, and its arrival is undoubtedly due to practical and mechanical reasons, stimulated by the backwardness of a people who cling to all forms of folk remedies. [. . .] The Chinese, furthermore, appears to have inoculated his descendants with the fatalism, apathy, and defects of the decrepit Orient" (279). While Mariátegui acknowledges that the Chinese in their homeland show moral discipline, cultural and philosophical tradition, and skill as farmers and artisans, he proceeds to minimize the cultural value and impact of Chinese theater in Peru, and to emphasize the vicious nature of coolies and their love for gambling and opium.

3. "Vino el médico amarillo / A darme medicina / Con una mano cetrina / Y la otra mano al bolsillo: / ¡Yo tengo allá en un rincón/ Un médico que no manca / Con una mano muy blanca / Y otra mano al corazón!"

4. In this essay, Martí reports on the Mohonk Conferences of 1883 that provided plots of reservation land to individual Indians.

5. "Otro de los de la convención ha visto a los indios acurrucarse en rondas a jugar la paga del año, y jugar de cada diez pesos nueve, como los chinos en los talleres de cigarrería de un presidio español, no bien reciben a la tarde del sábado el exceso de sus jornales sobre la faena que han de entregar al establecimiento" ("Los indios" n.p.).

6. "Lo recuerdo, y lo recuerdo con horror. Cuando el cólera recogía su haz de víctimas allí, no se envió el cadáver de un desventurado chino al hospital hasta que un paisano suyo no le picó una vena y brotó una gota, una gota de sangre negra, coagulada. Entonces, sólo entonces se declaró que el triste estaba enfermo. Entonces; y minutos después el triste moría" ("Presidio político" n.p.).

7. "Un funeral chino: los chinos en Nueva York" was originally published on December 16, 1888, in *La Nación*.

8. " ¡La libertad tiene sus bandidos! Y Li-In-Du no quiso ser de ellos, sino se empleó en traficar en cosas de su tierra, que es, con lavar ropa y servir de comer, en lo que por acá permiten a los chinos ocuparse. Porque si se ocupan en minas o en ferrocarriles, como a fieras los persiguen, los echan de sus cabañas a balazos, y los queman vivos" ("Un funeral chino" n.p.).

9. "Y con el mallete de masón le ha estado ablandando la cabeza al emperador chino" ("Un funeral chino" n.p.).

10. "Chino abate, sabichoso y melifluo"; "el chino de la tienda"; "sujeto a ración por el rico ignorante, que halla gusto en vengarse así de quien tiene habitada la cabeza" ("Un funeral chino" n.p.).

11. "Pero más es canijo y desgarbado, sin nobleza en la boca o la mirada, manso y deforme; o rastrea en vez de andar, combo y negruzco, con dos vidrios por ojos, y baboso del opio" ("Un funeral chino" n.p.).

12. "Enjutos e indiferentes chinos. El chino es el hijo infeliz del mundo antiguo: así estruja a los hombres el despotismo: como gusanos en cuba, se revuelcan sus siervos entre los vicios. Estatuas talladas en fango parecen los hijos de sociedades despóticas. No son sus vidas pebeteros de incienso: sino infecto humo de opio" ("Puente de Brooklyn" n.p.).

13. "En Cuba no hay temor a la guerra de razas. Hombre es más que blanco, más que mulato, más que negro. En los campos de batalla murieron por Cuba, han subido juntas por los aires, las almas de los blancos y de los negros" (*Ensayos y crónicas* 130).

14. "Los chinos eran grandes patriotas; no hay caso de que un chino haya traicionado nunca: un chino, aunque lo cojan, no hay peligro: 'no sabo,' nadie lo saca de su 'no sabo'" (*Obras completas* 593. Qtd Varela 10).

15. "No hay odio de razas, porque no hay razas" (*Ensayos y crónicas* 125).

16. "Insistir en las divisiones de raza, en las diferencias de raza, de un pueblo naturalmente dividido, es dificultar la ventura pública y la individual, que están en el mayor acercamiento de los factores que han de vivir en común" (*Ensayos y crónicas* 129).

17. "El mercader chino" is cited by Francisco Morán. Meza's full name was Ramón Meza y Suárez Inclán, but he often used the pseudonym R. E. Maz, an acronym of his name. He was also the author of two biographical studies on Julián del Casal and Eusebio Guiteras, the study *Homero: la Iliada y la Odisea*, the comedy *Una sesión de hipnotismo*, and the novels *Flores y calabazas* (1886), *Últimas páginas* (1891), *En un pueblo de la Florida* (1899), *Mi tío el empleado* (1960), *El duelo de mi vecino* (1961), and *Don Aniceto el tendero* (1889).

18. "Rompen con la armonía;" "Garabatos;" "Embadurnado;" "Se graban profundamente en la retina"; "Lastima los oídos el acompasado chirrido" ("Mercader chino" 5).

19. "Egoísmo"; "Al prisma estrecho de sus ideas" ("Mercader chino" 6).

20. "Infranqueable muralla, tras la cual se parapetó la China" ("Mercader chino" 5).

21. "Culto comprador de raza caucásica" (6).

22. The farces *La Marquesa Rosalinda* (1913) and *La cabeza del dragón* (1914) are the first works by Valle-Inclán where one can find the *esperpento*.

23. "¡Qué risas hubo cuando Carmela mandó a Assam que se mirara a un espejo que allí había! La cara se le acható, sus bigotes se le prolongaron, sus pequeños ojos semejaban una raya, sus hombros se cuadraron, sus piernas quedaron reducidas a una cuarta; se parecía al león de bronce que se engulle toda la correspondencia, bajo el arco de la casa de Correos, sin atragantarse por eso" (138).

24. "No era chino más que en la apariencia, que en todo lo demás era una persona decente" (134).

25. "Era tener blanco el color de la piel y ser cristiano como ellas" (138).

26. "Brujeros y médicos chinos eran los más mentados. Aquí hubo un médico de Cantón que se llamaba Chin. [. . .] Los pobres lo veían de lejos, porque él cobraba muy caro. Yo no dudo que él curara con yerbas de esas que se meten en pomos y se venden en las boticas" (85–86).

27. "Un negro congo o lucumí sabía más de medicina que un médico. ¡Que el médico chino! Sabían hasta cuándo una persona iba a morirse" (146).

28. "A ti no te salva ni el médico chino."

29. "Con semejante frase antológica hacía referencia a la fama adquirida por el médico culí Cham Bombia, un sabio de la flora y de la fauna" (235). Chuffat praises the philanthropy of the nineteenth-century Chinese physician Cham Bom-Bia [Dr. Juan Chambombián or Chang Pong Piang], who had studied botany in his country and knew the Cuban flora very well. According to the author, he would cure poor people without charge and became famous all over the island for his ability as a doctor, hence the saying, "Ni el médico chino lo salva" (Not even the Chinese physician can save him). The author also mentions the Chinese physician Kan Shi Kong, who was a great botanist and died without revealing his secrets to anyone.

30. "Era lo peor con lo que se podía casar una mujer, pero lo único a lo que podía aspirar una muchacha como ella, pobrecita y con el pelo duro" (31).

31. "En el fondo soñaba con aquellas paisanas silenciosas, con viajar a Cantón para buscar una esposa de su propia raza, y desquitarse con ella de todos los años que había tenido que conformarse con una mujer de piel oscura, que era lo único a lo que podía aspirar en Cuba" (206).

32. "En Cuba se necesitan braceros y los terratenientes ya no quieren más esclavitud negra, quieren blanquear, en este caso amarillear la población" (205).

33. According to the "Presencia china en Cuba" map (Baltar Rodríguez et al.) the Chinese societies that survive in Havana today are Casino Chung Wah, Min Chih Tang, Alianza Socialista China de Cuba (See Man), Chung Shan, Kow Kong, Lun Con Cun Sol, Lon Say Li, Wong Kong Ja Tong, Chang Weng Chung Tong, Yi Fong Toy Tong, Chi Tak Tong, Sue Yuen Tong, and On Teng Tong. Contemporary Chinese and Chinese Cubans may belong to several societies at the same time.

34. The "Presencia china en Cuba" map (Baltar Rodríguez et al.) explains that the Chinese societies responded to eight different types of affiliation: clan, regional

or by district, corporative or by guild, secret, political, artistic, sports-related, and national.

35. Kathleen López has studied the secret societies known as the Triad Lodges, which were accused of "blackmail, gambling, opium, and immigrant trafficking" (113). In contrast, she explains that regional associations provided "mutual aid, assisted with employment, extended credit, maintained hostels, mediated disputes, represented the Chinese 'colony' in the non-immigrant community, and initiated and coordinated fund-raising and charitable projects" (103). According to Chuffat Latour, the first Chinese society in Cuba, called Kit Yi Tong (The Union), was created in 1867 with the goal of uniting all Chinese residing in Havana. The following year another society, Hen Yi Tong (The Brothers), was founded for the same purpose. A third one, founded by Hakka men from the south of China, became Yi Seng Tong (Second Alliance); its objective was to unite all the Hakka on the island (Chuffat 18).

36. The Chung Wah Casino, as Kathleen López explains, is an umbrella organization that was "established in 1893 [in 1886, according to Scherer] under the influence of Chinese diplomats and acted as an auxiliary consulate, facilitating procedures for Chinese returning to China. It engaged in Chinese charitable, welfare, cultural, and educational missions. In 1902 Chinese Consul General Tan Qianchu purchased the huiguan building for US$40,000. Branches of the umbrella organization were established throughout Cuba, and representatives of the merchant community and various organizations assumed leadership on the board of directors" (103).

37. "Tugurio apestoso" (147).

38. Beatriz Varela, in her book *Lo chino en el habla cubana* (Chinese Influence in the Cuban Dialect), defines Chinese charades (26). These charades are depicted in several novels, including Ramón Meza's *Carmela*, Severo Sarduy's *Gestos* and *Maitreya*, José Lezama Lima's *Paradiso*, Miguel Barnet's *Gallego*, Cristina García's *Monkey Hunting*, and Zoé Valdés's *La eternidad del instante*.

39. As Beatriz Valera points out, the Chinese detective Chan Li Po in the popular detective story and radio soap opera *La serpiente roja*, written by Félix B. Caignet, always repeated the sentence "Tenga mucha pachencha" (have a lot of "pachienche") (18). Likewise, Méndez Capote points out the patience of the *chinos sederos* (Chinese silk traders), and Valdés, in *I Gave You All I Had*, states that the protagonist's peculiar way of walking has to do with this virtue in Chinese culture.

40. "El anciano, además, dotado de una gran paciencia, china por supuesto, escuchaba sin protestar su perorata cotidiana" (261). The topic of Chinese patience is also mentioned in Meza's *Carmela*, Rodríguez's *The Last Masquerade*, and Chuffat's *Apunte histórico de los chinos en Cuba*.

41. Silence is a pervasive topic in the *Tao Te Ching*: "One who knows does not speak; / One who speaks does not know. / He / Stopples the openings of his heart, / Closes his doors, / Diffuses the light, / Mingles with the dust / Files away his sharp points, / Unravels his tangles. / This is called "mysterious identity." / Therefore, / Neither can one attain intimacy with him, / Nor can one remain distant from him; / Neither can one profit from him, / Nor can one be harmed by him; / Neither can

one achieve honor through him, / Nor can one be debased by him. / Therefore, / He is esteemed by all under heaven" (Mair 25). Likewise, in "The Dharma of the Heart" we read: "There is only testimony of silence, it goes beyond thinking. Therefore it is said the Dharma cuts off the passage of words and puts an end to all forms of mental activities" (Kornfield 135). The Dharma is the Hindu and Buddhist equivalent to the Taoist Tao.

42. Antonio Ortega was born in Gijón, Spain, and died in Caracas, Venezuela. Besides being a writer, he worked as a journalist and as a biologist. He went into exile after the Spanish Civil War. He moved to France, then to Cuba and, in 1960, with the coming to power of Fidel Castro, he moved to Caracas. He wrote for cultural magazines in Cuba and in Venezuela. Besides the collection of short stories *Chino olvidado and Other Stories*, he published a novel, *Ready* (1946), and co-authored the novel *El caballito verde* (1956). "Chino olvidado," a short story, was first published in July 8, 1945, in *Bohemia*, a popular Cuban magazine.

43. "Mejor no saber nada. No entender nada. ('Chino no sabel nada. ¡Chino ser inolante!') Eso era lo mejor. ('La naturaleza no habla,' dijo el venerable Lao Tse). No hablaría, no entendería nada de lo que le dijeran. (Eso era algo así como cerrar los ojos: cómodo)" (106).

44. "Pero lo más doloroso era aquel desarraigo invencible, que ni el éxito económico que algunos alcanzaron habían podido mitigar. La única salvación para aquellos males había sido sostener una cultura de ghetto, y devolver silencio al desprecio, sonrisa a la burla" (177–78).

45. "Ninguno habló de eso ni de nada. Esto está jodido, yo no entiendo a los chinos, los cabrones se hacen los que no me entienden a mí" (157).

46. "Silenciosa soy mejor y puedo comportarme más humana ante el dolor de los otros. El que no habla sabe, aquel que habla demasiado ignora lo más importante, escuchar a los demás" (117).

47. Zoé Valdés has explained that, although most of the plot is fictional, two passages are based on real events: Mo Ying's voyage from China to Mexico and, from there, to Havana, and his decision to remain silent after Valdés's Irish grandmother left him. According to the author, Mo Ying chose to communicate with his family only via writing. After arriving in Mexico, he never saw his Chinese family again. Zoé Valdés only saw her grandfather from afar, but her mother told her much about him (Martínez n.p.).

Conclusion

1. Part of this conclusion was published as an essay titled "Chinesism and the Commodification of Chinese Cuban Culture," in the volume *Alternative Orientalisms in Latin America and Beyond* (Ed. Ignacio López-Calvo, Cambridge: Scholars Publishing, 2007).

2. "Pero no se trata de una India trascendental, metafísica o profunda, sino al contrario, una exaltación de la superficie y yo diría hasta de la pacotilla India. Yo creo, y me hubiera gustado que Octavio Paz estuviera de acuerdo—pienso que lo está—que

la única descodificación que podemos hacer en tanto que occidentales, que la única lectura no neurótica de la India que nos es posible a partir de nuestro logocentrismo es ésa que privilegia su superficie. El resto es traducción cristianizante, sincretismo, verdadera superficialidad" (Rodríguez Monegal, "Conversación," 318–19).

3. Prominent among these famous thinkers are the poet Li Po; the philosopher Lao-tzu; and the painter, writer, and calligrapher Wu Chen (1280–1354).

4. Among the authors and testimonialists studied here who have not been openly critical of Castro's regime are Regino Pedroso (who, after the revolution, became cultural attaché to the PRC); Arnaldo Correa; and Generals Armando Choy, Gustavo Chui, and Moisés Sío Wong. Leonardo Padura Fuentes is the only author included in this study who has dared to criticize Castro's policies while still living in Cuba.

5. The 2006 edition of Cubadisco also featured a lecture by Dr. Jesús Guanche Pérez entitled "The Chinese Presence in Cuba," and a traditional Chinese dance choreographed by Zhang Zheng, professor of classical dance in China (at the Dance Institute in Beijing).

6. Cristina Apón Peña, a Chinese Cuban who heads the social work program in Havana's Chinatown, has pointed out additional symbolic gestures: "In 2003, the Cuban and Chinese governments hosted a trip home for five of the [Chinese] immigrants, and plans are in the works to organize visits for about a dozen more" (Arrington n.p.). There is also an official celebration of "the historic October of China and Cuba" in Havana. Scientific forums, sociocultural activities, and sports events commemorate the anniversary of the creation of the PRC (October 1), the beginning of the Cuban wars of independence (October 10), and the Day of Cuban Culture (October 20).

7. However, along with new films dealing with African-rooted religions—such as the Spanish-Cuban-Venezuelan coproduction *Las profecías de Amanda* (1999), directed by Pastor Vega, and the Spanish-Cuban co-production *Miel para Oshún* (2001), by Humberto Solás—other Cuban films on the same topic were produced in the 1970s, such as Sergio Geral's *El otro Francisco* (1976) and Tomás Gutiérrez Alea's *La última cena* (1976).

8. Incidentally, in a house in the Callejón de Hamel where Salvador González's paintings are exhibited there is a figure of Buddha placed next to various images of Santería orishas. It is quite common to find figures of Buddha, with offerings of rice beside them, in Cuban homes.

9. Jesús Díaz has written several film scripts, among them *Clandestinos* (1986), *Barroco* (cowritten with Paul Leduc; 1987), and *Alicia en el pueblo de Maravillas* (cowritten with Daniel Díaz Torres; 1989). He has also directed documentaries such as *Cincuenticinco hermanos* (1978) and *En tierra de Sandino* (1979), as well as two films, *Polvo rojo* (1982) and *Lejanía* (1985). He was a professor of philosophy at the University of Havana (1962–1971) and founded the cultural magazine *El Caimán Barbudo* (1966–1967).

10. Perhaps reflecting the improvement of diplomatic and economic relations with the Chinese government, particularly after the disintegration of the Soviet Union and

the subsequent proclamation of the *Período especial*, Mandarin language courses are now being offered as part of the project to revitalize Havana's Chinatown. Cantonese phonetics courses were offered every other Saturday, but they have recently been cancelled. Scherer has pointed out the paradox of teaching Mandarin (or Pekingese, as they call it) as opposed to the Cantonese spoken by the coolies. When I asked several members of the Chinese community why they were being taught Mandarin instead of Cantonese, their answer was that they were interested in learning the language of Chinese tourists and diplomats. Mandarin courses are taught by a Chinese Cuban, Alberto Koc.

"Special Period in Peacetime" was the official name given to a steep economic decline during the first half of the 1990s. After the collapse of the Soviet Union and its Eastern European allies, Cuba lost 85 percent of its foreign trade and 80 percent of its ability to purchase goods abroad. Among other measures, the Cuban government opened up the tourist industry, imported millions of bicycles from China, and allowed the U.S. dollar to circulate freely. It also allowed some self-employment and deregulated certain prices in agricultural markets.

11. Napoleón Seuc described the fierce competition between Spanish and Chinese warehouses (85).

12. In this sense, Spivak states, "The postcolonial intellectuals learn that their privilege is their loss" (28).

13. "Un mundo en extinción" (22).

14. They celebrate the arrival of the Lunar Year (or Spring Holiday in January–February), Quing Ming Day (or Day of the Deceased in the first days of April), the Day of the Chinese Presence in Cuba (June 3), and the Day of the PRC (October 1). Likewise, each association celebrates the day of its venerated ancestor, the construction of the headquarters of the association, and the foundation of the society.

15. As recently as May 9, 2006, several elderly Sino-Cuban women performed in a brief Chinese theater play that included operatic singing. These women, known in Havana's Chinatown as "Las Divas," are the soprano Caridad Amarán (artistic name Jo Chan Lan [Autumn Orchid]); Georgina Wong (artistic name Wong Mei Yuk [Beautiful Jade]); Ana Li (Li Yit Go [Moon Swan]); and Elia Duarte (Chin Pak Lei [White Pear]). They were accompanied on the gong and cymbals by María del Carmen Li, and on the violin by Milagros Loo. Although no member of this women's theater company knew Chinese, they were able to learn the lines phonetically. Several performed male roles.

As part of the recovery of Chinese culture in Cuba, in the 1990s the Cuban Ministry of the Armed Forces created a medical exchange whereby China sent physicians to teach traditional medicine in Cuba for eighteen months, including acupuncture, massage, and herbal medicine. These doctors would go on Saturdays to the Chung Wah Casino to help native Chinese and their descendents. Similarly, after decades of prohibition, the lion dance, which was performed from 1930 to 1961, during both Chinese festivities and carnival, has been reinstated, thanks to the support of anthropologist Fernando Ortiz.

16. The publisher of this newspaper is Ángel Chiong and the editor is Guillermo Chiu. Although they have been trying to publish it bimonthly, the limited paper supply has made it very difficult to keep a regular schedule.

17. According to Cristina Apón Peña, a group of Chinese traditional healers formed by Chinese Cuban doctors and whose president is an allergist, Dr. Felipe Chao Barriero, has held eight different symposia.

Epilogue

1. Perhaps the most famous Cuban person of Chinese descent is Wifredo Lam (his full name was Wifredo Óscar de la Concepción Lam y Castillo), widely considered the best Cuban painter of all time. He was born in 1902 in Sagua la Grande, in the former province of Las Villas, and died in Paris in 1982. Michel Leiris has elaborated on the seclusion that characterized the Chinese community in Sagua la Grande: "the Estero River once traced the demarcation between Spanish and black districts, with the Chinese remaining as aliens not only excluded by the whites but marginal to the blacks as well" (v). Lam was the eighth child of a Cuban mulatta and a Chinese man from Canton who was hired as an agricultural laborer in Cuba and later became a merchant. Wifredo Lam never had a close relationship with his father, who was 84 years old when he was born (he died at the age of 108). Yet as a boy he was known to everyone as "the son of the *chino* Enrique" (v). Perhaps for this reason, as the titles of his Cubist paintings demonstrate, he was more concerned with motifs taken from African religion and folklore than with Chinese culture: "Ogue Oriza," "Malembo, God of the Crossroads," "The Altar for Elegua," "The Siren of the Niger," "Osum and Elegua for Yemayá," and "Oya." Other than the pencil portrait of his father, Lam "Enrique" Yam, that he sketched in 1914 when he was only twelve, the rest of his works do not seem to explicitly reflect the Chinese side of his heritage. However, some art historians have pointed out his imitation of Asian styles when he painted animals, as well as the presence of bamboo in some of his paintings, among other details. One of his biographers, Max-Pol Fouchet, has underscored Lam's preference for his mother's African culture: "However important the presence of his father—and of those ideograms he drew and hung on his walls—it seems that the reminiscences of his mother had a greater impact on the child. Particularly when she told him of one of her ancestors, a man called José Castilla" (32). Yet Lam never forgot his ethnically mixed origins, a fact revealed in the following lines (collected by Fouchet in 1972) where the artist depicts himself as the embodiment of hybridity and at the crossroads of various civilizations: "Slave-owners, slave suppliers, / And Slaves. / And while the lands of Africa are unpeopled, / Castilian Spain sends all her younger sons, / All her Arabs, all her Jews. [. . .] Later came the others, / Catalans, Galicians, / And, last of all, Chinese,/ Apart. Such are the ancestors / Wifredo Lam claims as his own, / For more than any man / He represents the heritage / Of the convulsion of mankind and the earth" (29). Similarly, although Nancy Morejón's mother was of Chinese and European ancestry, her poetry concentrates on topics dealing with the African heritage of her father.

2. "Con la Revolución, la mayoría de los chinos se fueron del país, sobre todo los más ricos. Los que se quedaron eran más pobres y la mayoría estaban casados."

3. "Yo fui miliciano veinte años y durante la crisis de octubre de 1960 estuve en la trinchera."

4. The Chinese embassy donated the big-screen television set and the air-conditioning in the Chung Wah Casino. They also provide presents for certain Chinese holidays (such as the Lunar New Year) and for the winners of the mahjong competition during the Festival of Overseas Chinese, invite members of the Chinese community to official dinners at the embassy, and have paid for trips back to China for some of them.

5. On my way to the Chung Wah Casino, I actually saw graffiti on a wall in Havana's Chinatown consisting of a Chinese name followed by the word "narra."

6. "Lo dicen sin pensarlo. En el fondo los cubanos no son malos."

7. "El barrio chino está cambiando."

8. "Le quitaba la suerte." The name is a Spanish adaptation of the Chinese word *machiok* (Ma: henequen [similar to maguey plant leaves] bird; Chiok: horse).

9. When Yuli Chung moved to Cuba, a neighbor told her not to stoop while she walked. After so many years of carrying heavy burdens, she had gotten used to that posture.

10. "Era como si el tiempo no pasara."

11. In this context, Joaquín Li describes in his testimony how he and his wife were matched: "our families did not know each other before the marriage. The matchmaker wrote down the names of three generations of ancestors on both sides on a piece of red paper. They were taken to the fortune-teller, who said that the union would be an auspicious one" (42).

12. The word for foreigner also means "devil" but, according to Yuli, they called her "La extranjerita" as a term of endearment.

13. "Tuve que aprender otra vez a llevar zapatos, a beber leche, a comer pan y a hablar español."

14. "No puedo sentir nostalgia por Cuba, ya que la Cuba que yo conocí no existe."

15. "Por mi experiencia, siempre he visto a la mujer chino-cubana como muy decidida, liberada del tutelaje del marido. Puedo citar como ejemplo a mi suegra que fue una mujer muy emprendedora con una gran habilidad para los negocios. Y, como ella, recuerdo otros dos casos. En la segunda generación, hubo chinas-cubanas profesionales: farmacéuticas, médicos, dentistas, etc."

16. "Más bien es tristeza porque se echa de menos todo lo que existía y lo que pudiera haber existido."

17. "Siempre vivimos en barrios habitados por cubanos."

18. "El cubano usaba ciertas palabras utilizadas por los chinos."

19. "Sólo un pequeño incidente de niña en el colegio, pero con sólo una pequeña conversación con la ofensora yo sola resolví el asunto. Creo que le enseñé una lección."

Bibliography

Adams, Henley C. "Fighting an Uphill Battle: Race, Politics, Power, and Institutionalization in Cuba." *Latin American Research Review* 29.3 (2004): 339–42.

Adler, Mortimer J., ed. *Hippocratic Writings.* Chicago: Encyclopaedia Britannica, 1993. Vol. 9 of *Great Books of the Western World.*

Aizenberg, Edna. "*La gesta del marrano* y el sefaradismo literario argentino." *La gesta literaria de Marcos Aguinis. Ensayos críticos.* Ed. Juana Alcira Arancibia. San José, Costa Rica: Instituto Literario y Cultural Hispánico, 1998. 45–54.

Almaguer, Tomás. *Racial Fault Lines: The Historical Origins of White Supremacy in California.* Berkeley and Los Angeles: University of California Press, 1994.

Ang, Ien. "Can One Say No to Chineseness?" *Modern Chinese Literary and Cultural Studies in the Age of Theory: Reimaging a Field.* Ed. Rey Chow. Durham and London: Duke University Press, 2000. 281–300.

———. *On Not Speaking Chinese: Living between Asia and the West.* London and New York: Routledge, 2001.

Arrington, Vanessa. "Havana's China Immigrants Keep Traditions." *Yahoo! News.* May 30, 2006. <http://news.yahoo.com/s/ap/20060530/ap_on_re_la_am_ca/cuba_chinese_elders;_ylt=AhQ7xklh5yrvqvGiwOlkKFq3IxIF;_ylu=X3oDMTBjMHVqMTQ4BHNlYwN5bnN1YmNhdA—>, accessed June 7, 2006.

Balán Sainz, María Elena. "El Barrio Chino visto por Carpentier." *Radio Reloj.* Havana, 1998. <http://www.nnc.cubaweb.cu/cultura/cultura41.htm>, accessed Aug. 1, 2005.

———. "Flora Fong: sensualidad tropical." *Radio Reloj.* Havana, 1998. <http://www.nnc.cubaweb.cu/cultura/cultura45.htm>, accessed Aug. 1, 2005.

Baltar Rodríguez, José. *Los chinos de Cuba: apuntes etnográficos.* Havana: Fundación Fernando Ortiz, 1997.

Baltar Rodríguez, José, Yrmina Eng Menéndez, et al. "Presencia china en Cuba." (map). Havana: Geo, 1999.

Barnet, Miguel. "Flora Fong's Painting." *Nube de otoño.* By Flora Fong. Havana: Grafispaço, 1997. 124–25.

———. *Gallego.* Barcelona: Sudamericana, 2002.

———. "La pintura de Flora Fong." *Nube de otoño.* By Flora Fong. Havana: Grafispaço, 1997. 77–78.

———. *Poemas chinos.* Havana: Unión, 1993.

Barnet, Miguel, and Esteban Montejo. *Biografía de un cimarrón.* Havana: Letras Cubanas, 1980.

———. *Biography of a Runaway Slave.* Trans. W. Nick Hill. Willimantic, Conn.: Curbstone Press, 1994.

Barriero, José. "Survival Stories." *The Cuba Reader: History, Culture, Politics.* Ed.

Aviva Chomsky, Barry Carr, and Pamela Maria Smorkaloff. Durham and London: Duke University Press, 2003. 28–36.
Behar, Ruth, dir., prod., and writer. *Adio Kerida*. DVD. Women Make Movies, 2002.
Bhabha, Homi. *The Location of Culture*. London and New York: Routledge, 2004.
———. "The Third Space." *Identity*. Ed. Jonathan Rutherford. London: Lawrence and Wishart, 1990. 207–21.
Blázquez, Agustín, and Jaums Sutton. "Barlovento: The Massacre of Cuban-Chinese." <http://www.nocastro.com/news/massacre.htm>, accessed July 11, 2003.
Bonnett, Alastair. *The Idea of the West: Culture, Politics and History*. New York: Palgrave Macmillan, 2004.
Bourdieu, Pierre. *Language and Symbolic Power*. Cambridge, Mass.: Harvard University Press, 2001.
Brock, Lisa, and Otis Cunningham. "Race and the Cuban Revolution: A Critique of Carlos Moore's *Castro, the Blacks, and Africa*." *AfroCubaNet*. 1991. <http://www.afrocubaweb.com/brock2.htm>, accessed Nov. 25, 2006.
Bulmer, Martin. "Race and Ethnicity." *Key Variables in Sociological Investigation*. Ed. R. G. Burgess. London: Routledge, 1986. 54–76.
Buruma, Ian, and Avishai Margalit. *Occidentalism: The West in the Eyes of Its Enemies*. New York: Penguin, 2004.
Cabrera, Lydia. *El monte, Igbo-Finda, Ewe Orisha, Vititi Nfinda (Notas sobre las religiones, la magia, las supersticiones y el folklore de los negros criollos y el pueblo de Cuba)*. Miami: Universal, 1992.
Cabrera Infante, Guillermo. *Tres tristes tigres*. Barcelona: Seix Barral, 1995.
Campilongo, Xiomara. "A 'chino' in Cuba: Cristina García's *Monkey Hunting*." *Alternative Orientalisms in Latin America and Beyond*. Ed. Ignacio López-Calvo. Cambridge: Cambridge Scholars Publishing, 2007. 113–23.
Carpentier, Alejo. *La música en Cuba*. Havana: Letras Cubanas, 1979.
Castro, Juan E. de. *Mestizo Nations: Culture, Race, and Conformity in Latin American Literature*. Tucson: University of Arizona Press, 2002.
"Castro se reúne con el Partido Comunista Chino." *El País.com*, Internacional. Apr. 21, 2007. <http://www.elpais.com/articulo/internacional/Castro/reune/Partido/Comunista/Chino/elpepuint/20070421elpepuint_8/Tes>, accessed Apr. 21, 2007.
César, Antonieta. "La pequeña gran alegría." <http://www.trabajadores.cubaweb.cu/sugerencias/estampas/lapequena.htm>, accessed Feb. 15, 2005.
Chang, Félix, and Gustavo Chang Suy. *Legítimas aspiraciones de la colonia china en Cuba*. Havana: El Fígaro, 1926.
Chaviano, Daína. *Casa de juegos*. Barcelona: Planeta, 1999.
———. *El hombre, la hembra y el hambre*. Barcelona: Planeta, 1998.
Chen, Xiaomei. *Occidentalism: A Theory of Counter-Discourse in Post-Mao China*. Lanham, Md: Rowman and Littlefield, 2002.
Chow, Rey. Introduction. *Modern Chinese Literary and Cultural Studies in the Age of*

Theory: Reimaging a Field. Ed. Rey Chow. Durham and London: Duke University Press, 2000. 1–25.

Choy, Armando, Gustavo Chui, and Moisés Sío Wong. *Our History Is Still Being Written: The Story of Three Chinese-Cuban Generals in the Cuban Revolution.* Ed. Mary-Alice Waters. New York: Pathfinder, 2005.

Chuffat Latour, Antonio. *Apunte histórico de los chinos en Cuba.* Havana: Molina, 1927.

Chun, Allen. "Fuck Chineseness: On the Ambiguities of Ethnicity as Culture as Identity." *Boundary 2* 23.2 (Summer 1996): 111–38.

Confucius. *The Essential Confucius.* Trans. and ed. Thomas Clearly. New York: Castle Books, 1992.

"A Conversation with Cristina García." *Asian Review of Books.* <www.asianreviewofbooks.com>, accessed Jan. 5, 2006.

Corbitt, Duvon Clough. *A Study of the Chinese in Cuba, 1847–1947.* Wilmore, Ky.: Asbury College, 1971.

Cornejo Polar, Antonio. "Indigenismo and Heterogeneous Literatures: Their Double Sociocultural Stature." *The Latin American Cultural Studies Reader.* Ed. Ana del Sarto, Alicia Ríos, and Abril Trigo. Durham and London: Duke University Press, 2004. 100–15.

———. "Mestizaje, Transculturation, Heterogeneity." *The Latin American Cultural Studies Reader.* Ed. Ana del Sarto, Alicia Ríos, and Abril Trigo. Durham and London: Duke University Press, 2004. 116–19.

Correa, Arnaldo. *Cold Havana Ground.* Trans. Marjorie Moore. New York: Akashic Books, 2003.

Cosano Alén, Reinaldo. "Frecuente el robo de huesos en cementerios cubanos." *Cubanet.org,* Jan. 23, 2003. <http://www.cubanet.org/CNews/y03/jan03/23a7.htm>, accessed Sept. 13, 2004.

Crespo Villate, Mercedes. *Mis imágenes.* Havana: Verde Olivo, 2000.

The Cuba Commission Report: A Hidden History of the Chinese in Cuba. Intro. Denise Helly. Baltimore: Johns Hopkins University Press, 1993.

Cuentos populares cubanos. Ed. Samuel Feijóo. Vol. 1. Havana: Universidad Central de Las Villas, 1960.

Cuentos populares cubanos de humor. Ed. Samuel Feijóo. Havana: Letras Cubanas, 1981.

Dana, Richard. "The Trade in Chinese Laborers." *The Cuba Reader: History, Culture, Politics.* Ed. Aviva Chomsky, Barry Carr, and Pamela Maria Smorkaloff. Durham and London: Duke University Press, 2003. 79–82.

Delgado de Torres, Lena. "Reformulating Nationalism in the African Diaspora: The Aponte Rebellion of 1812." *The New Centennial Review* 3.3 (Fall 2003): 27–46.

Derpich, Wilma E. *El otro lado azul: empresarios chinos en el Perú.* Lima: Fondo Editorial del Congreso del Perú, 1999.

Deznermio, Raúl. "Interview with Arnaldo Correa, author of *Cold Havana Ground* and *Spy's Fate.*" Akashic Books. <http://www.akashicbooks.com/arnaldointv. htm>, accessed June 12, 2005.

Díaz, Jesús. "Confesión." *Antología de cuento: concurso internacional Juan Rulfo, Premios 1984–1992.* Mexico City: Diana, 1993. 208–21.

Diccionario de la lengua española. 20th ed. Madrid: Espasa-Calpe, 1984.

Dubs, Homer H., and Robert S. Smith. "Chinese in Mexico City in 1635." *Far Eastern Quarterly* 1.4 (Aug. 1942): 387–89.

Eça de Queiroz, José María. *The Mandarin and Other Stories.* Trans. Richard Franko Goldman. Athens, Ohio: Ohio University Press, 1965.

Encyclopedia of Chinese Overseas. Singapore: Chinese Heritage Centre, 1998.

Espina Prieto, Rodrigo, and Pablo Rodríguez Ruiz. "Raza y desigualdad en la Cuba actual." *Temas* 45 (Jan.–Mar. 2006): 44–54.

Espinosa Luis, Mitzi. "Si tú pleguntá, a mí gusta hace cuento. 'If You Ask, I'll Be Happy to Tell You': Felipe Luis Narrates His Story." *The Chinese in the Caribbean.* Ed. Andrew R. Wilson. Princeton, N.J.: Markus Wiener Publishers, 2003. 129–44.

Fanon, Frantz. *The Wretched of the Earth.* Preface Jean-Paul Sartre. Trans. Constance Farrington. New York: Grove Press, 1968.

Felipe, Carlos. "El chino." *Teatro.* Havana: UNEAC, 1967. 45–103

Fernández Retamar, Roberto. "Caliban: Notes toward a Discussion of Culture in Our America." *The Latin American Cultural Studies Reader.* Ed. Ana del Sarto, Alicia Ríos, and Abril Trigo. Durham and London: Duke University Press, 2004. 83–99.

———. "Nuestra América y Occidente." *Casa de las Américas* 98 (1976): 36–57.

Ferreira, Ramón. "Bagazo." *Antología del cuento cubano contemporáneo.* Ed. Ambrosio Fornet. Mexico City: Era, 1967. 176–84.

Fong, Flora. *Nube de otoño.* Havana: Grafispaço, 1997.

Fouchet, Max-Pol. *Wifredo Lam.* New York: Rizzoli International Publications, 1976.

Freire, Paulo. *Pedagogía del oprimido.* Mexico City: Siglo XXI, 1990.

———. Pedagogy of the Oppressed. Trans. Myra Bergman Ramos. New York: Seabury Press, 1970.

Fuente, Jorge de la. "Critics' Comments." *Nube de otoño.* By Flora Fong. Havana: Grafispaço, 1997. 126.

Fuente, José Luis de la. "Las novelas de Mayra Montero: hacia una nueva magia." *Horizontes* 45.89 (Oct. 2003): 87–126.

Galván, Javier A. "Sugar and Slavery: The Bittersweet Chapter in the 19th-Century Cuba, 1817–1886." *Revista de Humanidades Tecnológico de Monterrey* 16 (2004): 211–31.

García, Cristina. *Monkey Hunting.* New York: A. A. Knopf, 2003.

García Canclini, Néstor. *Hybrid Cultures: Strategies for Entering and Leaving Modernity.* Minneapolis and London: University of Minnesota Press, 1995.

García-Castañón, Santiago. Introducción. *Verdadera relación de la grandeza del*

Reino de China. By Miguel de Luarca. Oviedo, Spain: Eco de Luarca, 2002. 19–42.

Geirola, Gustavo. "Chinos y japoneses en América Latina: Karen Tei Yamashita, Cristina García y Anna Kazumi Stahl." *Chasqui* 34.3 (Nov. 2005): 113–30.

Godfried, Eugène. "The Massacre of 1812: José Aponte y Ubarra Longstanding Racial Problems in Cuba." Oct. 19, 2006. <http://www.afrocubaweb.com/eugenegodfried/Aponte.htm>, accessed Nov. 19, 2006.

González, Ángel T. "La milicia china de Castro." Crónica. Supplement of *El Mundo*. <http://www.elmundo.es/suplementos/cronica/2005/505/1119132018.html>, accessed June 19, 2005.

González-Echevarría, Roberto. "Foreword." *Maitreya by Severo Sarduy*. Trans. Suzanne Jill-Levine. Hanover, N.H.: Ediciones del Norte, 1987.

Gordon, Peter. "Fusion Fiction: *Monkey Hunting* by Cristina García." *Asian Review of Books*, June 6, 2003. <http://www.asianreviewofbooks.com/arb/article.php?article=247>, accessed Dec. 10, 2004.

Goytisolo, Juan. Preface. *Orientalismo*. By Edward W. Said. Trans. María Luisa Fuentes. Barcelona: Debate, 2002.

Guanche Pérez, Jesús. "La cuestión 'racial' en Cuba actual: algunas consideraciones." *Papers* 52 (1997): 57–65.

——. "Juan Pérez de la Riva y los culíes chinos en Cuba." Cuba, una identità in movimento. <http://art.supereva.it/carlo260/culies.htm?p>, accessed June 20, 2004.

Guillén, Nicolás. "Crónica de Yucatán." *Revista Literaria Electrónica "El Navegante."* <http://www.elnavegante.com.mx/rev05/nicolas_guillen.html>, accessed June 20, 2004.

——. "Médico chino." *Sátira política (1949–1953). Obra poética, 1920–1972*. Vol. 1. Havana: Editorial de Arte y Literatura, 1974.

——. "Poema con niños." *Obra poética, 1920–1972*. Vol. 1. Havana: Editorial de Arte y Literatura, 1974. 262–68.

Gutiérrez, Ramón A. *When Jesus Came, the Corn Mothers Went Away: Marriage, Sexuality, and Power in New Mexico, 1500–1846*. Stanford: Stanford University Press, 1991.

Haviland, William A. *Cultural Anthropology*. Orlando, Fla.: Harcourt Brace, 1996.

Helly, Denise. Introduction. *The Cuba Commission Report: A Hidden History of the Chinese in Cuba*. Baltimore: Johns Hopkins University Press, 1993. 3–30.

Hernández Catá, Alfonso. *Cuatro libras de felicidad*. Madrid: Renacimiento, 1933.

——. *Cuentos y novelitas*. Ed. Salvador Bueno. Havana: Letras Cubanas, 1983.

Herrera, Manuel. "El pirotécnico Li-Shiao." *Cuentos cubanos*. Barcelona: Laia, 1983. 265–73.

Hu-DeHart, Evelyn. "Chinese Coolies and the Middle Passage, 1847 to 1888." *Other Middle Passages*. Ed. Marcus Rediker, Emma Christopher, and Cassandra Pybus. Berkeley: University of California Press, Forthcoming.

——. "Opium and Social Control: Coolies on the Plantations of Peru and Cuba." *Journal of Chinese Overseas* 1.2 (Nov. 2005): 169–83.

———. "Race Construction and Race Relations: Chinese and Blacks in Nineteenth-Century Cuba." *Alternative Orientalisms in Latin America and Beyond.* Ed. Ignacio López-Calvo. Cambridge: Cambridge Scholars Publishing, 2007. 82–94

———. "Transpacific Confrontation/Confrontación transpacífica." *Review: Literature and Arts of the Americas.* New York: Ameritas Society, 2006.

Jackson, Eric. "Panama's Chinese Community Celebrates a Birthday, Meets New Challenges." *Panama News,* May 22, 2004. <http://www.thepanamanews.com/pn/v_10/issue_09/community_01.html>, accessed Aug. 23, 2006.

Jameson, Frederic. "Third World Literature in the Era of Multinational Capitalism." *Social Text* 1 (1986): 67–90.

Jiménez Pastrana, Juan. *Los chinos en las luchas por la liberación cubana (1847–1930).* Havana: Instituto de Historia, 1963.

Johndrow, Donald Ray. "'Total' Reality in Severo Sarduy's Search for Lo Cubano." *Romance Notes* 13.3 (Spring 1972): 445–52.

Johnson, Cecil. *Communist China and Latin America (1959–1967).* New York and London: Columbia University Press, 1970.

Juan, Adelaida de. "Autumn Cloud." *Nube de otoño.* By Flora Fong. Havana: Grafispaço, 1997. 119–21.

———. "Nube de otoño." *Nube de otoño.* By Flora Fong. Havana: Grafispaço, 1997. 9–12.

Khan, Abrahim H. "Identity, Personhood, and Religion in the Caribbean Context." *Nation Dance: Religion, Identity, and Cultural Difference in the Caribbean.* Ed. Patrick Taylor. Bloomington and Indianapolis: Indiana University Press, 2001. 138–52.

Ko, Dorothy. "Bondage in Time: Footbinding and Fashion Theory." *Fashion Theory* 1.1 (March 1997): 3–28.

———. *Teachers of the Inner Chambers: Women and Culture in Seventeenth-Century China.* Stanford: Stanford University Press, 1994.

Kornfield, Jack, ed. *The Teachings of the Buddha.* New York: Barnes and Noble Books, 1999.

Kristeva, Julia. *Strangers to Ourselves.* Trans. Leon S. Rondiez. New York: Columbia University Press, 1991.

Kung, Chin. *Buddhism: The Wisdom of Compassion and Awakening.* Taiwan: Silent Voices, 2003.

Kushigian, Julia A. *Orientalism in the Hispanic Literary Tradition: In Dialogue with Borges, Paz, and Sarduy.* Albuquerque: University of New Mexico Press, 1991.

Lachatañeré, Rómulo. *Afro-Cuban Myths: Yemayá and Other Orishas.* Trans. Christine Ayorinde. Princeton, N.J.: Markus Wiener Publishers, 2004.

Lao-tzu. *Tao Te Ching: The Classic Book of Integrity and the Way.* Trans. and ed. Victor H. Mair. New York: Bantam Books, 1990.

Lee, Debbie. "Regino Pedroso and *Nosotros*: De-Colonization and Reconstruction of the Self." *PALARA* 6 (Fall 2002): 72–83.

———. *When East Meets West: An Examination of the Poetry of the Asian Diaspora in Spanish America*. Diss. University of Missouri–Columbia, 2002.

Lee Chan, Alejandro. "Chinos de la diáspora en las novelas de Isabel Allende, Mayra Montero y Cristina García." Diss. University of California, Los Angeles, 2005.

Leiris, Michel. *Wifredo Lam*. New York: Harry N. Abrams, 1970.

Lezama Lima, José. *Cartas (1939–1976)*. Ed. Eloísa Lezama Lima. Madrid: Orígenes, 1979.

———. "Juego de las decapitaciones." *Cuentos Cubanos*. Barcelona: Laia, 1983. 55–69.

———. *Paradiso*. Ed. Eloísa Lezama Lima. Madrid: Ediciones Cátedra, 1980.

———. *Paradiso*. Trans. Gregory Rabassa. Austin: University of Texas Press, 1988.

Li, Joaquín. "Paper Son Meets Father." *Being Chinese: Voices from the Diaspora*. Ed. Wei Djao. Tucson: University of Arizona Press, 2003. 42–46.

Lipski, John M. "El español de los braceros chinos y la problemática de lenguaje bozal." *Montalbán* 31 (1998): 101–39.

Look Lai, Walton. *The Chinese in the West Indies, 1806–1995: A Documentary History*. Kingston: University Press of the West Indies, 1998.

López, Kathleen. "'One Brings Another': The Formation of Early-Twentieth-Century Chinese Migrant Communities in Cuba." *The Chinese in the Caribbean*. Ed. Andrew R. Wilson. Princeton, N.J.: Markus Wiener Publishers, 2003. 93–128.

Luarca, Miguel de. *Verdadera relación de la grandeza del Reino de China*. Ed. Santiago García-Castañón. Oviedo, Spain: Eco de Luarca, 2002.

Luis, William. "De la oralidad a la escritura en *Me llamo Rigoberta Menchú*." *La memoria popular y sus transformaciones: a memória popular e as suas transformações*. Ed. Martín Lienhard. Madrid: Vervuert-Iberoamericana: 2000. 221–35.

———. *Literary Bondage: Slavery in Cuban Narrative*. Austin: University of Texas Press, 1990.

Ma, Sheng-mei. *Immigrant Subjectivities in Asian American and Asian Diaspora Literatures*. Albany: State University of New York Press, 1998.

Mair, Victor H. "Afterword." *Tao Te Ching: The Classic Book of Integrity and the Way*. By Lao-tzu. Trans. and ed. Victor H. Mair. New York: Bantam Books, 1990. 119–53.

Mañach, Jorge. *Indagación del choteo*. Miami: Mnemosyne Publishing Co., 1969.

Mariátegui, José Carlos. *Seven Interpretative Essays on Peruvian Reality*. Trans. Marjory Urquidi. Austin: University of Texas Press, 1974.

Martí, José. "Un funeral chino." *Portal José Martí*. 2007. <http://www.josemarti.cu/?q=oma&nid=500>, accessed Feb. 20, 2007.

———. "Los indios en los Estados Unidos." *Portal José Martí*. 2007. <http://www.josemarti.cu/files/Los%20indios%20en%20los%20EEUU.PDF>, accessed Feb. 2, 2007.

———. *José Martí: ensayos y crónicas*. Ed. José Olivio Jiménez. Madrid. Anaya, 1995.

———. *José Martí: Selected Writings*. Ed. and trans. Esther Allen. Intro. Roberto González Echevarría. New York: Penguin, 2002.
———. *Obras completas*. 2 vols. Havana: Lex, 1946.
———. "El presidio político en Cuba." *La página de José Martí*. <http://www.josemarti.org/jose_marti/obras/documentoshistoricos/presidiopolitico/presidio07.htm>, accessed Feb. 2, 2007.
———. "El puente de Brooklyn." *Cervantes Virtual*. <http://www.cervantesvirtual.com/servlet/SirveObras/04708307600403884199079/p0000036.htm#43>, accessed Feb. 20, 2007.
Martínez, Toni. "Zoé Valdés: 'nos pasamos la vida hablando, escribiendo y cada vez escuchamos menos.'" *Cubanet*. Nov. 3, 2004. <http://www.cubanet.org/CNews/y04/nov04/03o5.htm>, accessed Feb. 26, 2006.
Méndez Capote, Renée. *Memorias de una cubanita que nació con el siglo*. Havana: Gente Nueva, 1998.
Menzies, Gavin. *1421: The Year China Discovered America*. New York: Perennial, 2004.
Meyer, Andrew. "Anatomy of a Craze: Cuban Chinese Restaurants in New York." *The Chinese in the Caribbean*. Ed. Andrew R. Wilson. Princeton, N.J.: Markus Wiener Publishers, 2003. 145–58.
Meza, Ramón [R. E. Maz]. *Carmela*. Havana: Arte y Literatura, 1978.
———. "El mercader chino." *La Habana Elegante*, Apr. 10, 1887.
Mignolo, Walter D. "Posoccidentalismo: las epistemologías fronterizas y el dilema de los estudios (latinoamericanos) de áreas." *Revista Iberoamericana* 62.176–77 (July–Dec. 1996): 679–95.
Montero, Mayra. *Como un mensajero tuyo*. Barcelona: Tusquets, 1998.
———. "The Great Bonanza of the Antilles." Trans. Lizabeth Paravisini-Gebert. *Healing Cultures: Art and Religion as Curative Practices in the Caribbean and Its Diaspora*. Ed. Margarita Fernández Olmos and Lizabeth Paravisini-Gebert. New York: Palgrave, 2001. 195–201.
———. *The Messenger*. Trans. Edith Grossman. New York: Harper Flamingo, 1999.
Montesquieu, Charles de. *The Spirit of Laws*. Ed. Mortimer J. Adler. Chicago: Encyclopaedia Britannica, 1993. Vol. 35 of *Great Books of the Western World*.
Moore, Carlos. *Castro, the Blacks, and Africa (Afro-American Culture and Society)*. Los Angeles: Center for Afro-American Studies, University of California, 1988.
Morán, Francisco. "Volutas del deseo: hacia una lectura del orientalismo en el modernismo hispanoamericano." *Modern Language Notes* 120 (2005): 383–407.
Moss, Suzan. "Behind the Embargo: The Inclusive Nature of Afro-Cuban Dance Culture." <http://www.cubaupdate.org/cu0404_23_2.htm>, accessed July 23, 2006.
Nadie escuchaba. Co-dir., prod., and writers Néstor Almendros and Jorge Ulla. DVD. Facets Video, 1989.
"The Nature of Inheritance: A Conversation with Cristina García." *Atlantic Unbound*. April 11, 2003. <http://www.theatlantic.com/doc/prem/200304u/int2003-4-11>, accessed October 1, 2007.

Nelson, Bernard H. "The Slave Trade as a Factor in British Foreign Policy 1815–1862." *Journal of Negro History* 27.2 (Apr. 1942): 192–209.

Nogueras, Luis Rogelio. *La forma de las cosas que vendrán*. Havana: Letras Cubanas, 1989.

Novás Calvo, Lino. "Aquella noche salieron los muertos." *Cuentos cubanos contemporáneos*. Ed. José Antonio Portuondo. Mexico City: Leyenda, 1946. 147–80.

Nussa, Ele. "Critics' comments." *Nube de otoño*. Havana: Grafispaço, 1997. 126.

Okin, Susan Moller, ed. *Is Multiculturalism Bad for Women?* Princeton, N.J.: Princeton University Press, 1999.

Oppenheimer, Andrés. "U.S. Should Fear No 'China Threat'—For Now." *Miami Herald.com*. <http://www.keepmedia.com/pubs/MiamiHerald/2005/09/29/1030979?ba=m&bi=1&bp=12>, accessed Sept. 29, 2005.

Ortega, Antonio. "Chino olvidado." *Chino olvidado y otros cuentos*. Ed. Jorge Domingo Cuadriello. Seville, Spain: Biblioteca del Exilio, 2003. 101–20.

Ortiz, Fernando. *Contrapunteo cubano del tabaco y el azúcar (advertencia de sus contrastes agrarios, económicos, históricos y sociales, su etnografía y su transculturación)*. Foreword María Fernanda Ortiz Herrera. Intro. Bronislaw Malinowski. Madrid: CubaEspaña, 1999.

———. *Los negros brujos: apuntes para un estudio de etnología criminal*. Miami: New House Publishers, 1973.

———. "The Relations between Blacks and Whites in Cuba." *Phylon (1940–1956)* 5.1 (1944): 15–29.

———. "'Transculturation' and Cuba." *The Cuba Reader: History, Culture, Politics*. Ed. Aviva Chomsky, Barry Carr, and Pamela Maria Smorkaloff. Durham and London: Duke University Press, 2003. 26–27.

Padura Fuentes, Leonardo. *Adiós Hemingway y La cola de la serpiente*. Havana: Ediciones Unión, 2001.

———. *El viaje más largo*. Madrid: Plaza Mayor, 2002.

Pedroso, Regino. *El ciruelo de Yuan Pei Fu: poemas chinos*. Havana: P. Fernández y Compañía, 1955.

———. "Hermano negro." *Antología poética (1918–1938)*. Havana: Molina, 1939.

———. *Nosotros*. Havana: Letras Cubanas, 1984.

———. *Poemas*. Havana: Unión de Escritores y Artistas de Cuba, 1975.

Pellón, Gustavo. "Severo Sarduy's Strategy of Irony: Paradigmatic Indecision in Cobra and Maitreya." *Latin American Literary Review* 11.23 (Autumn–Winter 1983): 7–13.

Pérez de la Riva, Juan. "Demografía de los culíes chinos en Cuba (1853–74)." *Revista de la Biblioteca Nacional "José Martí"* 57.4 (1966): 13–16.

———. "A World Destroyed." *The Cuba Reader: History, Culture, Politics*. Ed. Aviva Chomsky, Barry Carr, and Pamela Maria Smorkaloff. Durham and London: Duke University Press, 2003. 20–25.

Pérez Firmat, Gustavo. "Riddles of the Sphincter: Another Look at the Cuban Choteo." *Diacritics* 14.4 (Winter 1984): 67–77.

Pérez Sarduy, Pedro. "An Open Letter to Carlos Moore." *AfroCubaWeb*. Summer 1990. <http://www.afrocubaweb.com/lettertocarlos.htm>, accessed Nov. 20, 2006.

———. "What Do Blacks Have in Cuba?" *AfroCubaWeb*. July 13, 1995. <http://www.afrocubaweb.com/whatdoblacks.htm>, accessed Nov. 20, 2006.

Pérez Sarduy, Pedro, and Jean Stubbs, eds. *Afro-Cuban Voices: On Race and Identity in Contemporary Cuba*. Gainesville: University Press of Florida, 2000.

Pérez Torres, Yazmín. "Regresando a la Guinea: historia, religión y mito en las novelas caribeñas de Mayra Montero." *Revista Iberoamericana* 54.186 (Jan.–Mar. 1999): 103–16.

Pogolotti, Graziella. "El huracán y su ojo." *Nube de otoño*. By Flora Fong. Havana: Grafispaço, 1997. 55–56.

———. "The Hurricane and Its Eye." *Nube de otoño*. By Flora Fong. Havana: Grafispaço, 1997. 123.

Ponte, Antonio José. "A petición de Ochún." *Cuentos de todas partes del imperio*. Angers: Éditions Deleatur, 2000. 43–46.

———. *Tales from the Cuban Empire*. Trans. Cola Franzen. San Francisco: City Lights, 2002.

Prieto, René. "The Ambiviolent Fiction of Severo Sarduy." *Symposium* 29.1 (1985): 49–60.

Quesada, Gonzalo de. *Páginas escogidas*. Havana: Instituto del Libro, 1968.

Rama, Ángel. "Literature and Culture." *The Latin American Cultural Studies Reader*. Ed. Ana del Sarto, Alicia Ríos, and Abril Trigo. Durham and London: Duke University Press, 2004. 120–52.

Ratliff, William. "Cuba and China: Why Is Economically Successful China Interested in the Economically Failed Cuba and Vice Versa?" May 25, 2006. <http://www.lanuevacuba.com/archivo/notic-06-05-2520.htm>, accessed June 7, 2007.

———. "Mirroring Taiwan: China and Cuba." *Jamestown Foundation* 6.10 (May 2006). <http://www.jamestown.org/publications_details.php?volume_id=415&&issue_id=3721>, accessed June 7, 2006.

Rénique, Gerardo. "Race, Region, and Nation: Sonora's Anti-Chinese Racism and Mexico's Postrevolutionary Nationalism, 1920s–1930s." *Race and Nation in Modern Latin America*. Ed. Nancy P. Appelbaum, Anne S. Macpherson, and Karin Alejandra Rosemblatt. Chapel Hill and London: University of North Carolina Press, 2003. 211–36.

Rivera, Ángel A. "Ética y estética de la compasión en Mayra Montero: aguaceros dispersos." *Atenea* 23.2 (Dec. 2003): 39–51.

Rodríguez, Antonio Orlando. *Aprendices de brujo*. New York: Rayo, 2005.

———. *The Last Masquerade*. Trans. Ernesto Mestre-Reed. New York: Rayo, 2005.

Rodríguez Monegal, Emir. *El arte de narrar*. Mexico City: Joaquín Mortiz, 1978.

———. "Conversación con Severo Sarduy." *Revista de Occidente* 31.93 (Dec. 1970): 315–43.

———. "Diálogo con Severo Sarduy: las estructuras de la narración." *Mundo Nuevo* August 1966: 15–26.

Rodríguez Pastor, Humberto. *Herederos del dragón: historia de la comunidad china en el Perú*. Lima: Fondo Editorial del Congreso del Perú, 2000.

Rojas, Rafael. *Isla sin fin: contribución a la crítica del nacionalismo cubano*. Miami: Ediciones Universal, 1988.

Said, Edward W. *Orientalism*. London: Penguin, 2003.

Santí, Enrico Mario. "Textual Politics: Severo Sarduy." *Latin American Literary Review* 8.16 (Spring–Summer 1980): 152–60.

Sarduy, Severo. *Barroco*. Buenos Aires: Sudamericana, 1974.

———. *Big Bang*. Barcelona: Tusquets, 1974.

———. *Cobra*. Buenos Aires: Sudamericana, 1974.

———. *Cobra and Maitreya*. Trans. Suzanne Jill Levine. Intro. James McCourt. Normal, Ill.: Dalkey Archive Press, 1995.

———. *Colibrí*. Barcelona: Argos Vergara, 1984.

———. *De donde son los cantantes*. Mexico City: Joaquín Mortiz, 1967.

———. *From Cuba with a Song*. Trans. Suzanne Jill Levine. Los Angeles: Sun and Moon Press, 1994.

———. *Gestos*. Barcelona: Seix Barral, 1963.

———. *Maitreya*. Barcelona: Seix Barral, 1978.

———. *Maitreya*. Trans. Suzanne Jill Levine. Foreword. Roberto González-Echevarría. Hanover, N.H.: Ediciones del Norte, 1987.

Sariol, Jorge. "Suerte, dicha y longevidad." *La Jiribilla: Revista Digital de Cultura Cubana* 239.3–9 (Dec. 2005). <http://www.lajiribilla.cu/2002/n75_octubre/1767_75.html>, accessed Dec. 10, 2005.

Sartorius, David. "My Vassals: Free-Colored Militias in Cuba and the Ends of Spanish Empire." *Journal of Colonialism and Colonial History* 5.2 (Fall 2004). <http://libproxy.library.unt.edu:2735/journals/journal_of_colonialism_and_colonial_history/v005/5.2sartorius.html#NOTE12>, accessed Nov. 19, 2006.

Scherer, Frank F. "A Culture of Erasure: Orientalism and Chineseness in Cuba, 1847–1997." Master's thesis. York University, Toronto, Ont., 2000.

———. "Sanfancón: Orientalism, Self-Orientalization, and 'Chinese Religion' in Cuba." *Nation Dance: Religion, Identity, and Cultural Difference in the Caribbean*. Ed. Patrick Taylor. Bloomington: Indiana University Press, 2001. 153–70.

Schurz, William Lytle. *The Manila Galleon*. New York: Dutton, 1939.

Seuc, Napoleón. *La colonia china de Cuba 1930–1960: antecedentes, memorias y vivencias*. Miami: Ahora Printing, 1998.

Siu, Lok C. D. *Memories of a Future Home: Diasporic Citizenship of Chinese in Panama*. Stanford, Calif.: Stanford University Press, 2005.

Smith, Robert Freeman. "Twentieth-Century Cuban Historiography." *Hispanic American Historical Review* 44.1 (Feb. 1964): 44–73.

Spence, Jonathan D. *The Chan's Great Continent: China in Western Minds*. New York: North and Co., 1998.

Spivak, Gayatri Chakravorty. "Can the Subaltern Speak?" *The Postcolonial Studies Reader*. Ed. Bill Ashcroft, Gareth Griffiths, and Helen Tiffin. London and New York: Routledge, 1997. 24–28.

Stewart, Watt. *Chinese Bondage in Peru*. Durham, N.C.: Duke University Press, 1951.

Suárez, José. "Cuba y el Mandarín de Eça de Queiroz." *Círculo* 12 (1983): 51–57.

Teixeira, José Roberto. "Chineses entrados no Brasil 1814–1842." *A China no Brasil: influências, marcas, ecos e sobrevivências chinesas na sociedade e na arte brasileiras*. Campinas, São Paulo: Ed. da Unicamp, 1999. 269–75.

Tu, Wei-ming. "Cultural China: The Periphery as the Center." *The Living Tree: The Changing Meaning of Being Chinese Today*. Ed. Tu Wei-ming. Stanford, Calif.: Stanford University Press, 1994. 1–34.

Turner, Elisa. "Chinese-Cuban Roots and Thrifting Prizes." *Miami Herald*, May 24, 2004. <http://www.cubanet.org/CNews/y04/may04/25e4.htm>, accessed June 4, 2005.

Vadillo, Alicia E. "La metáfora de Cuba en la novela *Maitreya* de Severo Sarduy." <http://www.ciicla.ucr.ac.cr/boletin25_05.htm>, accessed Sept. 2, 2004.

Valdés, Zoé. *La eternidad del instante*. Barcelona: Plaza y Janés, 2004.

———. *I Gave You All I Had*. Trans. Nadia Benabid. New York: Arcade Publishing, 1999.

———. *Querido primer novio*. Barcelona: Planeta, 1999.

———. *Te di la vida entera*. Barcelona: Planeta, 1996.

Varela, Beatriz. *Lo chino en el habla cubana*. Miami: Ediciones Universal, 1980.

Vasconcelos, José. *La raza cósmica* Mexico City: Porrúa, 2001.

Vaughan, Umi. "Shades of Race in Contemporary Cuba." Mar. 21, 2005. <http://www.walterlippmann.com/docs090.html>, accessed July 6, 2006.

Weiss, Judith A. "On the Trail of the (Un)Holy Serpent: *Cobra*, by Severo Sarduy." *Journal of Spanish Studies: Twentieth Century* 5.1 (Spring 1977): 57–69.

Wilson, Andrew R. "Introduction." *The Chinese in the Caribbean*. Ed. Andrew R. Wilson. Princeton, N.J.: Markus Wiener Publishers, 2003. vii–xxiii.

Wood, Frances. *Did Marco Polo Go to China?* Boulder, Colo.: Westview Press, 1996.

Yun, Lisa Li-Shen. "An Afro-Chinese Caribbean: Cultural Cartographies of Contrariness in the Work of Antonio Chuffat Latour, Margaret Cezair, and Patricia Powell." *Caribbean Quarterly* 50.2 (2004): 26–43.

"Zoé Valdés gana el premio Ciudad de Torrevieja." *Mujeres Hoy*, Espacios/Literatura. Apr. 10, 2004. <http://www.mujereshoy.com/secciones/2457.shtml>, accessed Dec. 8, 2005.

Chronological List of Works

Ch'en Lan Pin, *The Cuba Commission Report* (1877)
José María Eça de Queiroz, *O Mandarim* (1880)
José Martí, *Versos sencillos* (1881)
Ramón Meza, *Carmela* (1887)
Ramón Meza, "El mercader chino" (1887)
José Martí, "A Chinese Funeral" (1888)
José Martí, "My Race" (1893)
Alfonso Hernández Catá, "Los chinos" (1924)
Antonio Chuffat Latour, *Apunte histórico de los chinos en Cuba* (1927)
Regino Pedroso, *Nosotros* (1933)
Alfonso Hernández Catá, "Cuarenta y nueve chinos" (1933)
José Lezama Lima, "Juego de las decapitaciones" (1944)
Antonio Ortega, "Chino olvidado" (1945)
Carlos Felipe, *El chino* (1947)
Lydia Cabrera, *El monte: Igbo-Finda, Ewe Orisha, Vititi Nfinda* (1954)
Regino Pedroso, *El ciruelo de Yuan Pei Fu* (1955)
Cuentos populares cubanos. Ed. Samuel Feijóo (1960)
Renée Méndez Capote, *Memorias de una cubanita que nació con el siglo* (1963)
Miguel Barnet and Esteban Montejo, *Biography of a Runaway Slave* (1966)
Severo Sarduy, *De donde son los cantantes* (1967)
Severo Sarduy, *Cobra* (1972)
Severo Sarduy, *Maitreya* (1977)
Cuentos populares cubanos de humor. Ed. Samuel Feijóo (1981)
Miguel Barnet, *Gallego* (1981)
Luis Rogelio Nogueras, "Mirando un grabado erótico chino" (1989)
Jesús Díaz, "Confesión" (1991)
Miguel Barnet, *Poemas chinos* (1993)
Zoé Valdés, *I Gave You All I Had* (1996)
Flora Fong, *Nube de otoño* (1997)
Mayra Montero, *The Messenger* (1998)
Daína Chaviano, *El hombre, la hembra y el hambre* (1998)
Napoleón Seuc, *La colonia china de Cuba 1930–1960* (1998)
Leonardo Padura Fuentes, *La cola de la serpiente* (2001)
Antonio Orlando Rodríguez, *Aprendices de brujo* (2002)
Cristina García, *Monkey Hunting* (2003)
Arnaldo Correa, *Cold Havana Ground* (2003)
Joaquín Li, "Paper Son Meets Father" (2003)
Zoé Valdés, *La eternidad del instante* (2004)
Armando Choy, Gustavo Chui, and Moisés Sío Wong, *Our History Is Still Being Written* (2005)

Index

Abakuá Secret Society, 88, 101–2, 110, 189n35
Afro-Chinese, 81, 98, 120–22, 220
Apón Peña, Cristina, xiii, 15, 150, 154, 205n6, 207n17
Aponte y Ubarra, Antonio José, 11–12; and Aponte Conspiracy, 11–12, 15, 211, 213
Assimilation, 19, 24, 44, 105, 107, 109, 112, 114, 119, 121, 194n2

Barnet, Miguel, 29, 87, 171n1, 209; and *Biography of a Runaway Slave*, 21, 30–31, 42, 108, 188n25, 221; and *Gallego*, 53, 203n38, 221; and *Poemas chinos*, 70–71, 221
Barrio chino, 2, 13–16, 21–22, 54, 57, 71, 73, 76, 78, 88, 155, 185n35, 192n5, 208n7, 209
Batista, Juan Fulgencio, 14, 64, 124, 126, 169n28, 196n18
Bhabha, Homi, 21, 111, 154, 210
Bondage. *See* slavery
Brazil, 3, 5–6, 29, 154, 167n8
Buddha, 86, 97, 112, 116, 205n8, 214
Bueno, Salvador, 213

Cabrera, Lydia, 210, 221; and *El monte*, 102, 187n21, 188n25, 189n35, 190n37
Cabrera Infante, Guillermo, 20, 210
California, 5, 13–14, 21, 94, 155, 160, 167, 174n11, 192n5, 209
Carpentier, Alejo, 76, 186n16, 209, 210, 221; and *La música en Cuba*, 20
Castro, Fidel, 3, 14–17, 23, 44, 74–75, 88, 96, 105, 124–28, 132, 149, 160–61, 165n4, 169n27, 196n18, 197n23, 204n42, 205n4, 210
Castro, Juan de, xiii, 23, 106, 210, 213, 216
Castro, Raúl, 17
Chang, Josefina, 160
Chao, Luis, xiii, 156
Charada china, 108, 112, 142, 191n3
Chaviano, Daína, 190n44; and *Casa de juegos*, 191n48, 210, 222; and *El hombre, la hembra y el hambre*, 105, 150, 192n9, 210, 221
Chi ffa. See Charada China
China, ix, xi, xiii, 1–2, 4, 8–11, 13–21, 23, 32–34, 36, 38–41, 43–44, 46–47, 51, 63, 64, 67–74, 82–84, 86–88, 93–94, 100, 106, 111–14, 119–21, 124, 127–28, 132, 134, 138, 142, 148–50, 153–54, 156–60, 162, 165n2, 167n11, 168n14, 168n20, 170n33, 172n6, 173n14, 173n15, 176n26, 177n3, 179n22, 179n24, 182n1, 184n27, 188 n26, 189n32, 193n17, 196 n17, 196n22, 197n22, 199n39, 201n20, 203n35, 203n36, 204n47, 205n5, 205n6, 206n10, 206n15, 208n4, 209–10, 213–20; cultural China, 148–49, 220
China mulata. See Chinese Cuban women
Chinatown. *See barrio chino*
Chinese at war: cemetery, 39, 102, 112, 115, 188n31; cuisine, x, 20, 57, 78, 112, 115–16, 129, 142, 153, 163; dance, 68–69, 77, 205n5; lion dance, 48, 88, 151, 153–54, 170n42, 206n15; marriage, 10, 13, 44, 67, 73, 77, 95, 157, 159; marriage (arranged), 73, 157, 159–60, 181n16, 208n11; marriage (mixed), 34, 72, 88, 109, 140–41, 156; martial arts, 132, 153–54; nostalgia, 15, 22, 24, 45, 71, 83–85, 109–11, 142, 156–57, 161–62, 208n14; old sage, 69, 82–83, 85–87, 95, 139–40; opera, 78, 141–42, 178n11, 206n15; painting, 19, 24, 69–70, 74, 80, 84, 86–88, 113, 126, 132, 137–38, 144–45, 178n11, 184n29, 184n30, 205n3, 207n1, 209; patriotism, 96, 116, 122–32, 137, 195n16, 198n39, 201n14; patience, 75, 95, 142–43, 178, 188, 203n39, 203,n40; poetry, xii, 24, 40, 69, 74, 80–85, 87, 97–98, 113, 178n11, 179n18, 182n2, 183n5, 183n9, 183n17, 184n27, 205n3, 213, 214, 217; relations with blacks, 10, 21–22, 36,

Chinese at war—*continued*
    72, 75, 93, 99, 102, 104, 108–9, 115, 116, 121–24, 137, 140–41, 160, 214; religion, 21, 24, 44, 79, 85, 88–89, 93–94, 96, 98–105, 147, 157, 163, 173n15, 184n27, 187n24, 219; sexuality, 69–70, 84, 74–79, 111, 134, 141, 147–48, 179n21, 179n24, 221; silence, 46, 52–53, 55–56, 95, 143–44, 173n13, 203–4n41; smile, 46, 76, 85, 123, 143, 158; silk, ix–x, 2, 63, 84, 94, 178, 182n2, 203n39; suicide, 9, 12, 34, 36–37, 39–40, 42–44, 55–56, 75, 114, 159, 172n7, 172n9, 172n10, 188n30, 189n33; theater, 54–55, 67, 76, 78, 109, 132, 162, 171 n44, 175n21, 175n23, 200n2, 206n15; writing system, 65, 70, 71, 86–87, 89, 132, 177n6, 179n21, 179n25, 184n29, 207n1.
—societies, xiii, 13–14, 46, 48, 72, 89, 162, 167, 169n26, 169n32, 172n12; Lung Con Cun Sol (Lung Kong) Society, 104, 125, 133, 141, 142, 155, 157, 185n37, 185n3, 190n40, 202n33, 202n34, 203n35, 206n14; Ching Tak Tong Society, 156; Chung Wah Casino, xiii, 15, 95, 126–27, 142, 154, 156, 169n30, 169n32, 202n33, 203n36, 206n15, 208n4, 208n5. *See also* Chinese at war: cuisine; painting; religion; sexuality. *See also chinos mambises*
Chinese Cuban women, 79, 158, 160–61, 206n15; *china mulata*, 24, 74–76, 98, 109–10, 115, 139, 180n3
Chinese Exclusion Act, 14, 51, 136
Chineseism, 150
Chineseness, vii, 16, 25, 29, 51, 59, 64, 66, 77–80, 84, 86–87, 109, 113, 142, 148, 151, 163, 170n33, 209, 211, 219
Chinos mambises (Chinese rebels), 7, 14, 41, 50, 119, 121–25, 128–33, 197n29, 197–98n32, 198n35, 199n41
Chiu, Guillermo, xiii, 156, 207n16,
Chiu, Leandro, xiii, 185n3, 185n40
Chiu Wong, Alejandro, xiii, 154–55
Choy, León, xiii, 48, 139, 157
Choy Rodríguez, Armando, 123–24, 126, 205n4, 222
Chuffat Latour, Antonio, 54, 108, 119–23,

130, 140, 145, 152, 176n26, 191n3, 199n42, 199n43, 202n29, 203n35, 220–21; and *Apunte histórico de los chinos en Cuba*, 19, 23–24, 30, 45, 73, 96, 119–23, 128, 203n40, 211, 221
Chui Beltrán, Gustavo, 123–24, 205, 211, 222
Chung, Yuli, v, xiii, 154, 158–60, 191n1, 208n9, 208n12
Confucius, 73, 82, 84, 97, 172n6; and *Analects*, 35, 39, 93, 96, 211
Coolies, xi, 5–13, 21–22, 32–33, 34–44, 48, 62–65, 68, 70, 81–83, 100, 114, 120–21, 126, 129–31, 140–41, 149–51, 165n3, 166n8, 167n9, 167n10, 167n11, 169n25, 172n9, 176n26, 192n9, 198n34, 200n2, 206n10, 213; coolie trade, 5–6, 8, 10, 13, 22, 32–33, 81, 113, 167–68n12, 177n4
Corbitt, Duvon Clough, 5, 7, 10, 47, 168n21, 211
Cornejo Polar, Antonio, 106–7, 211
Correa, Arnaldo, 101, 105, 186, 205n4, 211; and *Cold Havana Ground*, 98, 101, 142, 169n26, 175n21, 186n14, 192n5, 196n21, 198n35, 211, 222
Cosio Sierra, Nicolás, 70; and "Algún día visitaré la China ancestral," 71
The Cuba Commission Report, 8–9, 11, 19, 23–25, 30–32, 34, 41, 43, 45, 51, 65, 70, 129, 145, 152, 167, 211, 213, 221
Cubanía. *See* Cubanness
Cubanidad. *See* Cubanness
Cubanness, 18, 23, 54, 87, 96, 101, 115, 119, 121–22, 132, 142, 148, 193
Cuban Revolution, 2, 3, 14, 22, 78, 81, 94, 124–28, 131–32, 151, 157, 160, 176n29, 195–96n17, 197n22, 210–11
Cultural Revolution, 74

Dana, Richard Henry, 10–11, 40, 107
De-ethnification, 113
Díaz, Jesús, 205n9; and "Confesión," 150
Divas, 206n15
Double consciousness, 24, 75, 82, 120, 148, 152
Double vision, 154

Eça de Queiroz, José María, 64, 170n41, 176n1, 176n2, 212, 220; and *O Mandarim*, 62–64, 221
Eng Herrera, Pedro, 20, 24, 80, 86, 88, 126–27, 137, 145
Eng Menéndez, Yrmina, xiii, 154, 209
Erasure. *See* Exclusion
Exclusion, vii, 13, 19, 25, 48, 73, 111, 134–35, 219
Exoticization, 67, 70, 146, 153. *See* Orientalism: self-orientalization; Orientalism: strategic self-orientalization

Fanon, Franz, 119–20, 145, 212
Feijóo, Samuel: and *Cuentos populares cubanos*, 49, 211; and *Cuentos populares cubanos de humor*, 47–48, 211, 221
Felipe, Carlos, 175n24; and "El chino," 54–56, 221
Fernández Retamar, Roberto, 18, 129, 134, 212
Fong, Flora, 19, 24, 70, 80, 86–88, 113, 145, 152, 155, 184n28, 184n30, 184n33, 184n34, 209, 212, 214, 218, 221
Footbinding, 65, 73, 76–77, 160, 165n2, 181n13, 181n14, 181n16, 214

Gambling, 33, 38, 41, 68, 108, 127, 135, 142, 200n2, 203n35
García, Cristina, xii, 95, 146–47, 149, 211, 213, 215–16; and *Monkey Hunting*, xii, 7, 20, 24–25, 40, 43, 74–75, 99, 110–14, 140–41, 143, 148–49, 178n11, 179n18, 188n30, 198n35, 203n38, 210, 212–13, 222
Grupo Promotor del Barrio Chino. *See* Havana Chinatown Promotional Group
Guanche Pérez, Jesús, 9, 40, 172n10, 205n5, 213
Guevara, Ernesto "Che," 88
Guillén, Nicolás, xii, 18, 70, 80, 182n2; and "Poema con niños," 182n3, 213

Havana Chinatown Promotional Group, 16, 149–50, 155, 169–70n32, 185n35
Hernández Catá, Alfonso, 174n10, 174n14; and "Los chinos," 51–52, 213, 221; and "Cuarenta y nueve chinos," 51–53, 213, 221
Herrera, Manuel: and "El pirotécnico Li-Shiao," 177, 213
Hu, Jintao, 1, 17,
Hu-DeHart, Evelyn, vii, x, xii–xiii, 5–6, 8–9, 33, 37–38, 169n24, 213
Hybridity, vii, 21, 27, 107, 110–11, 113, 116, 148, 207

I Ching, 105, 191n46

Jiang, Zemin, 17

Ko, Dorothy, 40, 73, 76
Kushigian, Julia A., 61, 64, 66, 78, 214,

Ladder Conspiracy, 12, 169n24
Lam, Wifredo, 19, 87, 145, 155, 207, 212, 215
Lao-tzu (Lao Tse), 82, 86, 97; and *Tao Te Ching*, 1, 29, 86, 143, 153, 184n27, 203n41, 215, 220
Lau, María, 24, 80, 86, 88–89
Lau Si, Ofede, xiii, 157
Lay, Amado, xiii, 161–162
Lay, Miriam Wenchang, xiii, 162–63
Leal, Eusebio, 16
Lezama Lima, José, 20, 153; and *Cartas, (1939–1976)*, 215; and "Juego de las decapitaciones," 64, 215, 221; and *Paradiso*, 181n17, 215
Li, Joaquín, 14, 162, 167n11, 173n1, 208n11, 222
Li, María del Carmen, xiii, 157, 206n15
López, Kathleen, 13, 15, 47, 112, 188n31, 203n35, 203n36
Luarca, Miguel de: and *Verdadera relación de la grandeza del Reino de China*, 72, 176n26, 179n22, 213, 215

Machado y Morales, Gerardo, 126, 196–97n22
Mair, Victor H., 66, 177n9, 215, 220
Mañach, Jorge, 48–49, 215
Mao, Zedong, 16–17, 74
Mariátegui, José Carlos, 200n2, 215

Martí, José, 18, 25, 48, 88, 96–98, 137, 171n43, 215–16, 221; and "Brooklyn Bridge," 136; and "A Chinese Funeral," 98, 135–36; and "The Indians in the United States," 135, 200n4; and "Our America," 134, 137; and "Political Prison in Cuba," 135; and "My Race," 136; and *Versos sencillos*, 135

Médico chino, 55, 74, 112, 135, 139–40, 182n3, 202n27, 202n28, 202n29, 206n15, 213

Méndez Capote, Renée, 131; and *Memorias de una cubanita que nació con el siglo*, 40, 140, 193n15, 198n38, 198n39, 203n39, 216, 221

Mestizaje, 18, 21, 23, 106–10, 112, 115–16, 134, 150, 154, 192n10, 211

Mexico, ix, x, xi, 5, 14, 109, 154, 165n3, 167n8, 204n47, 212, 218

Meza, Ramón, 201n17, 216, 221; and *Carmela*, 137, 203n38, 203n40; and "El mercader chino," 137–38

Miscegenation. See *mestizaje*

Montejo, Esteban: and *Biography of a Runaway Slave*, 21, 29–31, 42–44, 108, 139, 173n13, 188n25, 209, 221

Montero, Mayra, 94–95, 147–48, 170n41, 180n4, 186n16; and *Como un mensajero tuyo*, 74, 98–101, 140, 169n26, 186n16, 191n48, 212, 215–16, 218, 221

Nadie escuchaba, 24, 43–44, 173n16, 216

Nationalism, 13, 109, 150, 211, 218

New Spain. See Mexico

Nogueras, Luis Rogelio, 179n23, 217, 221; and "Mirando un grabado erótico chino," 70

Okin, Susan Moller, 77, 217

Opium, 4, 6, 33, 37–38, 41, 43, 54, 68, 82–83, 100–101, 127, 134, 136, 142, 200n2, 203n35, 213

Orientalism, vii, 7, 19, 24, 29, 46, 51, 55, 57, 61–67, 69–71, 77–80, 84, 86, 134, 136, 145, 148, 153, 176–77, 204n1, 213, 214, 216, 219, 219; self-orientalization, vii, 16, 24, 25, 46, 51, 80–81, 85–88, 94, 120, 145, 152, 219; strategic self-Orientalization, 16, 46, 85, 94, 145

Ortega, Antonio, 204n42, 217, 221; and "Chino olvidado," 143, 176n1

Ortiz, Fernando, 49, 106–7, 113, 134, 206n15, 217

Our History Is Still Being Written, 15, 23–24, 30, 123–26, 128–29, 145, 197n32, 211, 22

Padura Fuentes, Leonardo, 176n29, 191n10, 205n4, 217, 222; and *La cola de la Serpiente*, 56, 74–75, 104, 142–43, 147, 186n17, 189n33; and *El viaje más largo*, 128, 153–54

Palo Monte, 102, 188n30, 189n34, 189n35

Panama, 5, 52–53, 154, 167n8, 214, 219

Pedroso, Regino, xii, 19, 24, 80, 87, 105, 113, 119, 129, 145, 148, 152, 155, 182n2, 183n4; and *El ciruelo de Yuan Pei Fu*, 84–86, 96–98, 179n18, 184n27, 187n21, 205n4, 214, 221; and *Nosotros*, 80–83

Pérez de la Riva, Juan, 172n10, 213, 217

Período especial, 206

Peru, ix, xi, 5, 33, 36–38, 131, 154, 166n8, 168n12, 168n16, 172n9, 200n2, 211, 213, 215, 219, 220

Polo, Marco, 2, 63, 69, 165n2, 179n22, 220

Ponte, Antonio José: and "At the request of Ochún," 180n3

Post-national, 110

Quesada, Gonzalo de, 131, 197n29, 198n39

Racialization, 3, 20–21, 113, 129, 140, 148

Rama, Ángel, 107, 113

Regla de Osha. See Santería

Regla Mayombe. See Palo Monte

Rodríguez, Antonio Orlando, 175n23; and *Aprendices de brujo*, 54, 176n26, 187n24, 218, 222

Runaway slaves, 12, 21, 29, 31, 42–43, 169n22, 209. See also slavery

Said, Edward: and *Orientalism*, 61, 65, 77, 80, 148, 153, 213, 219

Sanfancón, 16, 67, 93–96, 100–101, 103–104,

109, 134, 140, 157, 161, 178, 185n37, 185n3, 188n29, 190n37, 190n40, 219
Santería, 93–95, 98–100, 102, 105, 109, 140, 150, 169n22, 185n1, 185n3, 185n5, 187n18, 187n23, 188n31, 192n7, 193n13, 205n8
Sarduy, Severo, xii, 18, 20, 24, 56, 61, 64–66, 77–79, 115, 146–47, 153, 175n21, 177n4, 182n19, 214, 217–21; and *Cobra*, 65–66, 79, 191n13; and *From Cuba with a Song*, xii, 66, 78, 115; and *Gestos*, 203n38; and *Maitreya*, 79, 116, 181n17, 203n38, 213
Scherer, Frank F., 14, 16, 51, 85, 87, 93–94, 96, 107, 110, 113, 124, 134, 141, 178, 203, 206, 219
Seuc, Napoleón, 152; and *La colonia china de Cuba 1930–1960*, 19, 45, 47, 54, 108, 127–28, 165n4, 170n34, 172n7, 193n16, 194n10, 195n10, 197n22, 197n29, 206n11, 219, 221
Sinicization, 23, 80, 84–86, 88, 112–13, 149
Sinophilia, 23, 149
Sinophobia, vii, 21, 45–46, 51, 56
Sío Wong, Moisés, 15–16, 20, 123–26, 129, 152, 196, 196n19, 196n22, 197n31, 199n42, 205n4, 211, 222
Slavery, x, xi, 5–13, 21, 24, 29–33, 36–37, 40–43, 61, 63, 73, 83–84, 93, 108, 112–13, 121–22, 128–29, 131, 136, 141,151, 160, 166n8, 167n9, 167n11, 168–69n21, 169n22, 169n23, 180n2, 186n17, 189n33, 197n32, 199n39, 207n1, 209, 212, 215–16, 221. *See also* runaway slaves

Spain, xi, 5–6, 8, 20, 32, 47, 49, 65, 101, 106, 119, 128, 130, 165n1, 168n16, 174n10, 197n32, 204n32, 207n1
Spence, Jonathan D., 39, 179n20, 179n22, 181n14, 219
Suárez, José, 62

Taino, 18, 134, 170n36, 182n19
Testimonial. *See Testimonio*
Testimonio, 8, 11, 14, 19, 22–23
Torture, 32, 35, 38–39, 65, 74, 177n5, 177n6
Transculturation, vii, 21, 24, 57, 65, 89, 104–16, 140, 157, 191n48, 191n3, 211, 217, Transnationalism, xi, 22

Valdés, Zoé, 20, 131, 148–49, 177n10, 192n4, 221–22; and *La eternidad del instante*, 15, 34, 51, 67–70, 76–77, 95–96, 114, 131–32, 140–44, 147–48, 173n13, 174n9, 173n26, 176n2, 178n13, 179n21, 181n16, 203n38, 203n47, 216, 220; and *I Gave You All I Had*, 74–75, 106, 108–10, 150, 153, 175n21, 180n8, 203n39; and *Querido primer novio*, 109
Varela, Beatriz, 20, 137, 173n2, 191n3, 201n14, 203n38, 220
Voodoo, 44, 98, 100

Whitening, 141
Wilson, Andrew R., 14, 18, 220
Wong, José, 126, 127, 196n22
Woong, José. *See* Wong, José
Wong, María del Carmen, xiii, 155

Ignacio López-Calvo is professor of Latin American literature at the University of California, Merced. He is the author of *Written in Exile: Chilean Fiction from 1973–Present* (2001); *Religión y militarismo en la obra de Marcos Aguinis 1963–2000* (2002); and *"God and Trujillo": Literary and Cultural Representations of the Dominican Dictator* (University Press of Florida, 2005).

www.ingramcontent.com/pod-product-compliance
Lightning Source LLC
Chambersburg PA
CBHW032315230426
43666CB00032B/182